Desktop Publishing for Educators Using Adobe™ PageMaker™

Macintosh and Windows Edition

Version 6.5

Desktop Publishing for Educators Using Adobe™ PageMaker™

Macintosh and Windows Edition

Version 6.5

Reza Azarmsa
Humboldt State University

Allyn and Bacon

Boston ■ London ■ Toronto ■ Sydney ■ Tokyo ■ Singapore

Copyright © 1998 by Allyn and Bacon
A Viacom Company
160 Gould Street
Needham Heights, Massachusetts 02194

ISBN 0-205-26626-6

Printed in the United States of America
10 9 8 7 6 5 4 3 2 1 00 99 98 97

Dedicated to my sister Ferri,
the baby of the family.

Contents

Part 2
Putting Desktop Publishing to Work Using Aldus PageMaker

Preface

Desktop publishing (DTP) is a phenomenon of desktop computing. Very few developments in microcomputers have grabbed the attention of computer users quite like desktop publishing. Desktop publishing began to be widespread when Apple Computer announced the LaserWriter laser printer in January 1985.

The term *desktop publishing* is quite recent. Paul Brainerd, "father" of the PageMaker software program, is credited with coining the phrase.[1] Simply, desktop publishing refers to the process of producing documents of near-typeset quality using equipment that can sit on a desktop. Users can combine text and illustrations (both graphics and photographs) in a document without the traditional paste-up procedure often used in print shops.

Desktop publishing systems use the principle known as WYSIWYG (pronounced wizzy-wig): What you see is what you get. As the user keys text and graphics into the computer, he or she can see exactly how the output will appear on the page before printing the final copy.

Another kind of software that contributed importantly to the new publishing process was the page description language *PostScript*. The PostScript language, used by laser printers for page description, makes these printers versatile type compositors. The PostScript interpreter allows the page composition language that controls the printer to combine text, drawings, and photographs for printing.

Desktop publishing systems, including a microcomputer, a laser printer, word processing software, a page layout program, and graphic arts software, make it easy to communicate graphically as well as textually. Research indicates that textual communication is processed primarily in the left lobe of the brain and graphic communication is processed primarily in the right lobe.[2] The combination of textual and graphic elements produces a powerful communications structure that facilitates simultaneous multichannel processing by both the left and right lobes of the brain. As a result, communication techniques that combine both textual and graphic elements produce effective results.

Research indicates that most people read typeset documents about 27 percent faster than they read nontypeset documents.[3] They also tend to view typeset documents as more credible, more persuasive, and more professional than nontypeset documents.

Desktop publishing is changing the way people produce documents. It enhances the individual's ability to control all or most of the process of producing printed materials. This potential means that multitalented people with writing, illustrating, editing, and designing skills can do the work effectively.

Desktop publishing provides users with a number of distinct advantages. In the hand of a knowledgeable user, desktop publishing equipment and software can produce superior-looking documents at a far lower cost than would otherwise be possible.

The potential benefits to students using desktop publishing are enormous. Students gain knowledge in a variety of disciplines—writing, typesetting, graphic design, printing, and computing. Controlling the publication process permits authors to become more involved with the visual impact of their ideas on the reader. The relationship between form and content may take on new meaning when authors integrate ideas with words, type style, graphics, and the other features involved in the production of publications with a high level of visual impact. Creating visually informative text gives the author a chance to gain a heightened sense of categories, divisions, and orderly progression.

The primary objective of this book is to provide a comprehensive introductory work on desktop publishing using Aldus PageMaker, particularly the use of PageMaker in schools. The text is enriched by basic elements of design and layout and is aimed primarily at educators, students who are working on their teaching credentials, and teacher inservice programs. Few educators are familiar with the new concept of desktop publishing, and few have access to a comprehensive book in this field.

The book consists of two parts. Part 1, "Basic Elements of Desktop Publishing," explains the basic concepts of desktop publishing, design elements, text elements, and ways to organize a publication and includes tips on enhancing design and layout. Part 2, "Putting Desktop Publishing to Work Using Adobe PageMaker," includes a tour of PageMaker and also is a guide to making a field-trip flyer, creating a brochure for school, creating a school newsletter, and creating a long document (a book). In part 2, the text concentrates on step-by-step, hands-on guidelines for creating flyers, brochures, newsletters, and long documents. With the help of these easy-to-use guidelines, users will be able to apply the learned skills immediately, regardless of which version of the PageMaker program they use.

In part 2, PageMaker is used to create desktop publishing documents because it is the most popular page layout program. Studies show that Adobe PageMaker has about 69% of the desktop publishing market compared to a 14% market share for Quark XPress and 8% for Ventura Publisher.[4]

Chapter 1 describes the concepts of desktop publishing. This chapter defines desktop publishing, shows material that can be produced by desktop publishing, describes the evolution of desktop publishing, explains desktop publishing systems, and discusses advantages of desktop publishing.

Chapter 2 addresses design elements. Elements such as simplicity, formal and informal balance, unity, and contrast are shown through examples.

Chapter 3 discusses typography, its importance in documents, its variations, and its format. Through examples, this chapter demonstrates different type styles, type weights, typefaces, and type formatting. Tips and tricks are offered for enhancing a document's quality.

Chapter 4 is a guideline to organizing a publication. It shows different ways to organize the overall display of the publication as well as to organize text. In this chapter, grids, columns, rules, boxes, and different shades of gray are exhibited as ways to organize the publication. Placing headlines, subheads, captions, and pullout text are shown as ways to help organize body copy.

Chapter 5 demonstrates the ways a document can be improved. This chapter warns against common mistakes to avoid and encourages techniques to improve the quality of both text and graphics.

Chapter 6 is a "tour" of PageMaker. In this chapter, readers get to know one of the leading desktop publishing programs and learn how to import and format text and graphics in a publication.

Chapter 7 is a step-by-step guide to creating a flyer. Flyers are considered one of the most used means of communication in schools. In this chapter, users learn how to develop a field-trip flyer as an example.

Chapter 8 shows the procedures for creating a promotional school brochure. The sample brochure is double-sided and trifolded. The materials in this chapter explain how to design each section of the brochure separately.

Chapter 9 presents step-by-step instructions for creating a four-page school newsletter. This chapter shows how to design newsletter master pages, a nameplate, headlines, how to make text "wrap" around graphics, and other PageMaker advanced features.

Chapter 10 provides a guideline for using PageMaker's unique features for creating a long document. This chapter shows how to plan, set up, and print a book, as well as how to create an automatic table of contents and index.

Chapter 11 describes the new technology of distributing a PageMaker publication electronically for the Internet access as well as creating hyperlinks to jump from one part of the document to another. This chapter concentrates on aspects of preparing, viewing, and distributing publications as PDF (Portable Document Format) or HTML (HyperText Markup Language) format.

The appendixes consist of a sample of clip art, a list of resources (books and periodicals) available in the field of desktop publishing, and a glossary of technical terms.

Conventions Used in This Book

Menu and dialog box names as well as selections from menus and dialog boxes appear in *italic* type.

Window names, tools, button, and keyboard keys have initial capitals and are in plain (roman) type.

All folder, file, menu, and tool names use upper and lowercase letters as they appear on-screen in PageMaker and on the DataDisk that accompanies this book.

DataDisk

The book is accompanied by a disk containing the materials necessary for the step-by-step, hands-on exercises in part 2. These exercises help the users to learn the program. This disk contains the following folders and files:

academic.txt
athletic.txt
balloons.eps
clubs.txt
eagle.eps
giraffe.eps
goel.txt
grid.pm4
kids.eps
lorem.txt
pen&ink.eps
poem.txt
tree4.eps
trophy.eps

Notes

1. John W. Seybold. "The Desktop-Publishing Phenomenon." *Byte* 12 (May 1987):149-165.

2. James B. Willams and Lawrence E. Murr. "Desktop Publishing: New Right Brain Documents." *Library Hi Tech* 5 (Spring 1987):7-13.

3. S. Tilden. *Harnessing Desktop Publishing: How to Let the New Technology Help You Do Your Job Better.* Pennington, NJ: Scott Tilden, 1987.

4. Jeanette Borzo. "PageMaker Users Fear Update Delay." *InfoWorld* 14 (August 17, 1992):1, 131.

Acknowledgments

I wish to express my appreciation to the following individuals and companies who generously contributed materials and granted permission to use them in this project: Mr. Peter Card, from Adobe, for his endless support; Mr. Steve Justice, from Dynamic Graphic, Inc., for clip art; Mr. Glenn Giaimo, from 3G Graphics, Inc., for clip art; Ms. Laura Johnson and Ms. Jennifer Madden, from T/Maker Company, for contributing clip art; Ms. Pam Richardson, from Ventana Press, for valuable books; Ms. Melissa Carlsen, from Mainstay, for Captivate software (Mac screen capture utility); Ms. Brenda Cheatham, from Quarterdeck, for HiJaack software (IBM/compatible screen capture utility); Mr. Steve Schoolman, from CAR, Inc., for Clipable art works; and Mr. Phil Bates, from Artbeats, for background graphics. Without the support of these individuals and companies, the completion of this project would have been impossible.

Special thanks go to Ms. Nancy Forsyth, Editor-in-Chief for education, from Allyn and Bacon, for her continuous and endless support.

Throughout this endeavor, Fah, Vishi, and Anna, my family, were constantly with me behind the scenes, helping, encouraging, believing in my effort. I cannot adequately thank them for their understanding.

Part 1

Basic Elements of Desktop Publishing

1

Understanding Desktop Publishing

Desktop publishing (DTP) provides the capability to produce reader-ready or camera-ready originals without the need for complicated prepress operations. The tools of production generally consist of a computer system and relevant software applications and are sufficiently compact to fit on a desktop. They provide the user with total control over the content and form of the publication. In general, prerequisite skills include a working knowledge of word processing, a general understanding of graphics, and a sense of what constitutes pleasing and functional layout and design.

The significance of desktop publishing is threefold. *First*, it provides the user with the tools to express thoughts and ideas in text, graphic, and sometimes photographic (halftone) form. These elements are pieces of the publication production process that have traditionally required the services of trade professionals to assemble into final form. *Second*, the user has immediate feedback on the appearance of the final publication. The page relationships of the elements, their sizes, and their physical characteristics are immediately visible and infinitely editable. *Third*, the paper output from the system is in finished form, ready for distribution to small numbers of readers or for further reproduction and subsequent mass distribution.

The Process of Desktop Publishing

The desktop publishing production process involves electronically placing text and graphics on a page and reproducing the page for distribution. Produce a newsletter, a proposal, a résumé, or a high school yearbook, and you follow the same procedures as publishers of books and magazines, albeit on a less elaborate scale. No matter the kind of document produced or the technique used, publishing procedure follows five basic steps:

1. Plan the publication.
2. Prepare the text.
3. Prepare the charts and illustrations.
4. Make up the publication's pages (prepare them for reproduction).
5. Reproduce the publication.

Desktop publishing computerizes and accelerates the publishing cycle. Often text is created in a software application and then edited. Charts, graphs, illustrations, rules (lines), boxes, or circles are drawn either with DTP built-in tools or by other application software. Text and charts are placed on the page and resized and reshaped according to the predetermined page specifications. When the page is complete, it may be produced on a computer printer and then can be reproduced on a photocopy machine or a commercial printing press. Figure 1.1 illustrates the process of desktop publishing.

> Desktop publishing technology has brought the power of the typeset word to virtually every computer user.

Materials Produced by Desktop Publishing

Desktop publishing has enjoyed quick acceptance in most areas of document production within business, industry, government, and education. It is a step beyond word processing, providing users with the capability to produce better-looking and more informationally-potent documents.

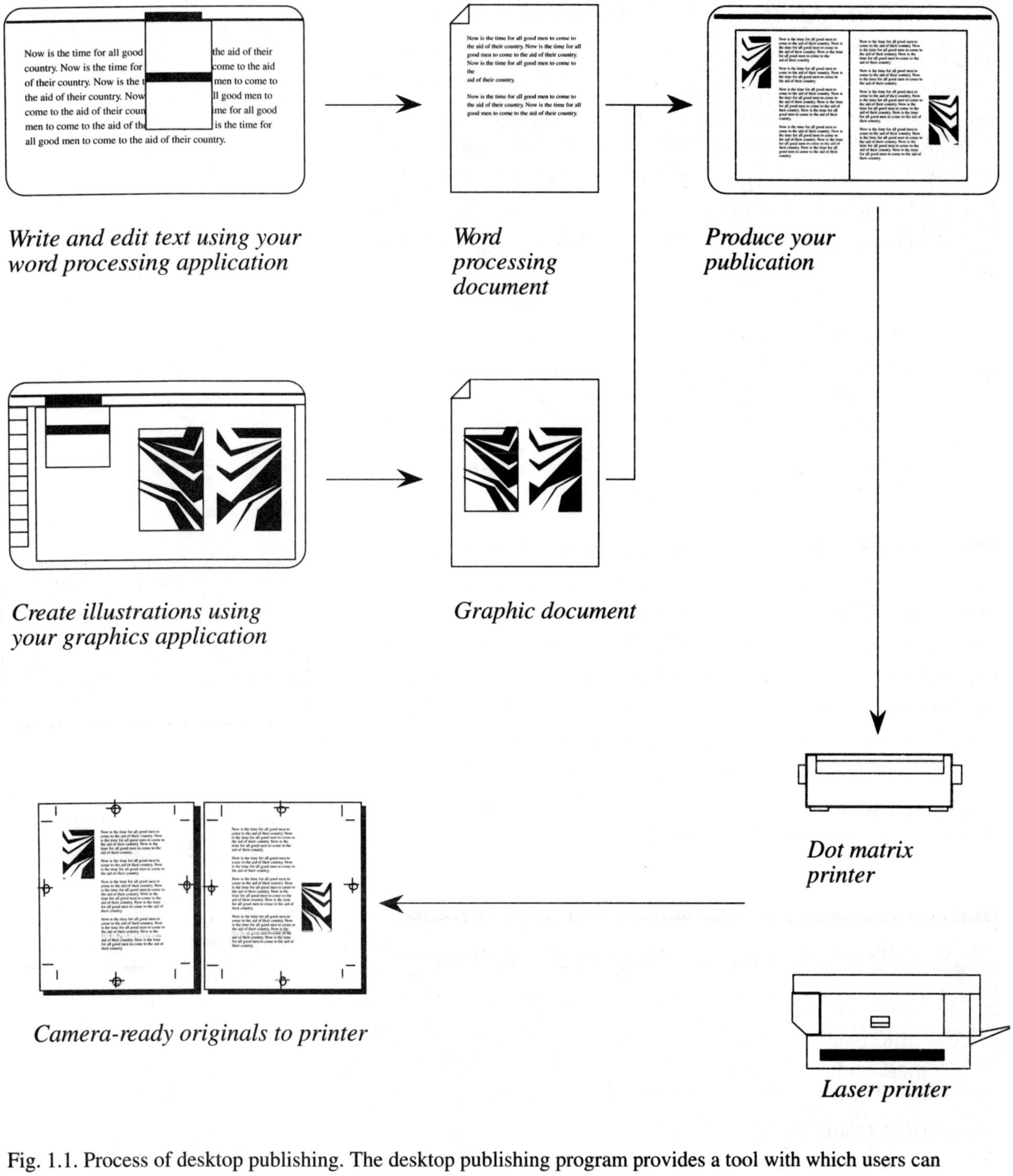

Fig. 1.1. Process of desktop publishing. The desktop publishing program provides a tool with which users can assemble text and illustrations into page format.

The following is a list of some of the materials that can be produced using desktop publishing.

books	brochures	bulletins
calendars	catalogs	certificates
charts	cover sheets	curriculum materials
diplomas	directories	documentation
flow charts	flyers	graphs
greeting cards	indexes	instructional materials
letterhead stationery	magazines	manuals
maps	memos	menus
nametags	newsletters	newspapers
notices	pamphlets	poetry
programs	proposals	prospectuses
résumés	schedules	signs
slides	statements	tabloids
testing materials	title pages	visual aids

Components of Desktop Publishing

Desktop publishing requires three basic components: a microcomputer with high-resolution monitor, page layout software, and a laser printer. Other peripherals and software packages are optional and can be added to the system later.

Microcomputer

A microcomputer (micro) is the most popular type of computer on the market. Since the late 1970s, when the microcomputer entered the market, sales have increased dramatically. It is estimated that in 1998 about 200 million micros will be in use in the United States. Major reasons for the micro's success are its low cost, ease of use, and general usefulness. The size and price of micros are decreasing as the speed and memory capacity are increasing. The speed at which micros process data is governed by timing circuits in the machine, and the pace of this internal electronic clock—the computer's "clock speed"—provides an indication of how quickly the processing is being done. Just a few years ago, a typical desktop computer's clock speed was 4 megahertz (MHz), or 4 million on/off cycles each second. Although that might seem like a blistering pace,

Computers are constantly changing. Some predict that desktop publishing will become a generic function of all desktop computers.

today's machines boast clock speeds as high as 160 megahertz. Faster machines, of course, carry higher pricetags. However, they can be well worth the additional cost when used for processing-intensive tasks such as the manipulation of fonts and graphics in page layouts and other desktop publishing and design applications.

Random access memory (RAM) can be thought of as the "working space" available within the computer. The more sophisticated a software package, the more RAM it is likely to require, so it is advisable to determine what software you will be using and how much RAM it needs before deciding how much memory your computer should have. Because RAM retains information only while the computer is on, your system will also include some means of "permanent" data storage—usually disk drives. So-called floppy disks are removable—and therefore transportable—data storage media, whereas "hard" or "fixed" disks are high-capacity information storage devices permanently installed either in or alongside the computer. In general, hard disk storage is considered essential in any type of professional production environment.

> The lowest price may not be the best price. Paying a bit more can be a wise investment, especially if you pay more to a dealer who will provide the support you need if you run into problems.

Both the size of RAM and the capacity of disk drives are measured in terms of the number of data characters, or bytes, that can be retained. These numbers are so large that for convenience they are expressed in multiples of 1,000 (kilobytes) or 1 million (megabytes). (Actually, a kilobyte equals 1,024 bytes, but in common conversation 1,000 is used.) Thus, a computer with 8 megabytes (8MB) of RAM has enough memory to manipulate approximately 8,000,000 pieces of data, and a 500 megabyte (500MB) hard disk can store about 500 million characters. Macintosh computers, IBM PS/2, and similar machines use 3-1/2" floppy disks with a capacity of 1.44 megabytes. The most common capacities for hard disk units currently are between 500 to 1,000 megabytes. Some desktop systems have capacities as high as 10 gigabyte. It has been said that there is no such thing as having too much hard disk capacity, and that is especially true with desktop publishing and design applications.

Fonts, clip art, scanned images, and the like are voracious consumers of disk space—so much so that a hard disk unit that stores information on removable cartridges may be advisable. Another situation calling for as much capacity as possible is the use of the hard disk as a file server on a network. In such an arrangement a single hard disk is shared by more than one computer, storing programs and data for many individual users.

It is essential to maintain a backup copy of the contents of a hard disk in case its data should be destroyed or damaged through either accidental erasure or a problem with the drive mechanism. The backup method used most often is copying all files from the hard disk onto either floppy disks or tape. Using floppy disks for backup can be a long and tedious process. Using tape for backup is quicker and easier but more expensive. A tape drive can cost as much or more than the hard disk it will be used to backup. But the tape drive can easily pay for itself in saved time and aggravation the very first time it is used to restore the contents of a damaged or accidentally erased hard disk drive.

> Expend as much time and effort as necessary to determine in advance what you will really be doing with your new system. Once you identify what you want your system to do, you will know what equipment and software you will need. And what you need is what to get!

Video Display

With the exception of the Macintosh Plus, Classic, and SE (which have built-in video displays), the computers used for desktop publishing require an external display device, or monitor, and a video board to drive the monitor. The variety and price range of computer displays are as varied as television sets. In general, the larger the display's cathode ray tube (CRT) and the higher the resolution (sharpness) and number of colors that can be displayed, the higher the cost. Single-page or dual-page monochrome displays are best for most black-and-white desktop publishing applications, whereas a color monitor is considered essential for any kind of desktop presentation work. When working with color, remember that there will be discrepancies between the accuracy and saturation of the color on the screen and the colors that come out on color printouts or film recorders.

Printer

Desktop publishing requires a laser printer for two reasons: l) to print text that appears near-typeset quality that it is appropriate for brochures, catalogs, and similar documents and 2) to print a combination of text and graphics in place on the page. Standard dot matrix and letter-quality printers cannot handle both tasks.

Laser printer *resolution* of 300 *dots per inch (dpi)* is a minimum to appear typeset to most readers; true typesetting quality has a resolution of 1,200 dpi and higher. In general, the higher the resolution, the more clearly defined the characters.

> Dots per inch (dpi) refers to digitized output from typesetting devices (laser printers and phototypesetters) and scanners—the greater the dpi, the higher the resolution.

Printers provide the final results of the production process. Regardless of the quality of the computer and software used to produce materials, it is the printer that determines how good your work will look on paper. Laser printers, which use a printing process that is similar to photocopying, are the current minimum standard for professional desktop publishing work. One of the major issues in selecting a laser printer is the question of PostScript compatibility.

PostScript

PostScript is a computer graphics language that describes pages of text and graphics and reproduces the descriptions on a printer, typesetting machine, or other output device. PostScript was developed by Adobe Systems of Palo Alto, California, for Apple's LaserWriter printer. PostScript is a widely accepted page description language for the Macintosh and other computers, such as the IBM PC series and compatibles.

PostScript describes pages by using mathematical formulas that represent shapes rather than by specifying individual pixels in a bit-mapped graphic image (the small dots that make up an image are known as picture elements, or *pixels*). PostScript translates images into the tiny dots that make up text, graphics, and halftones on printed pages. PostScript encodes typefaces into outlines (see fig. 1.2) that a laser printer reconstructs at the proper size and then fills in to solidify the outline. This approach has two clear advantages: Computer memory is conserved, and many different types of output devices can recreate the standard PostScript format at a wide range of resolutions.

PostScript's unique system of typeface definition creates characters in a wide variety of type styles and sizes. This approach can cut typesetting costs considerably, because typefaces are traditionally sold by the font (a set of characters of a single typeface, type style, and size). In other words, most typesetting machines require separate purchases for 9-point

Times Roman, 12-point Times Roman, 12-point Times Roman italic, and so forth. On the other hand, a single purchase gets you the Times Roman typeface for a PostScript system in all the major type styles—plain text, italic, bold, underline, outline, shadow, small caps, superscript, and subscript—and in virtually any type size (the Apple LaserWriter, for example, can produce any size from 3 points up). You don't pay separately for each variation.

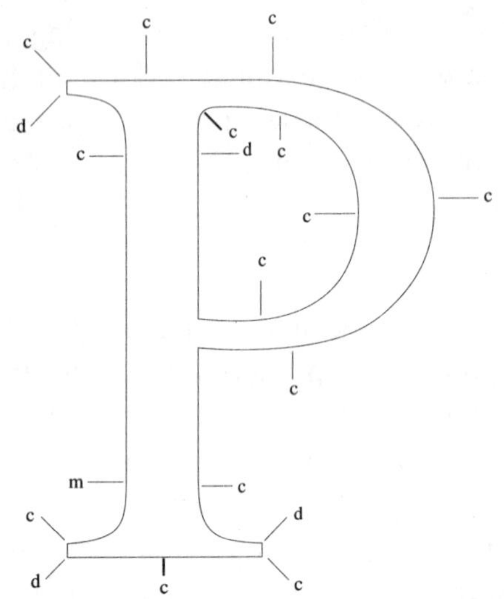

Fig. 1.2. PostScript outline of the letter P.

PostScript is a page description language developed by Adobe Systems and used by many laser printers and high-resolution typesetters.

It is also important to keep in mind that PostScript doesn't work only on printers. For example, you can write PostScript programs to create special graphics effects. Computers can use PostScript to describe text and graphics in a standardized common format that other computers or PostScript programmers can employ. Video displays can use PostScript to interpret page descriptions, convert the results into bit-mapped images, and display the images on a computer screen. PostScript provides a common language for various audiences and devices that precisely and concisely describes pages of information that contain text, graphics, or both.

PostScript has emerged as a standard among page description languages; many hardware and software companies now make PostScript-compatible products—from page layout and graphics software for the Macintosh and IBM PC to page printers and typesetting machines.

Page Makeup Programs

Although the race is on in the word processing camp to provide more page makeup tools and capabilities, page makeup programs are essential for producing sophisticated documents. Page makeup software brings text and graphics together on the page. It enables users to combine elements produced by word processing and graphics programs and typically offers much more flexible page formatting and typographical manipulation than do stand-alone word processors.

Software is your primary consideration. A computer that does not run the programs you need is out of the question, regardless of brand name or price.

When evaluating a page layout program, be sure that it will work properly in conjunction with the word processor and graphics programs you are using. PostScript support also is of major importance, and if you plan to incorporate scanned images, it is critical that the software support TIFF (Tagged Image File Format) EPS (Encapsulated PostScript), which is the most popular format for high-quality scanned images. Some page makeup programs (such as Adobe PageMaker) are better suited to free-form design applications, whereas others (such as QuarkXPress) are geared toward page-intensive projects such as books and technical journals.

Word Processing Software

TIFF represents Tagged Image File Format and EPS denotes Encapsulated PostScript.

A good word processing program is essential for the preparation of text to be incorporated into virtually any desktop publishing or design application. A word processor also can be used for day-to-day lesson plans, memos, and internal documents. Some of the newer word processing packages support multiple fonts and include limited page layout capabilities. No word processing program can match a good desktop publishing program, especially if your page layout requirements are at all sophisticated. The word processor program should work seamlessly with the page makeup program.

Presentation Packages

Presentation programs typically allow you to sketch out a presentation in an outline-style format, with the software automatically generating the proper layouts for overhead transparencies, 35mm photographic slides, and speaker handouts from the outline. Microsoft PowerPoint offers the ability to create business graphs and charts.

Type-handling capabilities are an important consideration in selecting a presentation program. Unfortunately, many of the currently available packages are seriously lacking in this regard. A presentation program is of little use if the type created in a dedicated graphic program will not work with other programs.

Presentation programs, such as Adobe Persuasion, also offers predetermined color combination schemes for backgrounds, type, and floating elements. This is an essential feature for those who have never dealt with the intricate issues of color coordination involved in preparing a professional presentation.

Graphics Programs

Graphics programs can be separated into three categories: *graphing and charting programs, painting programs,* and *illustration programs*. Graphing packages allow users to graph information extracted from a spreadsheet, and many graphing programs also allow data to be typed in directly. Painting programs are good for artistic applications but usually offer limited output quality. Illustration software usually takes full advantage of the resolution and capabilities of most printers and film recorders.

Command-driven software requires users to supply commands rather than select options from a screen menu.

Menu-driven software systems give users a list of selections and prompts from which to make choices.

When evaluating graphing programs, be sure to verify that the program can handle a full variety of chart types (pie, bar, column, scatter, etc.). If you are using a separate presentation program, make sure the two programs are compatible with each other.

The world of illustration software has essentially standardized on the PostScript format, making this a must-have capability for applications requiring professional reproduction quality. A new category of graphics program that is only just emerging is photo retouching software. These programs allow scanned images to be edited in fine detail, with the electronic equivalent of a retoucher's airbrush and fine brushes. Effective use of such software requires a higher degree of artistic skill than the standard graphics offerings, and these programs are best suited for graphics professionals.

Scanner

Scanners are used to transfer graphics (line art and continuous-tone photographs) and text into the computer. Once scanned into the computer, graphics can be manipulated with electronic retouching and enhancement tools, and text can be converted into editable copy through a process called OCR, or optical character recognition. Scanners are primarily differentiated by the ability to scan either loose sheets (sheet-fed) or bound materials (flatbed) and also by the number of dot-per-inch resolution they produce.

Color scanners are more expensive than their black-and-white counterparts, and software support for reproducing and separating color scans is only now beginning to solidify. For most purposes, scanned images are usually brought into page layout programs to be integrated with text and other forms of artwork.

> A scanner provides a great deal of control and flexibility when you design pages that have to accommodate numerous photographs or illustrations.

A vital consideration in evaluating the use of desktop scanners to create high-quality halftones (that are to be printed on a laser typesetter, for example) is the issue of cost-effectiveness. An image scanned with a resolution of 300 dots per inch and a full 256 shades of gray can take an inordinate amount of time to print out on a desktop system. It makes much more economic sense to have a continuous-tone photograph screened by traditional methods and then drop it onto a computer-generated page layout.

The advantage of scanning a photograph into the computer is that it can be finely retouched and manipulated using some of the sophisticated software currently available. But if large numbers of unretouched photographs need to be used in layouts and reproduced at high quality, it is advisable to carefully consider the cost versus the benefits of abandoning traditional methods in favor of electronic techniques.

Modem and Telecommunications Software

Modems are devices that enable computers at different locations to exchange data over standard telephone lines. Modems enable users to send and receive electronic mail, access online data services, and send documents to the district office or other schools, for example, for laser typesetting and film output.

Primary considerations when evaluating modems include compatibility with the Hayes command set (a de facto standard used by most telecommunications software), transmission speed (ranging from 9,600 to 28,800 baud), and ability to accurately send and receive data despite telephone line noise. The greater the speed and the greater the resistance to line noise, the higher the price of the modem.

Telecommunications software—sometimes called terminal emulation software—controls the modem and the communications process. As with other software, telecommunications programs offer differing features and degrees of sophistication at a wide variety of prices.

> In networked publishing, several interconnecting computers—either the same kind or different kinds—share information and resources.

A network is an interconnection of several computers at a single location through cabling, hardware interfaces, and software. There are various methods of networking that are specific to each basic type of computer and other methods that allow computers from various manufacturers to communicate and share information. *Ethernet* and *Token Ring* are popular networks for IBM PCs and compatibles, and *AppleTalk* is the standard for Macintosh computers.

In setting up a desktop publishing system, a school may not need all of the aforementioned components. The school may already have part of the desktop publishing system. Upgrading your production environment to the new desktop tools can be a rewarding and profitable experience, if approached with caution and intelligence.

Benefits of Desktop Publishing

Desktop publishing offers many advantages over the traditional printing process. Even though the initial costs of obtaining desktop publishing hardware and software are high, the system actually often saves money. In educational settings this is typically the case, especially when the time that the teacher and students are putting in to set up the layout is "free." Usually, the sense of accomplishment that comes with the finished product and the flexibility regarding the printing process are enough to justify that time. Additional potential benefits to desktop publishing include:

- Reduced typesetting time and costs
- Better-looking publications with improved readability, credibility, and prestige
- More control over the publishing process
- Increased convenience to designers
- Increased cooperation among students
- Possibility for electronic distribution

Reduced typesetting time and costs are a very tangible benefit of desktop publishing. Because word processing and page composition programs allow you to directly create and layout your documents, there is no need for a manual typesetting step. This eliminates typesetting costs and time. Typesetting can often take days and cost as much as $50 per page. For a school producing newsletters or brochures on a regular basis, typesetting costs and time can be a significant problem.

> In the hands of a knowledgeable user, desktop publishing equipment and software can produce superior-looking documents at far lower cost than would otherwise be possible.

Desktop publishing can result in better-quality publications because documents can be composed quickly, allowing more time for teachers and students to make revisions and additions. Many documents that would not merit the time and expense of printing by traditional methods can be produced in near-typeset form with desktop publishing equipment. If documents are created using a word processing program, it is a small additional step to compose and print them.

More control is achieved over the publishing process because the results are immediately available. This makes it much easier to try out ideas and see what various options look like. In addition, potential communication problems between the document designer and the printer are avoided because they often are the same person.

The availability of graphics and page composition programs makes design work much easier and faster. For example, a skilled artist can create technical illustrations much more productively using a computer than on paper. This is because it is possible to build up libraries of "clip art" that can be reused. Features such as automatic rescaling, rotating, and overlaying make the drawing process faster. Similarly, page layout can be accomplished much easier than manual paste-up due to features such as automatic pagination, line-spacing control, text wraparound, automatic hyphenation, and margin settings.

The process of preparing materials for desktop publishing layout involves cooperation by students. The students soon learn that the help of someone who is a graphic artist, a writer, or a designer can be of great value in a desktop publishing venture.

Finally, it is possible to send and exchange documents electronically, eliminating the time and costs of physical delivery. Suppose you are editing a newsletter that contains contributions from people all over the country. The articles can be transmitted to you from their personal computers to yours in a matter of minutes. You can then edit the articles, compose the newsletter, and transmit the complete newsletter to the printing site. Alternatively, the newsletter could be published electronically, meaning that people read it on their own computers as soon as it is made available.

Desktop publishing creates interesting written communications far beyond what can be created with an ordinary word processor. Some of the advantages of a desktop publishing program are as follows:

> The major advantages of desktop publishing are the reduced cost of producing quality productions and the ability to produce them in-house.

- Improves the appearance of documents
- Reduces the time and number of steps required to print pages
- Produces customized documents
- Produces camera-ready documents in a short time
- Reduces production costs
- Offers more capabilities and flexibilities
- Encourages creativity
- Increases productivity
- Makes the job more fun

Evolution of Desktop Publishing

A review of typesetting and printing advances offers a good starting point for understanding how desktop publishing builds on and streamlines traditional publishing methods.

Ancient Times

Publishing coincided with the development of written language. In ancient times, papyrus was used to produce printed material. Later, around the time of Jesus, the Chinese used bamboo to create a writing surface. Before the invention of the printing press, publications were hand-copied on pieces of paper or other writing surfaces. The first form of printing involved carving a message on a piece of stone or wood, coating it with some type of ink, and pressing that "plate" against a piece of paper. This method was mostly used for reproducing artwork rather than for printing characters.

Movable Type

The introduction of the printing press in the late 1400s led to more graceful, balanced type forms.

In the fifteenth century, Johannes Gutenberg's popularization of movable type became one of the milestones of European history—it reduced publishing time and expense so books became more plentiful. Until then, books had been hand-copied or printed from blocks of wood on which raised characters (letters, numbers, and punctuation marks) and illustrations were laboriously carved for each page. Movable type at that time involved small wooden blocks with individual characters that could be rearranged and used repeatedly. This wood type was later replaced by metal type for greater durability.

Linotype

The next important publishing innovation did not occur for four centuries. With the invention of the Linotype machine in the 1880s, publishers could set an entire line of type at once rather than only character by character. Although the process entailed melting lead, it reduced publishing costs and production time.

Offset Printing and Phototypesetting

In the 1950s and 1960s, the publishing process transformed from the "hot type" process involving molten lead into a photographic "cold type" process that is faster and cleaner. At this time, several photographic printing processes were introduced that used a flat plate rather than the raised type of earlier methods. The most important new process was *offset printing,* which is widely used today. Offset printing was soon joined by computer-based *phototypesetting,* which projects images of columns of text onto photosensitive paper. The paper is developed, cut into sections, and pasted onto a sheet of heavy paper to produce a *camera-ready page mechanical*—a paste-up of the complete page for offset printing. Illustrations are sized photographically and added as needed.

By the early 1980s, staff overhead presented a problem for a growing segment of the publishing industry: businesses, government offices, and educational institutions that had become major publishers of brochures, books, catalogs, and other phototypeset publications. The advent of microcomputers and software development introduced desktop publishing in 1985. This new development gave businesses and educational institutions an affordable publishing system anyone could learn to use. For some, bringing publishing to the desktop is known as the *second publishing revolution.*

Desktop Publishing

The term *desktop publishing* is credited to Paul Brainerd of Aldus Corporation, the father of PageMaker. DTP actually originated in 1973, when an experimental multifunction workstation was developed at the Xerox Palo Alto Research Center (PARC). The workstation was called Alto. Because its designers had graphics applications in mind, the Alto had a high-resolution bit-mapped display screen and a mouse pointing device.

> A bit map is a representation of characters or graphics as a series of square dots or pixels.

Altos were assigned to a few selected sites, including the White House, the House of Representatives, the Senate, a few universities (especially Stanford), and several undisclosed locations in the United States and Europe. The large base of users provided input as to what was right and what was wrong with the Alto and with the various software packages that had been developed for it. These packages included Bravo, Gypsy, Markup, Draw, SIL, and Laurel—for text editing and formatting, creating pictures and diagrams, and providing electronic mail by means of a central file server.

None of the Alto machines were ever commercially viable on cost grounds, and there was no affordable printer. Apple Computers, inspired by the PARC systems, designed and marketed the Lisa desktop microcomputer. This unit, released by Apple in 1983, had a high-resolution screen, a mouse, a WIMP (windows, icons, mice, and pointers) interface, and high-capacity hard and floppy drives. Lisa was discontinued in 1984 when Apple produced the first Macintosh, which led to a family of microcomputers that further extended the idea of an integrated suite of applications emulating the original PARC systems. The following year Apple produced a laser printer with an output resolution of 300 dots per inch (dpi), which is generally considered to have started the DTP revolution. This printer had a plain-paper typesetter using a raster image processor (RIP), which gave a resolution approximating professionally published documents. At 300 dpi a letter-size page requires about 1MB of storage to be set up in the RIP for printing manipulations.

Some consider publishing with the desktop computers as a second publishing revolution.

The fact is that the new technology has spawned a host of desktop publishers who are publishing—writing, producing, and distributing—to a readership, and the publishing process has suddenly become democratized and affordable beyond the dreams of only a few years ago.

Macintosh computers get credit for desktop publishing as we perceive it today. But nowadays desktop publishing is not limited to Macs. Windows-based computers are, in some respects, an ideal platform for the development of a desktop publishing system because they are popular, powerful, and open. Using a Windows-based computer, the user must specify what kind of graphics board is availablet.

Until recently, the interval between the development of new technologies and their introduction into education has been quite considerable. However, it is now increasingly apparent that new developments are appearing in the classroom sooner rather than later. In the case of DTP, where some of the essential tools, such as text and graphics processing, are already providing effective curriculum experiences, the interval has been extremely short. Expectations have already been raised by the early release of packages that claim to be DTP systems because they provide simple manipulations of both text and graphics on a single page. A particular selling point of such systems in schools has been their facility to design pages of a newspaper.

Desktop publishing is increasingly popular in the writing classroom for several reasons. By using desktop publishing, students gain experience in a variety of disciplines such as writing, typesetting, graphic design, printing, and computing. Desktop publishing represents a revolutionary literacy tool for schools because it encourages students to create and publish manuscripts of high quality. Yet desktop publishing does not exist very widely in schools, partly because of the expense involved and the computer expertise needed. To keep computers and writing in proper balance, desktop publishing should be introduced in special courses designed to teach writing and desktop publishing, such as journalism courses, writing for publication courses, or literary magazine courses. Desktop publishing brings students into a new relationship with the written word. If desktop publishing is introduced thoughtfully into the curriculum, it can improve students' reading and writing skills while providing opportunities for students to acquire computer publishing abilities that are increasingly valued outside the classroom.

> Desktop publishing helps students express their imaginations on paper in new ways.

2

Design

The success of many desktop publishing materials can be attributed in large measure to the quality and effectiveness of the graphic design. These are achieved through organizing preliminary thoughts, planning, and applying the techniques outlined in this chapter.

Many persons who develop desktop publishing materials have little or no professional art background. To avoid producing poor graphic materials, they can consider a number of practical suggestions and guiding principles and then apply these as the need arises.

Design Principles

Effective graphic design is based on knowing the building blocks of design and when to use them. In graphic design, everything is relative. Tools and techniques that work in one situation will not necessarily work in another. For example, it is impossible to define the exact layout for informal balance or the appropriate color for a newsletter or book cover.

In creating a visual, important design considerations are best faced by starting with a preliminary sketch of the intended visual. This is referred to as a *rough layout.* At the rough layout stage, little attention is paid to rendering the artistic details, but careful consideration is given to effective design.

Graphic design must be seen as a means of communication rather than mere decoration. There should be a logical reason for the way you employ every graphic tool. That tool should relate to the idea it expresses as well as to the environment in which the final product will appear. The following guidelines provide a framework for effective graphic design.

Planning

Design must be planned with consideration for the intended audience. What is the basic message, and what format will be used (newspaper, bulletin, poster)? The more you define your project's purpose and environment, the better you will do. You should also consider the size and dimensions of the publication in addition to the resources, skills, techniques, materials, and facilities that you can employ to produce the publication.

Planning is the basis for effective design.

It is useful to develop a grid or choose a predesigned one in template form (fig. 2.1). The grid adds continuity to a publication by defining where margins, rules, columns, and other elements should be on each page.

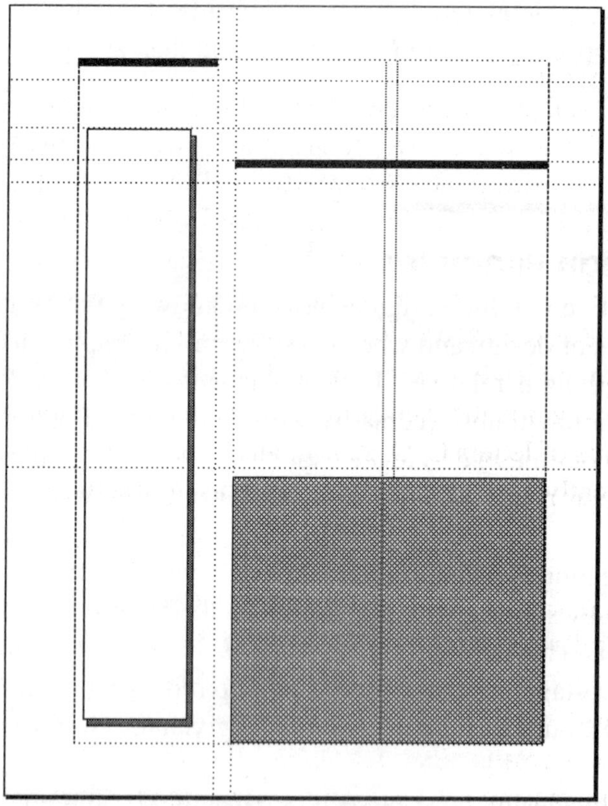

Fig. 2.1. A grid contributes to the continuity of a publication.

Publications may be designed by drawing *thumbnail* sketches. A thumbnail sketch is a rough sketch of a page design (fig. 2.2). This technique helps students visualize the final product.

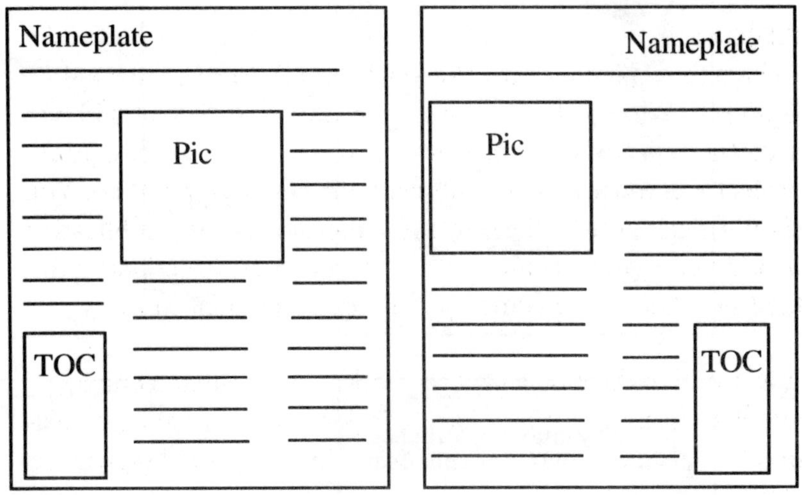

Fig. 2.2. Thumbnail sketches.

Organization

The visual and verbal elements of the design should be arranged in a pattern that captures the viewer's attention and directs it toward the relevant details. The manipulation of line and space are the designer's primary tools. The arrangement should be clear enough to attract and focus attention quickly. A configuration pattern is usually found in effective design. It may be established by the directional cues that are developed to guide the viewer to see details in proper sequence. Certain patterns guide the viewer's eye throughout the publication. The patterns of letters C, O, Z, I, L, and T, as seen in figure 2.3, are frequently used as underlying patterns in design.

Simplicity

Generally speaking, the fewer elements in the design, the more pleasing it is to the eye. Simplicity is the first rule of design (see fig. 2.4). Drawings should be bold, simple, and contain only key details. Picture symbols should be outlined. Use simple, easy-to-read lettering systems and a minimum of different type styles in the same visual or series of visuals (see fig. 2.5).

Fig. 2.3. From the top, left to right, the C, O, Z, I, L, and T patterns.

Keep it simple, student (KISS).

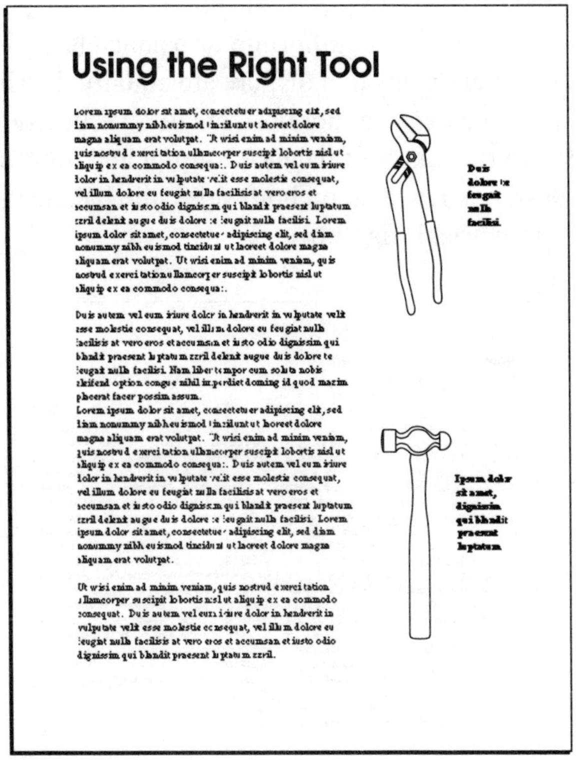

Fig. 2.4. "White space" around page elements.

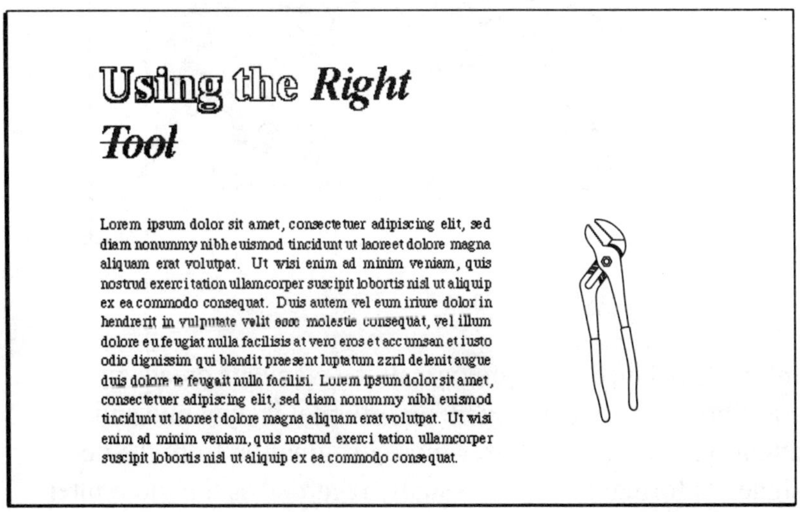

Fig. 2.5. Limit your type styles.

Balance

A psychological sense of equilibrium or balance is achieved when the design elements in a display are equally distributed on each side of the axis—either horizontally, vertically, or both. There are two kinds of balance: *formal* and *informal.* When the design is repeated on both sides, the balance is formal or symmetrical (fig. 2.6).

> Formal balance, if used too much, becomes monotonous.

Fig. 2.6. Formal balance.

Informal balance is asymmetrical; the elements create an equilibrium without being alike. Informal is dynamic and attention-getting. It requires more imagination from the designer. Informal balance is usually regarded as the more interesting choice (fig. 2.7).

There are an infinite number of possible designs in informal composition.

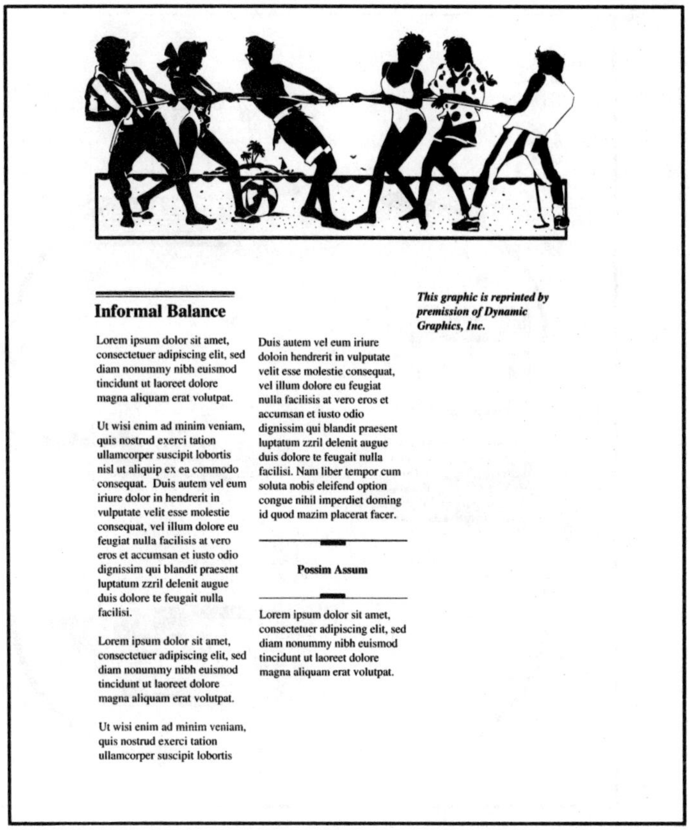

Informal Balance

Lorem ipsum dolor sit amet, consectetuer adipiscing elit, sed diam nonummy nibh euismod tincidunt ut laoreet dolore magna aliquam erat volutpat.

Ut wisi enim ad minim veniam, quis nostrud exerci tation ullamcorper suscipit lobortis nisl ut aliquip ex ea commodo consequat. Duis autem vel eum iriure dolor in hendrerit in vulputate velit esse molestie consequat, vel illum dolore eu feugiat nulla facilisis at vero eros et accumsan et iusto odio dignissim qui blandit praesent luptatum zzril delenit augue duis dolore te feugait nulla facilisi.

Lorem ipsum dolor sit amet, consectetuer adipiscing elit, sed diam nonummy nibh euismod tincidunt ut laoreet dolore magna aliquam erat volutpat.

Ut wisi enim ad minim veniam, quis nostrud exerci tation ullamcorper suscipit lobortis

Duis autem vel eum iriure doloin hendrerit in vulputate velit esse molestie consequat, vel illum dolore eu feugiat nulla facilisis at vero eros et accumsan et iusto odio dignissim qui blandit praesent luptatum zzril delenit augue duis dolore te feugait nulla facilisi. Nam liber tempor cum soluta nobis eleifend option congue nihil imperdiet doming id quod mazim placerat facer.

Possim Assum

Lorem ipsum dolor sit amet, consectetuer adipiscing elit, sed diam nonummy nibh euismod tincidunt ut laoreet dolore magna aliquam erat volutpat.

This graphic is reprinted by premission of Dynamic Graphics, Inc.

Fig. 2.7. Informal balance.

Unity

Unity is the relationship that exists among the elements of a visual. These elements function together to provide a single dominant visual to capture the reader's attention. Unity can be achieved by overlapping elements, by using pointing devices such as arrows, and by employing visual tools (lines, shape, color, texture, and space). The single dominant visual helps organize the reader's eye movement throughout the publication (fig. 2.8).

Emphasis

Through the use of size, relationships, perspective, lines, and such visual tools as color and space, emphasis can be given to the most important elements in the publication. Figures 2.9 and 2.10 show examples of emphasis.

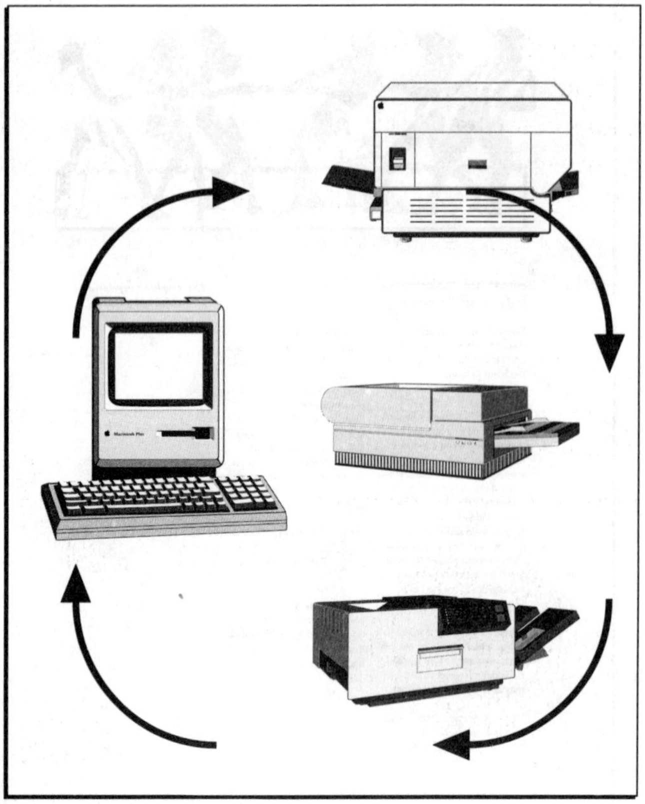

Fig. 2.8. Unity.

Visual tools such as line, shape, color, texture, and space help to unify a design.

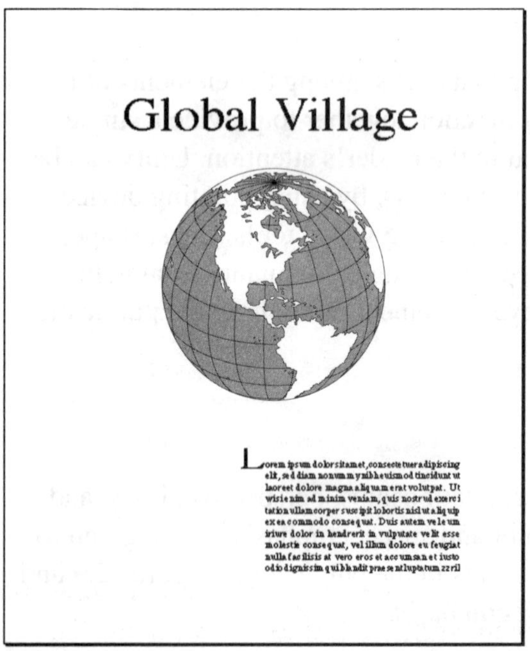

Fig. 2.9. Using size for emphasis.

Fig. 2.10. Using white space for emphasis.

Contrast

Any element that is different from those surrounding it will tend to stand out. The contrast or variation may be in terms of size, shape, color, or orientation. Contrast also refers to the relative amount of space devoted to text, artwork, and white space. You can create a high-impact publication with definite light and dark areas as well as lots of white space and illustrations. Figure 2.11 shows an example of contrast.

> Add visual contrast to your design to prevent monotony.

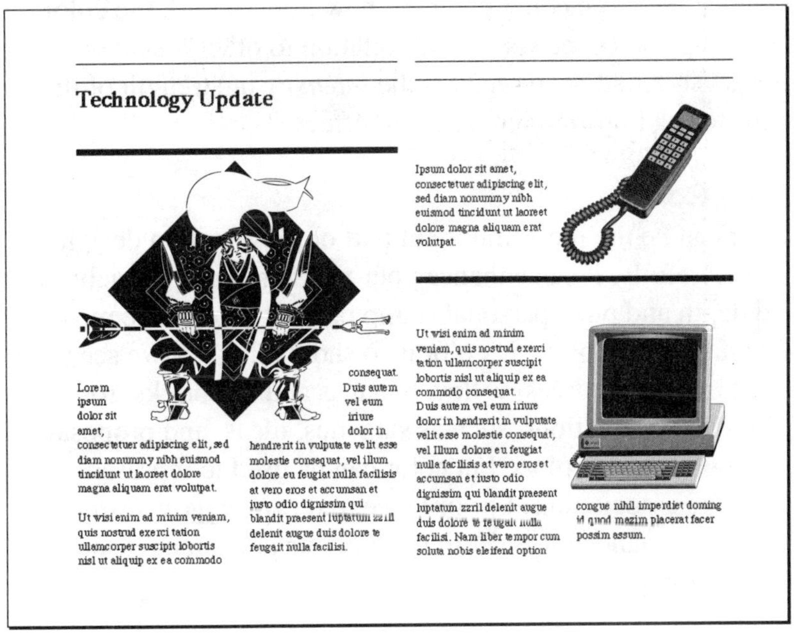

Technology Update

Lorem ipsum dolor sit amet, consectetuer adipiscing elit, sed diam nonummy nibh euismod tincidunt ut laoreet dolore magna aliquam erat volutpat.

Ut wisi enim ad minim veniam, quis nostrud exerci tation ullamcorper suscipit lobortis nisl ut aliquip ex ea commodo consequat. Duis autem vel eum iriure dolor in hendrerit in vulputate velit esse molestie consequat, vel illum dolore eu feugiat nulla facilisis at vero eros et accumsan et iusto odio dignissim qui blandit praesent luptatum zzril delenit augue duis dolore te feugait nulla facilisi.

Ipsum dolor sit amet, consectetuer adipiscing elit, sed diam nonummy nibh euismod tincidunt ut laoreet dolore magna aliquam erat volutpat.

Ut wisi enim ad minim veniam, quis nostrud exerci tation ullamcorper suscipit lobortis nisl ut aliquip ex ea commodo consequat. Duis autem vel eum iriure dolor in hendrerit in vulputate velit esse molestie consequat, vel Illum dolore eu feugiat nulla facilisis at vero eros et accumsan et iusto odio dignissim qui blandit praesent luptatum zzril delenit augue duis dolore te feugait nulla facilisi. Nam liber tempor cum soluta nobis eleifend option congue nihil imperdiet doming id quod mazim placerat facer possim assum.

Fig. 2.11. Contrast attracts attention.

Color

Color is an important adjunct to most visuals. Careful use of color plays an important role:

- To heighten the realism of the image by depicting its actual colors
- To point out similarities and differences and to highlight important emphasis
- To create a particular emotional response

Contemporary research in the psychology of motivation reveals that different colors stimulate more than the visual sense. They have "taste": Blue is sweet, orange is edible. They have "smell": Pink, lavender, yellow, and green smell best. Colors also have psychological connotations: Dark red and brown evoke masculine images of earth, wood, and leather; gold, silver, and black suggest the prestige and status associated with wealth.[1]

A highlight of color draws the eye immediately.

When selecting colors for visual materials, attention should be given to their elements. The *hue,* which is the specific color (red, blue, and so on), should be considered. Another element is the *value* of the color, meaning how light or dark the color should appear in the visual with relation to other visual elements. The final component is the *intensity* or strength of the color for its impact or coordinated effect.

Using Color

Color can be the most important part of presentation design. Used carefully, it can enhance your message, provide richness and depth and put a personal stamp on your work. The most obvious reason for using color is to show things as we see them in nature—green trees, yellow bananas and red bricks, for example. Abstractions, such as statistics, ideas, and proposals, have no intrinsic colors, but color can be used to represent symbolic associations. For instance, red can suggest warning, danger or financial loss. Following points are some reasons for using color.

- Advertisers try to establish associations of certain colors with consumer products, sports teams and such. You can apply the same logic by developing identifying color schemes for your presentation.
- Use color to distinguish between like and unlike elements. To clarify a flow chart, show file names in red and program names in blue. Color can distinguish elements or classes of information.
- Indicate the importance or progression of data by increasing the value and saturation level. Light-to-dark or gray-to-bright sequences are excellent ways to represent levels of importance. Use a chromatic or a rainbow series to show a graduated sequence.
- You can draw attention to elements in your presentation by choosing colors that are either brighter or lighter than the rest. Suppose you want to emphasize some of the

words in a list. On a dark-gray, blue or black back ground, use light yellow or cream as your main text color. For contrast, select full yellow (brighter) or white (lighter) as the emphasis color. Do not try to emphasize too much at once with several different colors; they may cancel each other out.

Color can set a mood; it can even evoke an era; it can be in or out of fashion.

- Be sensitive to cultural biases as well. Some people cannot accept pink as a serious color. That does not mean that pinks are not valid presentation colors. Pink is actually a serviceable color, but be aware of personal prejudices.
- The setting, the subject matter and the audience's previ ous experience can create certain expectations. Weigh all factors involved and decide whether audience expectation is reason enough to develop a color presentation.
- Don not sacrifice readability for pleasing color. Legibility takes precedence over all else in presentation materials, and poor color choices can interfere with it Colors do not perform the same way under all conditions: pure blue on dark grounds is extremely hard to read, but blue on white is fine. This isn't an opinion; it is a fact of human vision. Base your color choices on what works well for the audience rather than on personal taste.

The Color Wheel

Include color when you can identify exactly how it will help get your points across and tell your story. Make your colors serve your content.

You are probably familiar with the color wheel showing the range of colors and their relationships to each other. Primary and secondary colors alternate to form the circle. We are used to thinking of red, blue and yellow as the primary colors and green, orange and purple as the secondary colors. Complementary colors are ranged opposite each other on the color wheel. The three sets of complements each pair a primary with a secondary color. Figure 2.12 shows the color wheel.

In graphics, there are two methods of mixing colors. The first mixes colors of projected light—on your computer screen, for example. The second method mixes colors of pigment, like the ink on a printed page. The differences between the two methods make it very difficult to match what you see on the screen with "hard copy" printed on paper or film.

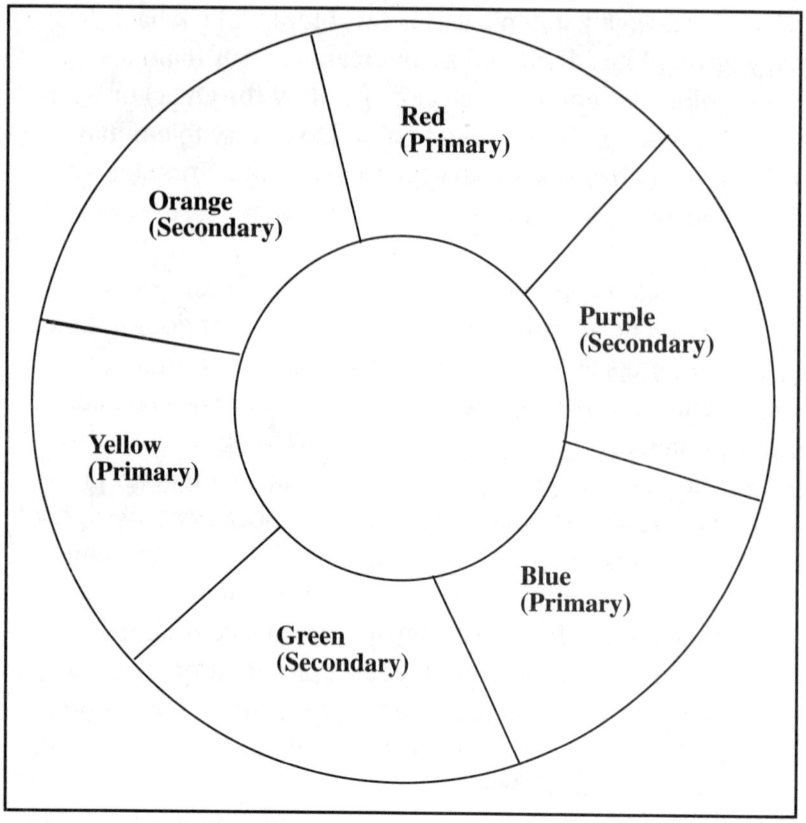

Figure 2.12. The color wheel.

Whether it is projected light or an opaque substance, a color can be described by its properties or qualities—its *hue, value* (or lightness) and *saturation*. Each color within the spectrum or around the color wheel is a hue (e.g., red or green). Value refers to the shade or the degree to which a color approaches black or white. Saturation is the intensity of a given hue.

Colors on Computer

The color you see on your computer screen is created by mixing red, green and blue (RGB) light. As more colors are added, the image approaches white; as colors are taken away, the image approaches black. The color receptors in our eyes are sensitive to the additive primaries; that is the way we perceive the light around us.

Computer color is mixed in RGB; pigment on paper or film is mixed in CYM (cyan, yellow, and magenta). If you make a color picture on screen and output it to paper, your system must translate the colors from additive to subtractive mode in order to move from colors of light to pigment colors. The translation can cause minor (or major) discrepancies between screen colors and output colors. Be prepared for this shift, first by identifying the degree to which it occurs on your particular setup, and second by choosing flexible palettes that do not depend too much on precision in order to work well. If your output is color film, you will probably notice less shift than if you are working on paper.

Color-on-Color

It is hard to predict how a given color will perform without considering its background and its neighbors. Black or white grounds are the easiest to start with, but most people want to graduate to more elaborate schemes early on. Following is some guidelines.

- Spectral neighbors are hues that sit side by side within the spectrum. Blue and green, red and orange, and yellow and green all hold hands in the rainbow. Use these pairs for shadowing or to suggest dimension.

  The contrast between spectral neighbors is low, so avoid these pairs when you need a distinct visual boundary between touching elements, such as type on a colored area or on wedges of a pie graph. Choose them for low-contrast situations and subtle effects.

- Colors opposite one another on the color wheel are very far apart visually and, if fully saturated, will actually appear to move or vibrate when placed side by side, a phenomenon that is especially noticeable when the colors touch. Sometimes complements even create glow or halo effects when they touch on film. If you must use comple ments as neighbors, reduce the saturation of one or both of the colors, or use a thin white or black outline to minimize the effect.

- A triad is a group of three primaries, three secondaries or any other set of three hues equally spaced around the color wheel. Triads have uniform visual distribution and are considered to be pleasing to the eye. Blue/red/yellow and orange/green/purple are triads.

- Contrasting colors differ markedly from one another—primarily in value. Black with white provides the greatest contrast. Being able to read text and small symbols depends on some degree of contrast between figure and ground. That is why most printed material is black on white. White on black is good for slides, but the white may be too bright for extended viewing. Colors can help alleviate eye fatigue.

  Hues with low values contrast well with white or light grounds; hues with high values contrast well with black; and some low-value and high-value hues work well together. For example, pure yellow reads fine on pure blue. However, the combination of cyan and orange does not work well because both are mid-value hues.

> The smaller a graphic element is, the more contrast is needed for readability. Small type is the best example. As type size increases, its contrast requirements decrease. Therefore, a large, bold line of type should generally be relatively low in contrast.

- Pure blue or black is a difficult combination to use successfully because of blue's position in the spectrum and the nature of human vision. When small graphic elements such as type, thin lines or intricate symbols are displayed in blue on black, the edges appear to be fuzzy. The human eye has a smaller member of blue receptors than red and green ones, and most of these receptors are distributed outside the focal point of the retina. For this reason, it is a good idea to avoid placing small blue elements on black.

- When a colored foreground element extends across several background colors, be aware of how each fore ground/background combination will perform. A straight line can seem to become thicker or thinner as it crosses color boundaries. Complex images with elaborate palettes can create color-oncolor problems.

Graduated Color

Graduated or ramped color is a special effect that allows one color to dissolve into another with no discernible break. Software products differ in regard to graduated color features. Some let the user specify two end colors; others add a color specification for the middle. Users sometimes choose the number of steps to use in creating the blend. With other systems, this is handled automatically by the software. Color can ramp horizontally, vertically or radially or in some other way, according to individual program features.

Graduated color is an appealing, easy way to lend depth to a picture. People are attracted to the impression of process, transition and motion associated with graduated color. Backgrounds that ramp from top to bottom suggest a horizon and the vault of the sky. Traditionally, colors have been tricky to blend by manual methods like airbrush, but computers are ideal for this purpose. Whenever you come upon an easy way to do what used to be difficult, it can seem like magic. In the excitement, you may forget your usual good judgment and go overboard. Color graduations can fall into this category.

One way to minimize the complications of graduated color is to make the graduation as subtle as possible. Fading from dark blue to black, for instance, is effective, and most foreground colors that read well on black also work well on blue. Spectral neighbors also make subtle blends; or try altering only the saturation or value of a single hue. Do not make life hard for yourself by trying to use wide ranges of hue, value or saturation.

Using Black and White

Since you will not always be working in color, it is good to be skilled at telling your story in black and white, too. Aside from a few technical considerations, the principles are much the same, whether your palette is monochrome or multicolor. Contrast, figure/ground definition and readability still top the list of design goals. Black and white means shades of gray as well. The illusion of gray is created with various black-and-white patterns. These patterns range from finely spaced dots to representational repeats of brick walls, with an infinite number of intermediate choices.

In commercial printing, ink density for a tint color is controlled by sandwiching a screen between the negative and printing plates. This screen stops light where the printer does not want ink to print, and lets light through where ink is desired. When a density of 50 percent is desired, the screen allows light through only half the image area and stops it from hitting the other half. The screen acts as a light stencil. Screen densities are determined by the percent of coverage; resolution is determined by the number of dots per inch— typically 85 to 150. Although this technology carve from the commercial printer's need to control ink coverage on paper, most desktop graphics programs incorporate some of these techniques for producing gray values on laser printer output.

Specifying screen densities is easy enough to do. Eighty percent is very dark, and 20 percent is light. If you need to use several shades of gray, do not use more than five values, including black, since people cannot easily read any more than that. Also, be aware that people do not see precisely a percent of density progression: 70 percent and 80 percent look almost the same, but 20 percent looks decidedly different from 30 percent. Figure 2.13 illustrates an example of shades of gray.

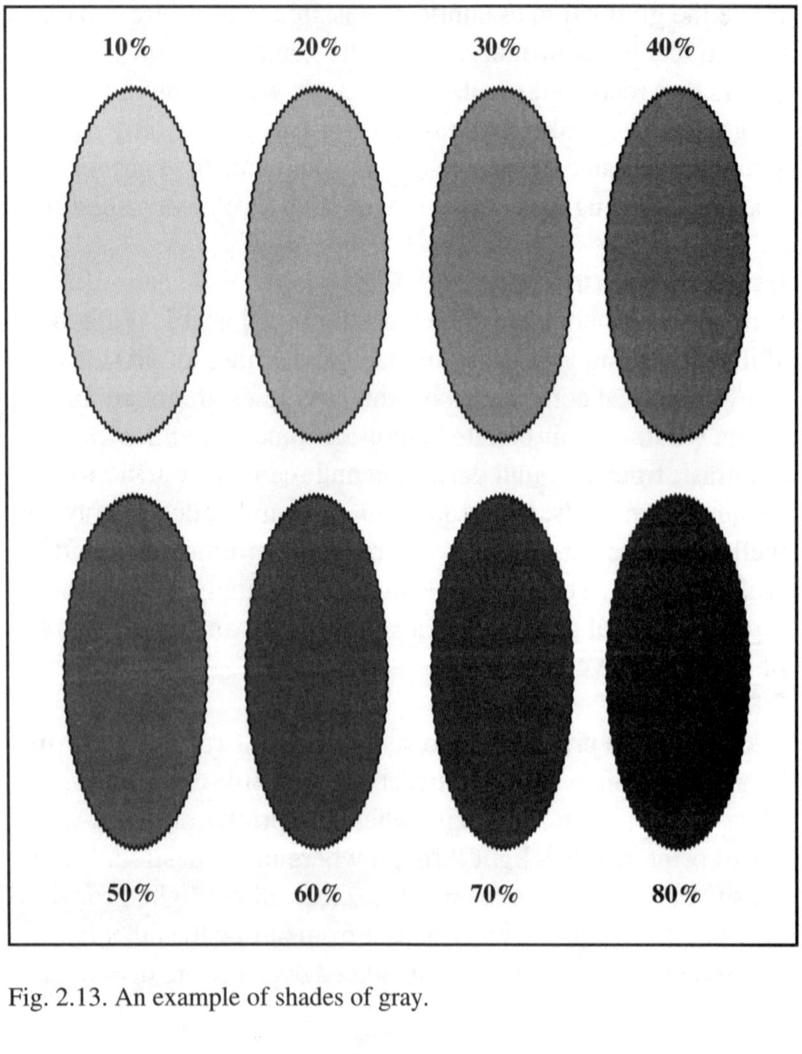

Fig. 2.13. An example of shades of gray.

Texture

Texture is a visual element that may serve as a replacement for the sense of touch. Texture can be used to give emphasis, to create separation, or to enhance unity (fig. 2.14).

Fig. 2.14.Texture enhances the image.

The feel for design is perhaps caught and not taught. Examine some of the graphic materials that are part of your everyday world—magazine advertisements, outdoor billboards, television titles and commercials, and so on. You can find many ideas for designing your own materials by studying the arrangement of elements in such commercial displays. Imitation and practice are the best ways to develop graphic design skills.

Notes

1. Robert Heinich. *Instructional Media and the New Technology of Instruction*. 2d ed. New York: John Wiley & Sons, 1985.

3

Typography

Type is nothing more than letters, and everybody has worked with letters most of his or her life. First we see typography in books, and perhaps packaging. Then advertising, brochures, parts lists, and manuals became part of our typographic experience. Today, typographic communication in the form of newsletters, annuals, reports, and proposals has been added to our typographic exposure.

As an educator, you probably have a sense for what looks good in type, what is easiest to read, and what is accomplished by the most effective graphic communication. You know when a B looks like a B and when it does not. You know that if a typewriter malfunctions and sets letters so close to each other that the letters begin to overlap, the end result will be difficult to read. Consciously or subconsciously, you have gained knowledge regarding typographic communication. Of course, being familiar with typographic communication from a reader's viewpoint does not make one a typographer. It is, however, a very important step in the right direction.

Type Style

Type style is the range of shapes and thicknesses within a typeface family. Type style makes it possible to create legible text in a quick and consistent manner and adds emphasis to the text as well. Letters may be changed and arranged to create an interesting and highly effective document. Using a variety of type styles often adds to the effectiveness of a publication. Words can be **bold**, *italic*, shadow, outline, underlined, and so on.

> Use bold for emphasis, not italic.

Type style can be modified to add contrast or emphasis to a publication. The various options, many available in QuarkXPress, are discussed in the following sections.

A typeface is the design for a family of characters and symbols that share a common style, such as Times or Avant Garde. A font is the specific size and variety of the actual letter or character in that family, for example, 12 point Times Bold or 10 point Avant Garde Italic.

Type Weights

Weight refers to the thickness of the lines that make up letters and varies from light to heavy or even black (fig. 3.1). Although a single typeface may exist in a variety of weights, no typeface currently offers every weight, and weights are not consistent from one typeface to another.

Type Style	Thin
Type Style	Light
Type Style	Book
Type Style	**Bold**
Type Style	**Extra bold**
Type Style	**Heavy**
Type Style	**Black**

Fig. 3.1. Different type weights.

Oblique

Oblique type is a slanted version of a roman typeface. The letters maintain their original forms except for the slant (fig. 3.2). This style is useful for emphasizing a word or passage.

Plain style

Oblique normal

Oblique bold

Fig. 3.2. Oblique type.

Italic

Italic letters have a different shape from oblique. This style is designed with letters that slant toward the right. The type is not only slanted, but also made scriptlike, or cursive (fig. 3.3). This is true for many serifed typefaces such as Times.

Plain style

Italic normal

Italic bold

Fig. 3.3. Italic type.

Outline

Outline is used to add emphasis to a passage of type. Outline is most often used for headlines or situations requiring large type sizes. It is generally less effective and muddier in smaller sizes (fig. 3.4).

> Outline or Shadow type styles are ornamental fonts. If you do use them, do it for a few short words that stand alone on the page, such as a headline or logo.

Outline 12 points

Outline 18 Points

Outline 24 Points

Fig. 3.4. Outline type.

Underline

Like outline, underlining is used to add emphasis (fig. 3.5). Underlined type is often used in newsletters and newspapers for denoting the title of a novel or other creative work.

> Do not underline unless there is a very specific need for it. Underlining is a throwback to the typewriter and lends an unprofessional look to your document.

Plain underline

Bold underline

Outline underline

Fig. 3.5. Underlined type.

Strikethrough

Strikethrough is a type style that draws a line through the text (fig. 3.6). This type style is used to indicate that text meaning, as in a legal contract, has been deleted from the paragraph.

> Too many typefaces and styles on the same page can turn your document into a ransom note.

~~Strikethrough~~

Fig. 3.6. Strikethrough type style.

Reverse Type

Reverse type is white letters on a black, dark, or color background (fig. 3.7). This type style is very useful for headlines or short sentences set in large, sans serif, upper- and lowercase type.

Reverse type

Fig. 3.7. Reverse type on black background.

Shadow Type

Shadow type is just what its name implies: Each letter has "shadow" lines (fig. 3.8). Shadow type tends to vary in quality depending on the size of the font; larger type sizes generally look better.

Shadow Type

Fig. 3.8. Shadow type.

Screened Type

To "screen" type is to replace its otherwise black form with a series of very small dots. The actual *number* of dots within each square inch of a screen remains constant no matter how light or dark the screen appears. The *size* of the dots is what determines the shade of the screen. Therefore, the percentage by which a screen is measured is equal to the amount of space covered by dots. A 0% screen produces completely white type, and a 100% screen produces completely black type. A 10% screen prints so lightly from imagesetters that it is nearly invisible. Figure 3.9 shows different shades of gray.

10% Screened type

20% Screened type

40% Screened type

60% Screened type

80% Screened type

Fig. 3.9. Different screened type.

> Screened types often work best when your publication is produced on a high-resolution phototypesetter.

Rotated Type

Type could be rotated at progressively steeper angles, starting at 0° (no rotation) and ending at 90° counterclockwise (fig. 3.10). Type also can be rotated clockwise beginning at 0° and continuing to 90°.

Clockwise rotation

Clockwise rotation

Clockwise rotation

Clockwise rotation

Clockwise rotation

Clockwise rotation

Clockwise rotation

Counterclockwise rotation

Counterclockwise rotation

Counterclockwise rotation

Counterclockwise rotation

Counterclockwise rotation

Counterclockwise rotation

Fig. 3.10. Rotated type.

Reflected Type

Most drawing programs allow you to reflect type (fig. 3.11). Reflecting type horizontally produces a standard mirror image. Reflecting type vertically produces an upside-down mirror image. When reflected both horizontally and vertically, the reflection is upside-down but otherwise normal.

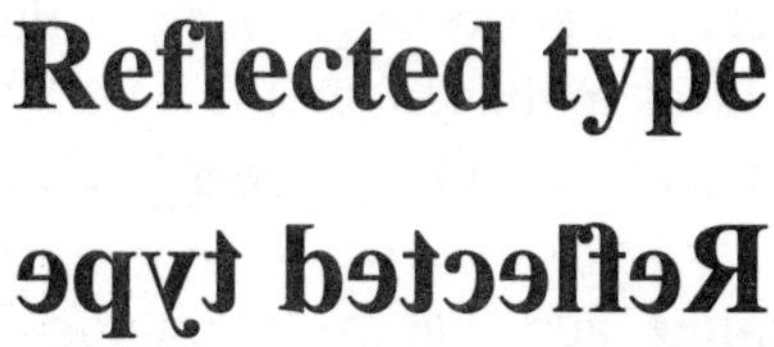

Fig. 3.11. Reflected type.

> Use decorative types for situations in which type is more ornamental than informational.

Projected Type

Projection is a special effect that adds emphasis to the text. Projected type can go in six directions (fig. 3.12). It is possible to make streamers progress in any direction.

Fig. 3.12. Projected type.

Special Effects

For many typefaces, a variety of stylistic alterations exist as separate fonts. Some of these special effect type styles such as thin outline and fat outline are available through the typeface (fig. 3.13). Others can be created by high-end drawing programs.

Fig. 3.13. Special effects type styles.

Additional Type Considerations

Typeface

Since the invention of movable type nearly 500 years ago until recently, about 20 different typefaces were available. The advent of computers and desktop publishing added more than 100 different typefaces to the list, and it is still growing. A typeface is classified as *serif* or *sans serif.*

The serif, or cross-line, added at the beginning and end of a stroke probably dates from early Rome. The serif was either a way to get a clean cut at the end of a chiseled stroke or an imitation of brush-written letter forms. The serif first appeared in ancient Roman monuments, where the letters were chiseled in stone. Later on, serifs appeared in the handwritten manuscripts prepared with quill pens by medieval scribes. Serif, or roman, typefaces are useful in text because the serifs help distinguish individual letters and provide continuity for the reader's eye. Figure 3.14 shows examples of serif typefaces.

Avoid combining two serif or two sans serif fonts on the same page.

M	M	M	M
Times	**Bookman**	**New Century School - book**	**Palatino**

Fig. 3.14. Serif typefaces.

In French sans means "without." Sans serif typefaces have no serifs. In sans serif typefaces the strokes of the letters are usually of nearly even thickness, which tends to give them a very austere, mechanical appearance. This even, mechanical look works against sans serif faces when they are used in text applications. Their uniform strokes tend to melt together before the human eye.

Sans serif typefaces are most useful in large point sizes—in newspaper headlines, book titles, advertisements, and chapter headings—or in small bursts that are designed to contrast with surrounding serif type. Sans serif type is typically used for signs because of the simplicity of its letter forms and because it does not seem to taper at a distance. These same characteristics make sans serif type useful for highlighting amid serif type, especially in listing, directory, and catalog formats. Figure 3.15 shows examples of sans serif typefaces.

M	M	M	M
Avant Garde	Helvetica	LITHOS	Franklin Gothic

Fig. 3.15. Sans serif typefaces.

Leading

Leading, or line spacing, is used to improve the appearance and readability of your publication. Leading (pronounced *ledding*) originally referred to the practice of placing small strips of lead between lines of type to make a page more readable. Although the job is no longer done with actual lead, the purpose and process are basically the same. Leading for lines of type specifies the distance from the baseline of one line to the baseline of the next line. It is usually at least the height of the font to prevent the bottoms of the letters on the top line from printing over the tops of the letters on the bottom line.

> Use minimal leading for short lines of text and increase the leading as the line length increases.

For smaller sizes of type, line spacing is often set one or two points (approximately 20%) greater than the type size to increase legibility. For example, if the type size is 12 points, the recommended leading is 14 points and usually is shown as 12/14 (12-point type with 14-point leading). Figure 3.16 demonstrates the same typeface and type size with different leading.

It flew from a green and sunny valley into a limpid blue sky. With its flight, the depth of the wet valley with its sleepy wildflowers and roar of water falling was gradually erased from its memory. The heat and the brightness of the sun penetrated its colorful wings, making them naked numb.

It flew from a green and sunny valley into a limpid blue sky. With its flight, the depth of the wet valley with its sleepy wildflowers and roar of water falling was gradually erased from its memory. The heat and the brightness of the sun penetrated its colorful wings, making them naked numb.

Fig. 3.16. Different leadings result in different effects for the same typeface and the same type size.

Too much space between certain letters can reduce the readability of a word.

Headlines, on the other hand, improve in appearance and readability when leading is reduced. Leading should make your headline appear as a unit.

Leading that is too spacious makes the reader's eyes wander at the end of one line trying to find the beginning of the next line. Closed leading can be used as a design tool. Sometimes you might want to tighten leading so that descenders from one line of type touch the ascenders from the line below. Figure 3.17 shows tight leading.

Educator's Handbook
to Desktop Publishing

Educator's Handbook
to Desktop Publishing

Fig. 3.17. Tight leading improves the appearance of the type.

Most software packages offer automatic leading, whereas some packages, such as QuarkXPress, in addition to "auto leading" allow manual leading.

Word Spacing

Word spacing refers to the amount of space between words in a line of type. When words are closer together, more words can be included on each line. Word spacing increases or decreases the density of type. In certain situations, that also can reduce the number of hyphenated words. If you reduce word spacing too much, however, the text becomes difficult to read. In figure 3.18 different word spacing is shown.

Desktop publishing helps students

Desktop publishing helps students

Desktop publishing helps students

Desktop publishing helps students

Fig. 3.18. Different word spacing creates different effects.

Paragraph Spacing

Adding space between paragraphs enhances readability and makes each paragraph more like a self-contained unit. Paragraph spacing can be adjusted in many software packages. Figure 3.19 shows different spacing between paragraphs.

> Adding space between paragraphs makes it easier for the reader to find the next paragraph and creates a sense of openness on the page.

The butterfly, in the heart of the pure blue sky, heard the roar of the green valley's waterfall and its hunger for sleep on an unknown wild-flower was making its wings numb and heavy.

The valley, with its towering waterfall and flower-strewn cliffs, grew small beneath its wings. It felt the heavy load of the water's spray, carried by the gay breeze, on its wing. It saw the world like a green and swelling wave.

The butterfly, in the heart of the pure blue sky, heard the roar of the green valley's waterfall and its hunger for sleep on an unknown wild-flower was making its wings numb and heavy.

The valley, with its towering waterfall and flower-strewn cliffs, grew small beneath its wings. It felt the heavy load of the water's spray, carried by the gay breeze, on its wing. It saw the world like a green and swelling wave.

Fig. 3.19. Paragraph spacing enhances readability.

Text Alignment

Text alignment determines how lines of text are placed between the right and left margins. Lines can be flush left (aligned on the left and ragged on the right), flush right (aligned on the right and ragged on the left), justified (aligned on both the left and the right), or centered. Figure 3.20 shows different text alignment. This book uses flush left/ragged right text.

Flush-left alignment with a ragged right edge provides an "open," informal feeling.

The butterfly, in the heart of
the pure blue sky, heard the
roar of the green valley's
waterfall and its hunger for
sleep on an unknown
wildflower was making its
wings numb and heavy.

The butterfly, in the heart of
the pure blue sky, heard the
roar of the green valley's
waterfall and its hunger for
sleep on an unknown
wildflower was making its
wings numb and heavy.

The butterfly, in the heart of
the pure blue sky, heard the
roar of the green valley's wa-
terfall and its hunger for sleep
on an unknown wildflower was
making its wings numb and
heavy.

The butterfly, in the heart of
the pure blue sky, heard the
roar of the green valley's
waterfall and its hunger for
sleep on an unknown
wildflower was making its
wings numb and heavy.

Fig. 3.20. Flush left, flush right, justified, and centered text.

Often text is organized flush left. This style creates an informal, contemporary, and open publication where each word is separated by equal space. Hyphenation is kept to a minimum. Western readers normally read from left to right; therefore, flush right/ragged left should be used cautiously. When flush right/ragged left is used, readers tend to slow their reading speed and spend more time identifying words by putting together individual letters.

Justified type, or flush left/flush right, because the text is forced together to fit in a line, is considered more difficult to read. Also, justified text contains more hyphenated words. Centered text is useful for short headlines. If a centered headline is more than three or four lines, however, readers have to search for the beginning of each line.

Because justified columns are uniform in length, they can "darken" a page by eliminating the white space surrounding the ragged edges of text.

Text does not always have to be presented in either justified or ragged right blocks. Often, it is desirable to "wrap" copy around the contours of a graphic (fig. 3.21).

The butterfly, in the heart of the pure blue sky, heard the roar of the green valley's waterfall and its hunger for sleep on an unknown wildflower was making its wings numb and heavy. The valley, with its towering waterfall and flower-strewn cliffs, grew small beneath its wings. It felt the heavy load of the water's spray, carried by the gay breeze, on its wing. It saw the world like a green and swelling wave.

Fig. 3.21. Text wrapped around a graphic.

Indention

An indent is the amount of space a given line or paragraph is inset from the normal margin of a paragraph or from the column guides. Software packages offer automatic and manual indent options. Indention enhances readability—especially when there is a large number of consecutive paragraphs on a page. The first line of a paragraph can have an *indent* or *outdent*. First-line indent is the most common. In this style, the first line of each paragraph is indented from the left margin (fig. 3.22).

Wide columns with large type usually require deeper indents than narrow columns with smaller type.

The butterfly, in the heart of the pure blue sky, heard the roar of the green valley's waterfall and its hunger for sleep on an unknown wildflower was making its wings numb and heavy.

The valley, with its towering waterfall and flower-strewn cliffs, grew small beneath its wings. It felt the heavy load of the water's spray, carried by the gay breeze, on its wing. It saw the world like a green and swelling wave.

Fig. 3.22. A first-line indent.

Hanging indent, or outdenting the first line, is the opposite of the first-line indent. In this style, the first line in a paragraph is at the left margin and the rest of lines in the paragraph are indented from the left margin. Hanging indents are useful in bibliographical references and directory listings—the telephone book and a yearbook are typical examples (fig. 3.23).

Azarmsa, Reza. *Desktop Publishing with QuarkXPress for Windows.* Needham Height, MA: Allyn & Bacon, 1996.

Azarmsa, Reza. *Desktop Publishing with PageMaker for Windows.* Needham Height, MA: Allyn & Bacon, 1996.

Fig. 3.23. Outdents.

Tabs

Tabs are used to align text at a particular location on the page, allowing great flexibility in formatting text. Most desktop publishing packages, including QuarkXPress, space words and letters proportionally. Therefore, it is recommended to use tabs rather than spaces to align text; otherwise, the printed text will be uneven. Tabs are especially useful in creating tables and columns (fig. 3.24).

Tabs should be proportionated to column widths.

List of Some of the Materials That Can Be Produced Using DTP

books	brochures	bulletins
calendars	catalogs	certificates
charts	cover sheets	curriculum materials
diplomas	directories	documentation
flow charts	flyers	graphs
greeting cards	indexes	instructional materials
letterhead stationery	magazines	manuals
maps	memos	menus
nametags	newsletters	newspapers
notices	pamphlets	poetry
posters	presentations	press releases
programs	proposals	prospectuses
résumés	schedules	signs
slides	statements	tabloids
testing materials	title pages	visual aids

Fig. 3.24. Tabs are used to create this table.

Line Length

The length of a line of text, also known as the *column width*, can affect readability and the overall look of a publication. The line length can be as narrow as one letter or as wide as the boundaries of the paper. If a line of text is too long, a reader may become weary. If a line is too short, the text may give a choppy appearance and may be difficult to read.

A good rule of thumb is to relate line length to type size: The bigger the type size, the longer the line length can be. An appropriate line length enhances the appearance of the publication and increases its readability. A good-sized line, depending upon the type of document, should be from 8 to 15 words long. Figure 3.25 shows different line lengths.

> Compared to the rest of the page, type size should always be proportionate to the importance of your message and the amount of white space available.

The butterfly, in the heart of
the pure blue sky, heard the
roar of the green valley's
waterfall and its hunger for
sleep on an unknown wild-
flower was making its wings
numb and heavy.

The butterfly, in the heart of the pure blue sky, heard
the roar of the green valley's waterfall and its hunger
for sleep on an unknown wildflower was making its
wings numb and heavy.

Fig. 3.25. The longer the line length, the larger the type should be.

Hyphenation

Hyphenation is the placing of a hyphen into a word so the word can be broken between two lines of text. Hyphenation can improve the appearance of your publication by helping you avoid particularly unequal line lengths in flush left/ragged right text and unsightly word spacing in justified text (fig. 3.26). Hyphenation is an area of trade-offs. A break in the middle of a

The butterfly, in the
heart of the pure blue
sky, heard the roar of
the green valley's wa-
terfall and its hunger
for sleep on an un-
known wildflower was
making its wings numb
and heavy. The valley,
with its towering wa-
terfall and flower-strewn
cliffs, grew small be-
neath its wings.

The butterfly, in the heart
of the pure blue sky, heard
the roar of the green
valley's waterfall and its
hunger for sleep on an
unknown wildflower was
making its wings numb
and heavy. The valley,
with its towering waterfall
and flower-strewn cliffs,
grew small beneath its
wings.

Fig. 3.26. Hyphenation in justified text (left) compared to ragged-right text (right).

word slows down reading. Desktop publishing programs offer different hyphenation options. You can have the program hyphenate the entire publication automatically or you can turn off the automatic hyphenation and hyphenate your document manually.

Drop Capital

An enlarged first character at the beginning of a paragraph that extends (drops) into the following lines of text is known as a drop capital. A drop capital breaks up large blocks of text. Typically, drop capitals are used to begin a chapter or section in a book or magazine. Drop capitals provide an important visual transition between the headline and body copy (fig. 3.27).

> The drop capital is a simple, yet powerful tool for grabbing the reader's attention.

The butterfly, in the heart of the pure blue sky, heard the roar of the green valley's waterfall and its hunger for sleep on an unknown wildflower was making its wings numb and heavy. The valley, with its towering waterfall and flower-strewn cliffs, grew small beneath its wings.

Fig. 3.27. A drop capital adds visual effect to a block of text.

Drop capitals can have the same or different character attributes, such as font, size, and style, as the rest of the text in the paragraph. Figure 3.28 shows a drop capital of different font and style.

The butterfly, in the heart of the pure blue sky, heard the roar of the green valley's waterfall and its hunger for sleep on an unknown wildflower was making its wings numb and heavy. The valley, with its towering waterfall and flower-strewn cliffs, grew small beneath its wings.

Fig. 3.28. A drop capital of different font and style.

Stick-Up Capital

An enlarged initial letter that extends above the body text is called a stick-up capital (fig. 3.29). A stick-up capital is used as a graphic element to draw attention to the beginning of a story or chapter.

The butterfly, in the heart of the pure blue sky, heard the roar of the green valley's waterfall and its hunger for sleep on an unknown wildflower was making its wings numb and heavy. The valley, with its towering waterfall and flower-strewn cliffs, grew small beneath its wings.

Fig. 3.29. A stick-up capital.

Type Size

The type size of a letter (also called height or point size) is measured by its vertical height, in points. One point is equal to one-twelfth of a pica, which in turn is almost exactly one-sixth of an inch. Therefore, there are 72 points per inch. Figure 3.30 illustrates the type size anatomy.

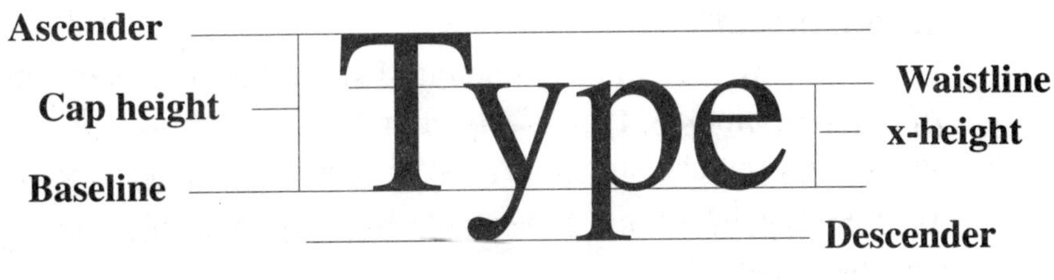

Fig. 3.30. Type size anatomy.

Small type floating in an ocean of white space is lost to the reader's attention. Large type crammed into a small or tight space becomes too imbalanced and difficult to read.

Point is normally abbreviated "pt." For example, 72-pt. type would measure 72 points from the top of its ascender to the bottom of its descender. This means that x-heights, as well as ascenders and descenders, will vary in size for different fonts even though their point sizes are the same. Except for f, j, l, and t, the body of lowercase letters rises to the x-height. Figure 3.31 examines different type sizes.

12 Points
14 Points
18 Points
24 Points
30 Points
48 Points
60 Points
72 Points

Fig. 3.31. Type size (points).

Letterspacing

Letterspacing refers to the amount of space between each letter of a line or block of type. Each letter consists not only of the letter itself but also a tiny amount of space before and after the letter called the left-side and right-side bearing.

> Reducing the space between letter pairs, or kerning, can improve the clarity and readability of a given word or group of words.

In general, it is desirable to keep the letterspacing range to a minimum, as wide spacing fluctuations give an uneven look to the page. Also, larger typefaces call for tighter letterspacing (fig. 3.32). Some software packages allow you to control the letterspacing.

Letterspacing
Letterspacing
Letterspacing

Fig. 3.32. Letterspacing.

Kerning

Kerning means the adjustment of space between pairs of characters to create visually even text that is easy to read. Most of the popular desktop publishing programs are capable of adding or subtracting space between characters in minuscule increments. Certain pairs of letters appear to be separated by too much space. According to the Adobe type catalog *Font & Function,* (fall 1989), the table below shows the pairs that have a hard time "getting along" (fig. 3.33).

Kerning can help balance the space between pairs of characters.

AO	**Aw**	**TA**	**Ve**	**YA**	**ex**	**wa**
AT	**FA**	**Ta**	**Vo**	**Ya**	**ey**	**we**
AV	**Ka**	**Te**	**Vu**	**Ye**	**ov**	**wo**
AW	**Ke**	**To**	**Vy**	**Yo**	**ow**	**xc**
AY	**Ko**	**Tr**	**WA**	**Yu**	**ox**	**xe**
Ac	**LY**	**Tu**	**Wa**	**av**	**oy**	**xo**
Ad	**Ly**	**Tv**	**We**	**aw**	**rw**	**ya**
Ae	**OV**	**Tw**	**Wo**	**ay**	**ry**	**yc**
Ao	**OW**	**Ty**	**Wr**	**ev**	**va**	**yr**
Au	**OX**	**VA**	**Wu**	**ew**	**vo**	**yo**
Av	**PA**	**Va**	**Wy**			

Fig. 3.33. Kerning table.

Too much word spacing breaks the line into separate elements, inhibiting reading. It also creates gaps within columns. When word spacing is greater than line spacing, reading is difficult because the eye tends to move from top to bottom instead of from left to right. Spacing between words also affects your type's appearance. Kern word spaces in harmony with letterspaces to create evenness and balance within a line or block of type.

Whether the typeface is extended or condensed, serif or sans serif, thoughtful kerning can make all the difference in the world. But if you apply the same kerning values to two different styles of type, you could see vastly different results. For example, condensed faces become even harder to read when kerned tightly, whereas extended faces, because they are naturally more open and more readable, can be kerned closer together. Figure 3.34 shows examples of kerning for the Times Roman and Avant Garde fonts.

ANYWAY Normal Times Roman

ANYWAY Kerned Times Roman

ANYWAY Normal Avant Garde

ANYWAY Kerned Avant Garde

Fig. 3.34. Kerned text in Times Roman and Avant Garde.

A Few Simple Rules

Once you know the basic typographic rules and have had a little firsthand experience with preparing simple typographic communication, it becomes relatively easy to produce a variety of documents.

Think of italics as a sort of typographic windshield wipers. They serve a very important function when it is appropriate to use them, but they can be very distracting if used all the time.

Use just one font family per job the first few times. Set the main body of copy in the 10- or 12-point size of the basic weight of the typeface. Add emphasis with bold, and set off main titles by using boldface that is a point size or two larger. When you feel the need to expriment a little, try mixing Helvetica and Times Roman in a single document. Use Times Roman for the main text (because it produces more readable copy), and continue to add emphasis with Times Roman bold. Try Helvetica for the section headings, titles, and/or subheads.

A surprising amount of beautiful and efficient communication can be created with just your printer's core fonts. More than 80% of all printed communication is set with just these two typefaces, and this includes lots of very creative and sophisticated graphic design work.

Type is a tool. Learn to use it, and a variety of typographic communications capabilities are opened up for you. With current technology you or your students can create documents that communicate attractively and efficiently.

4

Publication Organizers

The major purpose of publication organizers is to organize the publication, guide readers throughout the publication, enhance the effect of the publication, assist readers in quickly locating desired information, and place emphasis on the main idea of the publication.

Grids

A series of nonprinting vertical and horizontal lines used to determine placement of text and graphics on the page is referred to as a grid (see fig. 4.1).

> Grids divide your page into smaller, digestible sections that enable your reader to move more easily from point to point.

Fig. 4.1. A grid is a series of nonprinting horizontal and vertical lines.

The grid specifies such design elements as:

- Number and size of columns per page
- Space between columns
- Placement of headlines
- Placement and size of photographs and illustrations
- Size of bottom, top, and side margins

In other words, a grid accounts for every element of design and layout. It determines, for example, whether you can go beyond column boundaries to run a photo into a margin or even "bleed" the photo. The grid is the design and layout foundation on which the publication is built. Without a grid the publication may look unplanned (fig. 4.2). Once you have a grid, putting pages together becomes a logical, planned process.

A "bleed" is any photo or illustration that runs off the edge of the page.

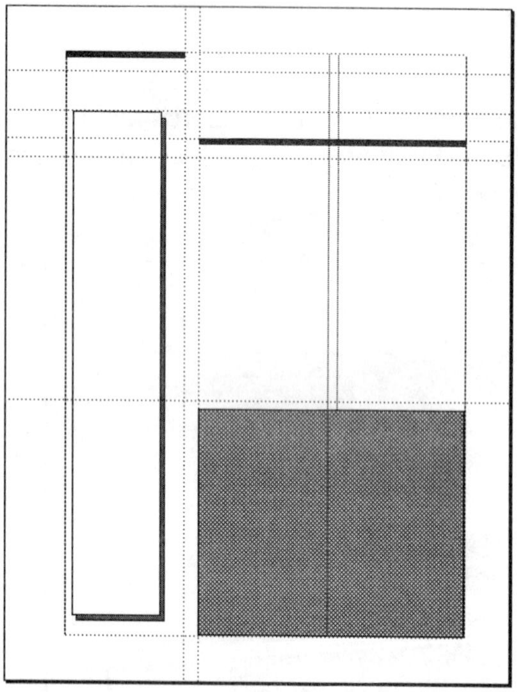

Fig. 4.2. A grid helps the consistency of a publication.

A well-constructed grid can make a lot of decisions for you, such as where to place the headlines, text, and art and how to handle the many details that inevitably turn up. A grid gives a publication a planned, cohesive look and helps ensure consistency from one page to the next. It also sets visual ground rules that everyone involved in putting together the publication can follow. This is especially important in designing a group project at schools such as a newsletter or a yearbook.

Most desktop publishing packages have the capability to create customized grids. They also offer predesigned grids (templates) that can be modified as needed.

The Page Anatomy

A printed page consists of many elements arranged so the page attracts readers and assists readers in easily picking up the main ideas. The printed page has a vocabulary that enables editors, designers, layout artists, and printers to communicate clearly. You may not see all of the page elements on one page, but each page will have some of them (fig. 4.3a, fig. 4.3b).

Columns

Text in newsletters and newspapers usually is arranged in one or more columns. Certain rules determine the placement, width, and number of columns, and columns can be set in different formats.

Columns form the foundation of your pages.

Generally, column format and width should be chosen according to functional needs. Newspaper stories, which are meant to be read quickly, are set in narrow columns. There is not much demand for left-to right eye movement: The reader's eye moves rapidly down the columns. By contrast, the type in a novel is usually set in one large column on the page: It is more relaxing to read a single column of text than to read many short lines. However, if a line of text is very wide and the eye has to travel too far, reading will be tiring and slow.

Normally, five-column format is used for classified ads; three- or four-column format is used for newspaper or newsy-look publications; two- or three-column format is used for magazines; and one-column format (occasionally two or three) is used for newsletters, reports, and papers.

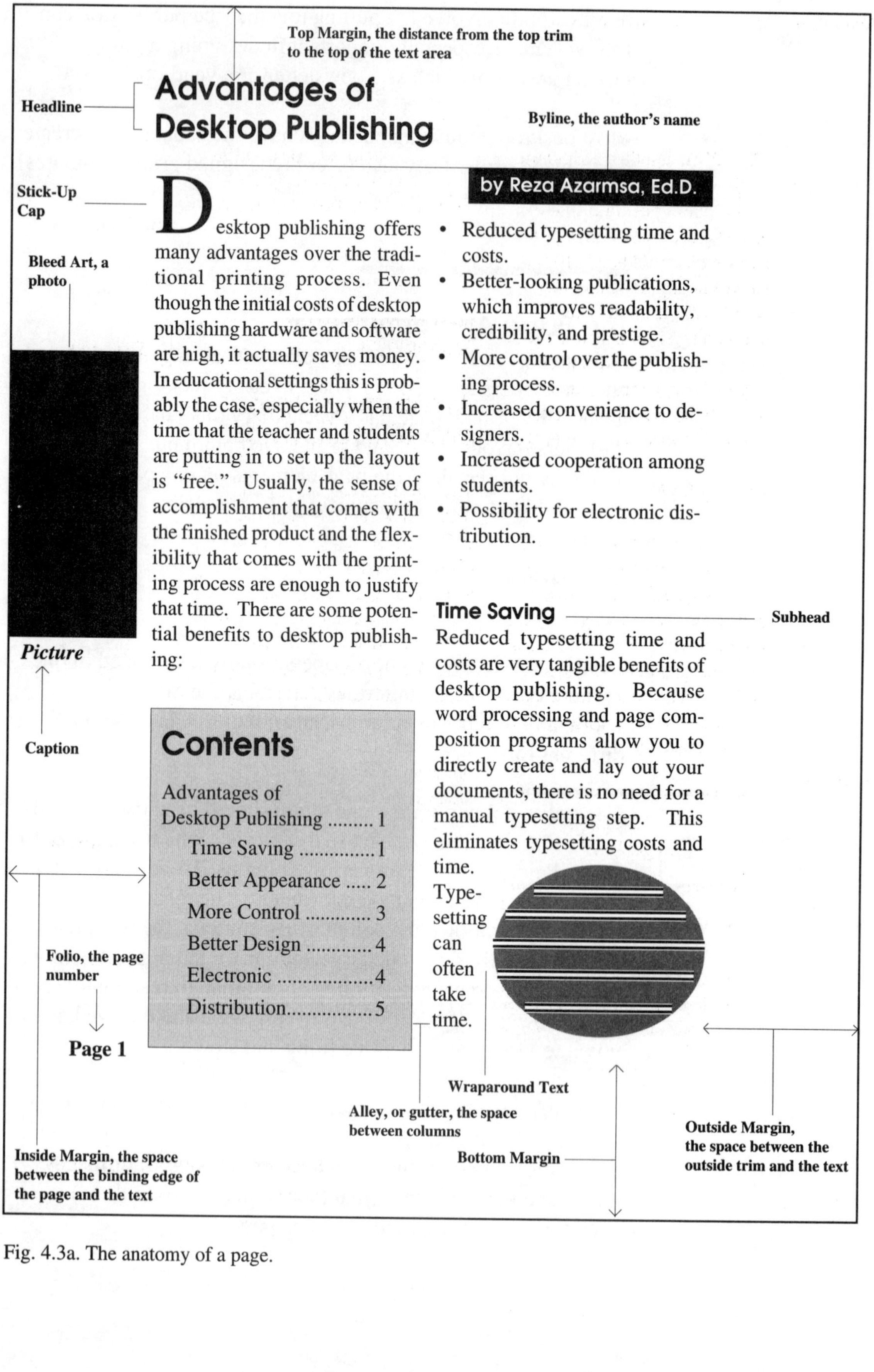

Advantages of Desktop Publishing

by Reza Azarmsa, Ed.D.

Desktop publishing offers many advantages over the traditional printing process. Even though the initial costs of desktop publishing hardware and software are high, it actually saves money. In educational settings this is probably the case, especially when the time that the teacher and students are putting in to set up the layout is "free." Usually, the sense of accomplishment that comes with the finished product and the flexibility that comes with the printing process are enough to justify that time. There are some potential benefits to desktop publishing:

- Reduced typesetting time and costs.
- Better-looking publications, which improves readability, credibility, and prestige.
- More control over the publishing process.
- Increased convenience to designers.
- Increased cooperation among students.
- Possibility for electronic distribution.

Time Saving

Reduced typesetting time and costs are very tangible benefits of desktop publishing. Because word processing and page composition programs allow you to directly create and lay out your documents, there is no need for a manual typesetting step. This eliminates typesetting costs and time. Typesetting can often take time.

Picture

Contents

Page 1

Fig. 4.3a. The anatomy of a page.

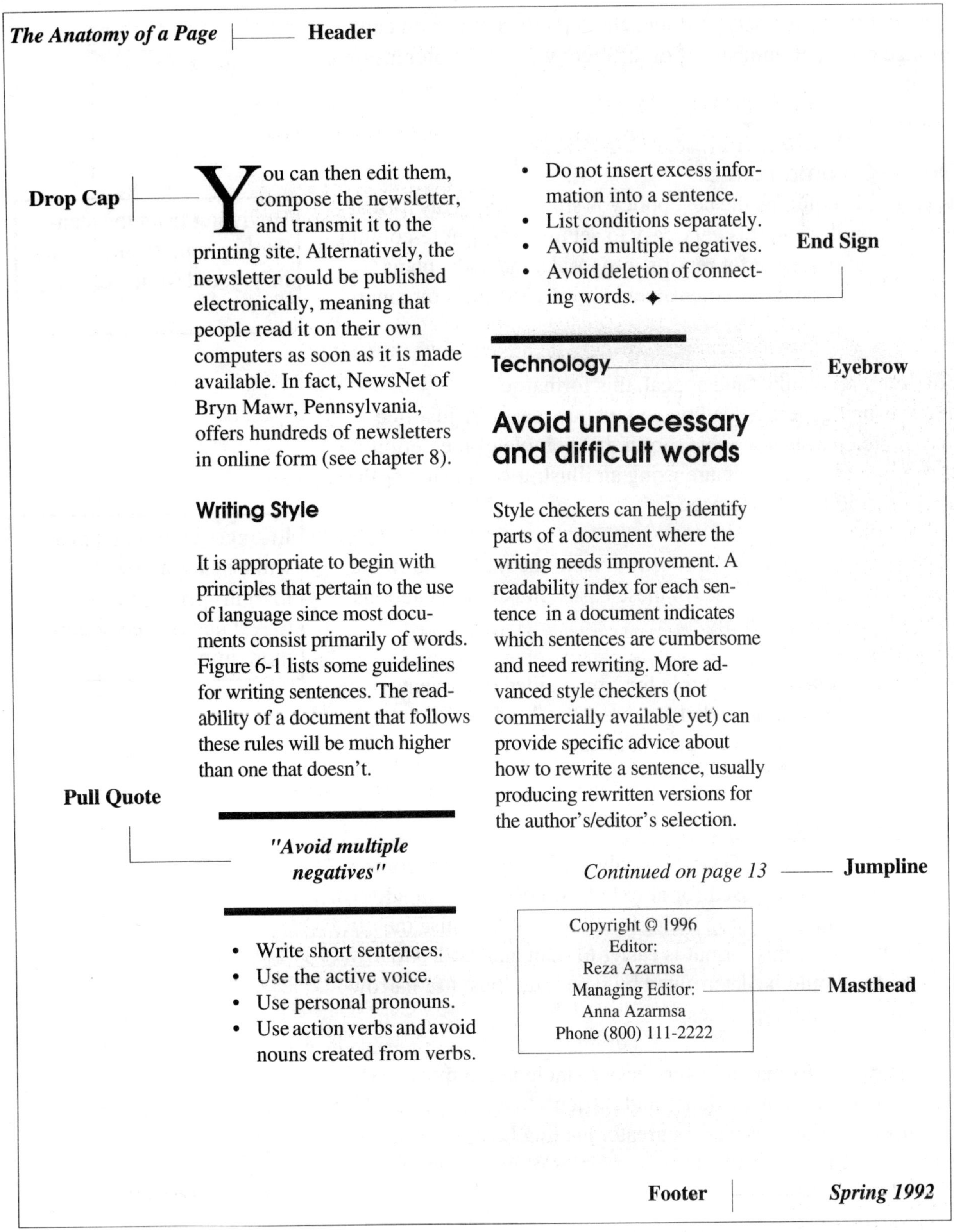

The Anatomy of a Page

You can then edit them, compose the newsletter, and transmit it to the printing site. Alternatively, the newsletter could be published electronically, meaning that people read it on their own computers as soon as it is made available. In fact, NewsNet of Bryn Mawr, Pennsylvania, offers hundreds of newsletters in online form (see chapter 8).

Writing Style

It is appropriate to begin with principles that pertain to the use of language since most documents consist primarily of words. Figure 6-1 lists some guidelines for writing sentences. The readability of a document that follows these rules will be much higher than one that doesn't.

"Avoid multiple negatives"

- Write short sentences.
- Use the active voice.
- Use personal pronouns.
- Use action verbs and avoid nouns created from verbs.
- Do not insert excess information into a sentence.
- List conditions separately.
- Avoid multiple negatives.
- Avoid deletion of connecting words. ✦

Technology

Avoid unnecessary and difficult words

Style checkers can help identify parts of a document where the writing needs improvement. A readability index for each sentence in a document indicates which sentences are cumbersome and need rewriting. More advanced style checkers (not commercially available yet) can provide specific advice about how to rewrite a sentence, usually producing rewritten versions for the author's/editor's selection.

Continued on page 13

Copyright © 1996
Editor:
Reza Azarmsa
Managing Editor:
Anna Azarmsa
Phone (800) 111-2222

Spring 1992

Fig. 4.3b. The anatomy of a page.

Although these formats predominate in publications, you can arrange different numbers of or different widths of columns on a page.

Single-Column Format

With single columns the best policy is simplicity. This format is very popular and it is very easy to set up. The single-column format is appropriate for reports, proposals, manuals, plans, press releases, announcements, and various internal communications.

> Deviating from the standard column formats can help you design a distinct look.

For better readability and appeal, this format requires wide margins and generous leading and white areas. Use justified text to create a strong right margin that completes the definition of the image area. If you are using an illustration, push it to the top or the bottom of the page.

> In single-column format, white space and wide margins give the eye room to rest and make the copy more inviting.

In some cases, you can run illustrations in the middle or on the side of a one-column page. In these cases, illustration captions should be placed carefully.

Wide-margin layout is suitable for single-sided documents that are either stapled or intended for three-ring binders. Figure 4.4 shows examples of one-column publication.

Two-Column Format

With the popularity of DTP, two-column format is very common, and it is mostly used for newsletters, bulletins, annual reports, brochures, catalog listings, and menus. Because the line is shortened, this format is easier to scan and read. Column width should be determined by type size; thus, use narrow columns for small type sizes.

In two-column format, it is very easy to include too much text and create pages that are dense and difficult to read. Wider margins and gutters as well as greater leading help increase the readability. Figure 4.5 illustrates examples of two-column format.

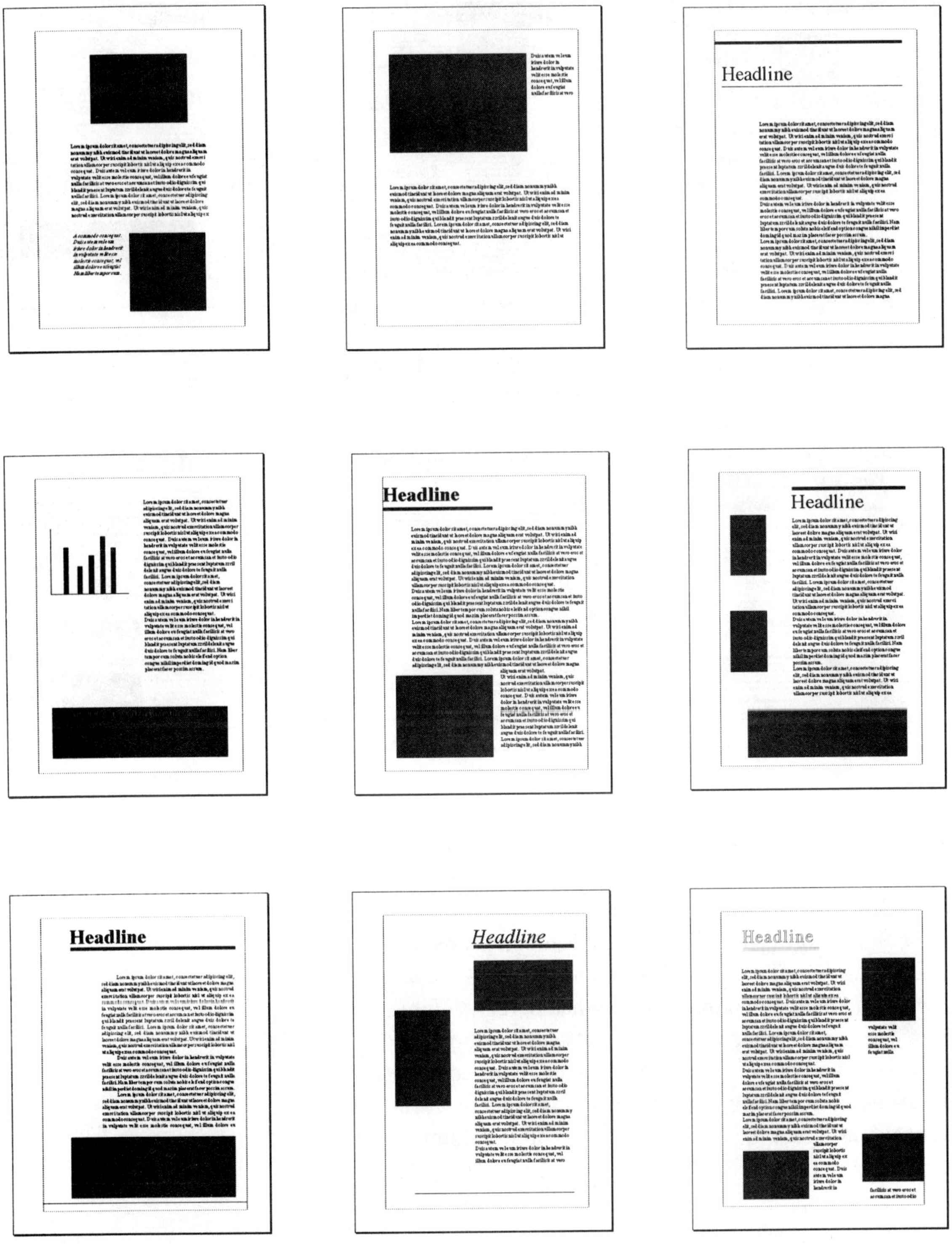

Fig. 4.4. Examples of one-column text publications.

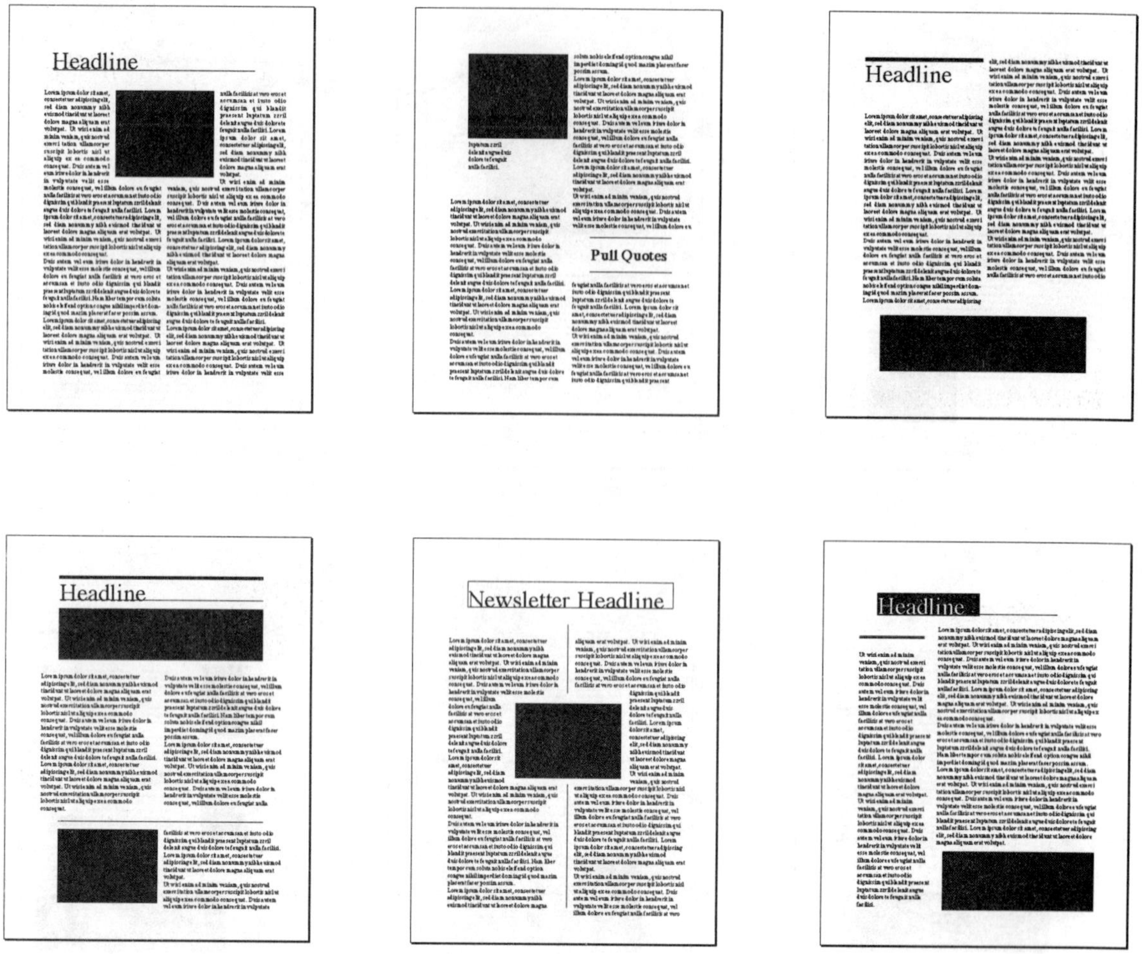

Fig. 4.5. Examples of two-column format.

Three-Column Format

Three-column format offers the most design options, and this makes it very popular for magazines, newspapers, newsletters, catalogs, and annual reports. This format is very flexible and allows you to plan your visual elements such as boxed copy, illustrations, and headlines across any one, two, or even three columns without having to worry about alignment over the text columns. See figure 4.6 for examples of three-column publication.

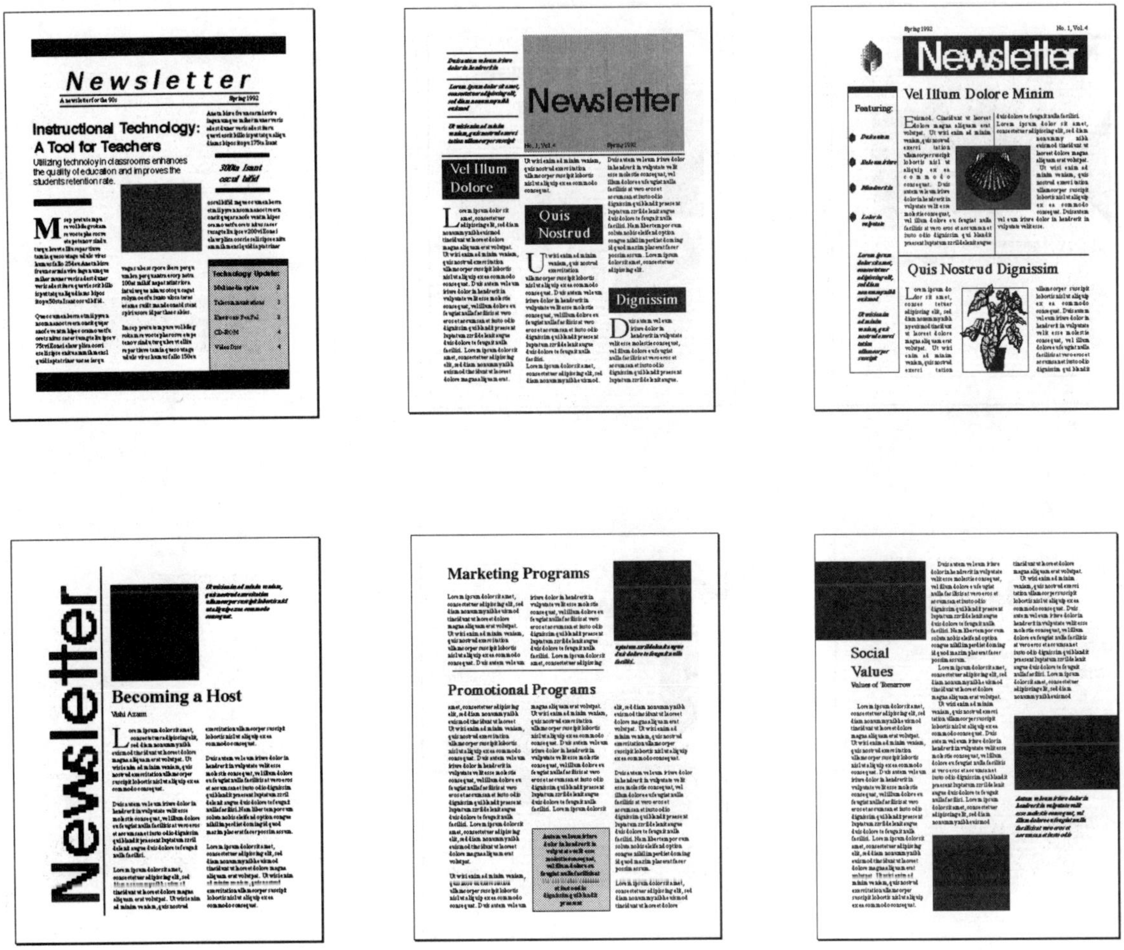

Fig. 4.6. Examples of three-column format.

Mixed-Column Format

All columns on a page do not have to be the same width. Good-looking publications can be created by using a variety of column widths. The column widths and variations can be changed for different sections of a publication or even different parts of a page.

The mixed-column format provides accommodation for different kinds of materials, allows for a varied page design, and can inspire creativity. Because of its flexibility, the mixed-column format is common for newspapers, newsletters, annual reports, and bulletins. Figure 4.7 shows samples of mixed-column publication.

Fig. 4.7. Examples of mixed-column publication.

Rules

Many DTP software packages make available a wide variety of rules, or lines. These rules can be used to highlight a block of text, enhance readability, draw attention, and separate topics within a publication. Rules also can be used to enliven the layout and organize materials on the page.

> Rules often are used to separate one part of a publication from another.

Rules are either horizontal or vertical. Horizontal rules are used to separate topics within a column or a page and to draw attention to pullout quotes. Horizontal rules are often used to guide the eye and make it easy to find the next line, especially in a table (fig. 4.8).

Fig. 4.8. Horizontal rules and a pullout quote separated by rules.

Vertical rules often are used to separate columns in a publication with lots of body copy, especially when nonjustified type is used (fig. 4.9).

Rules serve to create strong organization, which guides the eye from place to place.

Rules are designed according to their weight, or thickness. Desktop publishing packages offer a variety of rules of different weights. The weight is normally measured by points. (There are 72 points in 1 inch.) A good thickness of rules should be determined by the size of surrounding white space and the size of the typeface. Rules also are available with different combinations and styles (fig. 4.10).

Rules are available with a variety of endings and arrows (fig. 4.11). Controlling line endings is most useful when a line meets with another line or shape. Arrows are useful for flow charts and for labeling drawings.

Fig. 4.9. Vertical rules.

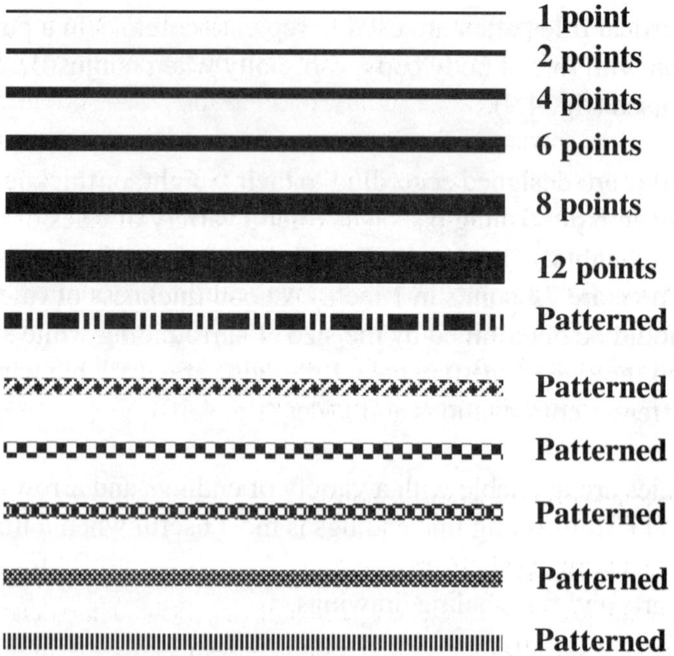

If rules are too thick, they can interfere with reading. If rules are too thin, they lack effectiveness.

Fig. 4.10. Rules with different weights and styles.

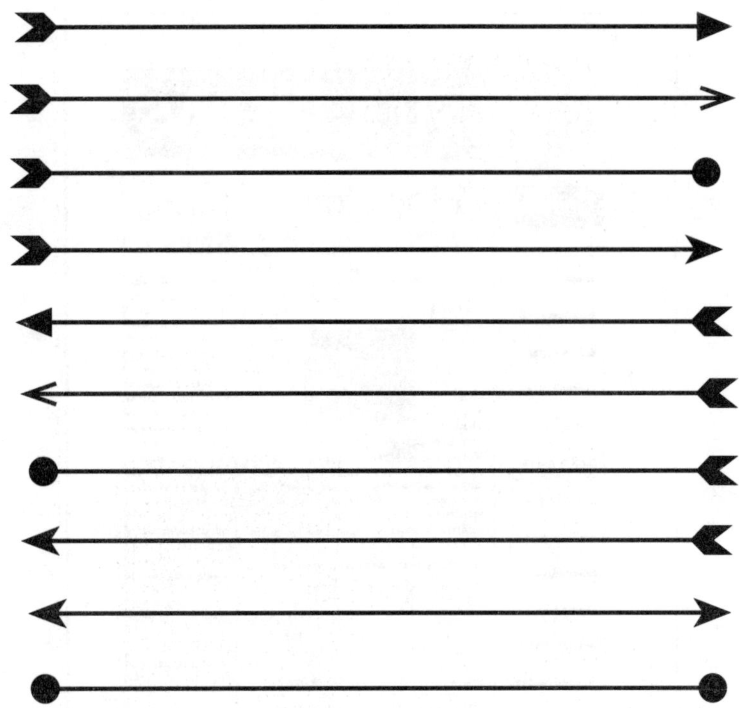

Fig. 4.11. Rules with different endings.

Boxes

> Use boxes for emphasis or to separate parts of a publication.

Text is often placed in a box to set it apart from the rest of the page in a publication. Boxes can also frame different types of illustrations, such as graphics, photographs, and schematics, to give a consistent look. Boxes are very useful in organizing and departmentalizing a page. Putting a box around a word in a title or a section of an article makes that element stand out. You also can use a box to completely surround an article or story. Boxes often are used to isolate publication information, such as a table of contents, addresses and telephone numbers, or coupons (fig. 4.12). Boxes are available in various line weights, corners, and decorative designs (fig. 4.13).

Screens and Patterns

Screens are composed of a series of tiny dots. These dots form a grid of parallel lines. A screen is measured by the number of lines per inch (LPI). The lightness or darkness of a screen is

Fig. 4.12. Boxes are used to separate information in a publication.

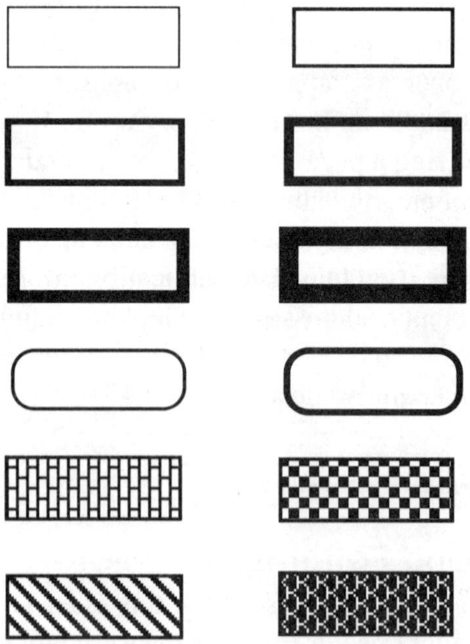

Thick boxes tend to darken the page.

Fig. 4.13. Variations of boxes.

measured in percentages, where 0% is white and 100% is black. Patterns consist of a series of lines either in a parallel sequence or forming a cross-hatch. Like screens, patterns are measured in LPI and percentages.

Boxes can be filled with different screens or patterns and the filled boxes can be used to highlight text and illustrations (fig. 4.14).

Screens add contrast and can enhance the readability of the publication.

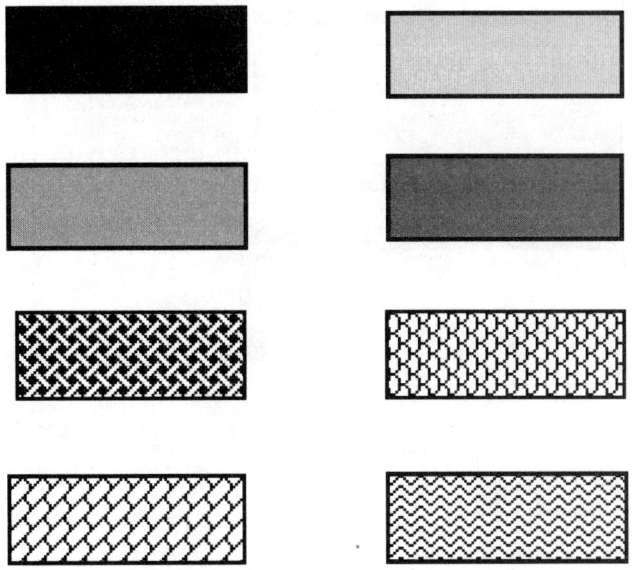

Fig. 4.14. A box filled with screen and pattern overlays.

Drop-Shadow Boxes

Drop-shadow boxes add depth and richness to charts, graphs, text, and photographs. They are most often used for highlighting text. The main purpose of a drop-shadow box is to lend a three-dimensional effect to the flat page and to draw the reader's attention to that area.

Drop-shadow boxes involve two similarly sized shapes, one offset from the other. The shadow can be designed with screen shadows or a black shadow (fig. 4.15). In some DTP programs, drop-shadow boxes are available as characters that can be inserted like text for use in checklists or forms. However, text cannot be placed inside such boxes.

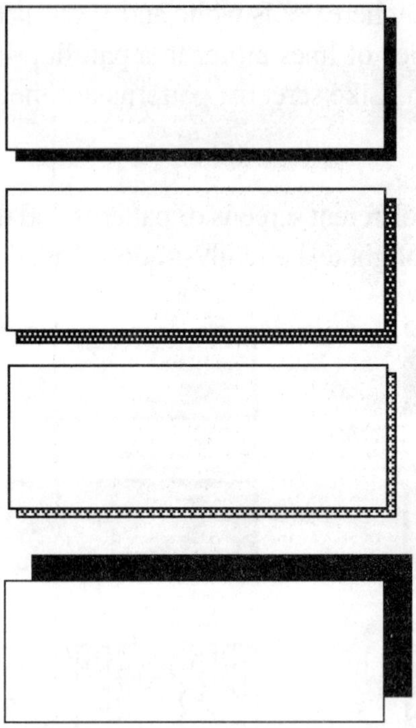

Fig. 4.15. Drop-shadow boxes with different shadow techniques.

Text Organization

Text organization helps readers better understand the meaning and the purposes of your publication. The size, position, and style of a line or block of text determine its application and connotation. For example, a phrase or a sentence positioned at the top of a page and set in large boldface is viewed as a headline. The same phrase or sentence placed under a picture in small italics would be considered a caption (fig. 4.16).

Headlines should be as short and concise as possible so their meaning can be understood quickly.

A headline is used to convey the most important information within the article and to attract prospective readers. Headlines help readers decide whether to read an article. Most people who see an article never read beyond its headline.

It is imperative that a headline pack as much information into as few words as possible. It must communicate as it attracts. Headlines should be clearly differentiated from body copy.

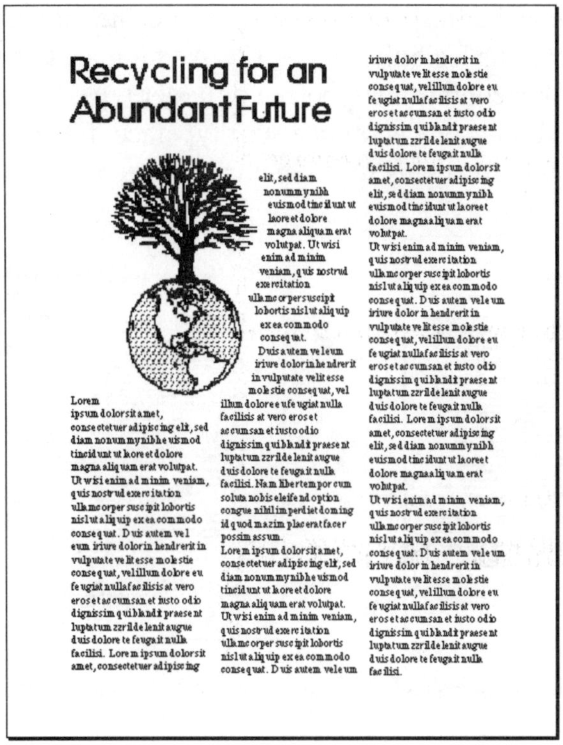

> The greater the difference between headline and body copy, the easier it is to read.

Fig. 4.16. A headline used as a caption.

A headline may be flush left, flush right, or centered without detracting from its legibility (fig. 4.17). Add impact to headlines by using a contrasting typeface or larger type. For example, if the body copy is set in a serif typeface, for the headline you should use a sans serif typeface.

Fig. 4.17. a) Headline flush left, b) Headline flush right, and c) Headline centered.

Subheads

A subhead is a secondary, smaller headline. Its purpose is to convey additional information and provide additional incentive. Subheads break up body copy into manageable segments, and improve appearance and enhance readability by providing a transition between headlines and body copy. They can also provide transitions between sections of an article. Their main role is often as design elements that prevent a long article from seeming so foreboding. Subheads are often set in boldface, allowing readers to quickly locate desired information (fig. 4. 18). To draw attention, subheads can be set apart from the body copy by placement, typeface, size, alignment, or rules (fig. 4. 19).

> Subheads provide a rest station for the eye.

Captions

A caption explains an illustration or photograph. Captions are the best-read part of a publication. The fact that many people who have not read the body copy will look at the pictures implies that a caption should be more than a label. A caption should add information that is not necessarily included in the body copy. See figures 4.20 and 4.21 for different caption placement.

> A caption can summarize important points.

Fig. 4.18. Subheads.

> Check that type styles and sizes are consistent for headlines, subheads, captions, and other copy.

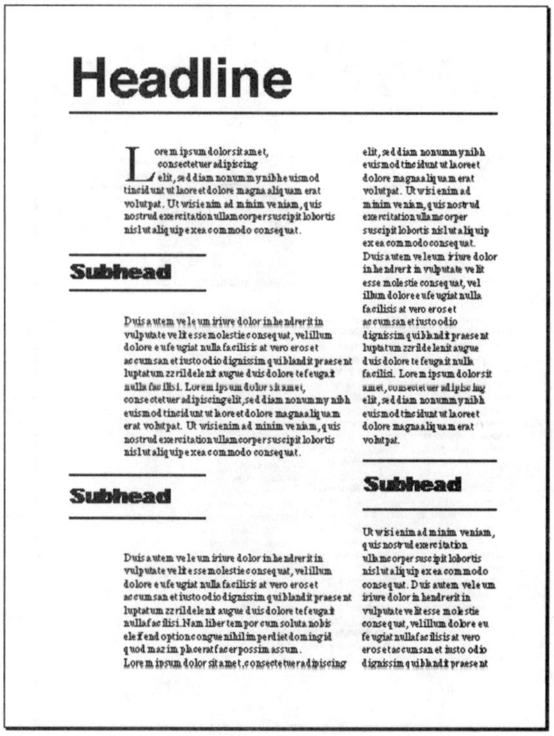

Fig. 4.19. Subheads placed on the side.

Fig. 4.20. Figure caption on bottom.

Captions should be styled or formatted the same way throughout a publication.

Fig. 4.21. Figure caption on side.

Pullout Text

Also called a breakout, a pull quote, or a blurb, pullout text is a phrase or sentence excerpted from the body copy and set in larger type (fig. 4.22). Pullout text should be positioned to attract attention to a specific portion of the document.

Pullouts are especially useful for keeping readers interested.

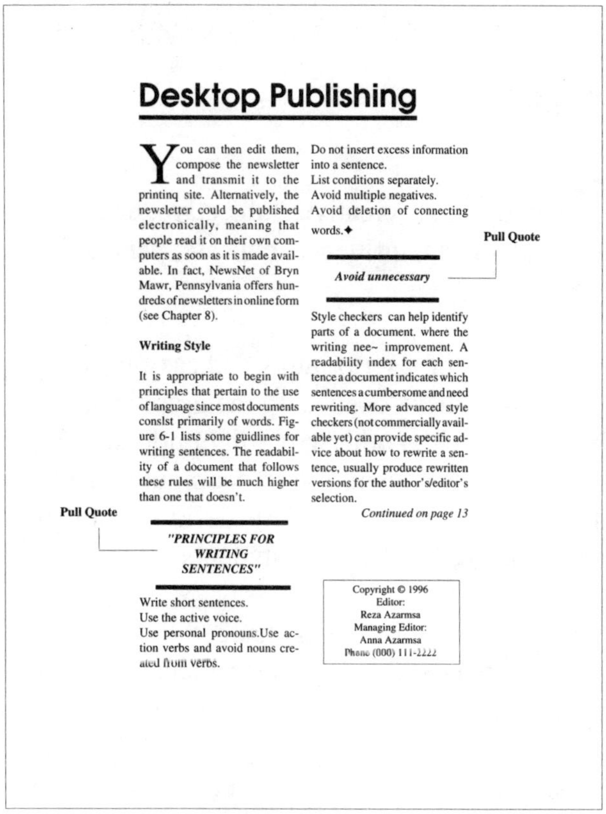

Desktop Publishing

You can then edit them, compose the newsletter and transmit it to the printinq site. Alternatively, the newsletter could be published electronically, meaning that people read it on their own computers as soon as it is made available. In fact, NewsNet of Bryn Mawr, Pennsylvania offers hundreds of newsletters in online form (see Chapter 8).

Writing Style

It is appropriate to begin with principles that pertain to the use of language since most documents conslst primarily of words. Figure 6-1 lists some guidlines for writing sentences. The readability of a document that follows these rules will be much higher than one that doesn't.

Pull Quote

"PRINCIPLES FOR WRITING SENTENCES"

Write short sentences.
Use the active voice.
Use personal pronouns.Use action verbs and avoid nouns created from verbs.

Do not insert excess information into a sentence.
List conditions separately.
Avoid multiple negatives.
Avoid deletion of connecting words.✦

Pull Quote

Avoid unnecessary

Style checkers can help identify parts of a document. where the writing nee~ improvement. A readability index for each sentence a document indicates which sentences a cumbersome and need rewriting. More advanced style checkers (not commercially available yet) can provide specific advice about how to rewrite a sentence, usually produce rewritten versions for the author's/editor's selection.

Continued on page 13

Copyright © 1996
Editor:
Reza Azarmsa
Managing Editor:
Anna Azarmsa
Phone (000) 111-2222

Fig. 4.22. Pullout text.

Publication organizers guide readers' eyes from one point to another in a document and alert them to what is of primary importance and what is supplemental. Effective use of the various organizing elements can make layout easier and enhance the look of a publication.

Organize for clarity. A well-organized publication draws reader attention in an orderly fashion. Appropriate use of columns, rules, headlines, illustrations, and spacing focuses its message.

5

Improving Your Product

Graphic design is creative, subjective, and personal: Its functions are to inform, influence, educate, persuade, and entertain.

The widespread use of laser printers and easy-to-use graphics and layout software have opened up the graphic arts to thousands of enthusiasts who otherwise might not have explored these disciplines. The advent of microcomputers and their prevalent use in education have made desktop publishing readily available to educators and students.

During its short history, DTP has changed the look of many of the things we read. Desktop publishing theoretically allows any student to become a typographer, paste-up artist, editor, writer, compositor, and graphic artist, once specialized skills practiced only by people with years of training and experience behind them. Of course, an untrained student cannot be expected to instantly acquire and use all these skills effectively. The availability of desktop publishing must be accompanied by an attention to detail that leads to good design. With the tips contained in this chapter, every beginning student can produce a good-looking document.

> A few basic design techniques can improve a publication's appearance, focus reader attention, and create a positive effect.

A publication is made up of two elements—words and pictures. Here we examine some of the practical approaches that make both most effective.

Ways to Improve Text

The primary function of words is to communicate instantly and effectively. A difference in type style not only helps to attract the reader's eye but also helps to organize information in terms of importance.

The most fundamental distinction between typefaces is that they are either serif or sans serif. Serif is a typeface with a line or curve projecting from the ends of the lines that makes up a letter. Sans serif is a typeface without finishing strokes at the ends of the characters (fig. 5.1). (For more information on typefaces and type styles, see chapter 3, "Typography.")

M	M
Serif	**San Serif**

Fig. 5.1. Serif and sans serif type.

> Avoid fancy typefaces: Their overuse can impair the basic communication function of words.

Serif projections are believed to help the eye jump from character to character. Serif text is ideal for main text or body copy. Nevertheless, sans serif typefaces (often used by popular tabloid newspapers), because of their simplicity, can handle virtually any kind of letterspacing.

Avoid Too Many Typefaces

Desktop publishing manufacturers loaded their software with typefaces. In practice, this abundance can create an absolute disaster in terms of good typographic design, and overloads of typefaces should be avoided.

As a general rule, two typefaces (a headline face and a body copy face) are adequate for most page designs. A variety of textures and styles can be conveyed by your choice of leading (the space between lines of type), weight (bold, light, or thin), size, and alteration of spacing between letters.

Match the Typeface to the Message

Every typeface has a character that either helps to deliver your message, harms the delivery, or is neutral. Once you have determined the character you want your printed message to possess to be most effective, select a typeface to match. There are masculine, feminine, delicate, rugged, Victorian, colonial, avant garde, formal, informal, high-tech, and Oriental typefaces (fig. 5.2).

Rock bottom prices

FOURTH OF JULY CELEBRATION

Fig. 5.2. Sample typefaces.

Avoid Fancy Typefaces

Although you want distinctive type, do not choose a typeface that is too elaborate. Fancy typefaces can be very difficult to read (fig. 5.3).

CONGRATULATIONS

CONGRATULATIONS

Fig. 5.3. Fancy typefaces.

Avoid All Caps

Uppercase type has its uses, but use of only caps slows down readers. Some typefaces cannot be set in all caps (fig. 5.4).

> **Headlines can be set in all uppercase, but limit uppercase headlines to a few words.**

HAPPY BIRTHDAY

CONGRATULATIONS

Fig. 5.4. All caps can be difficult to read.

Avoid Large Blocks of Text in Italic or Bold

Try not to set a great deal of text in italic or bold, particularly if you are using small type (fig. 5.5). Also, italic's small size in all caps tends to fit badly and is thus more difficult to read (fig. 5.6).

> Use italic and bold text for emphasis.

The butterfly, in the heart of the pure blue sky, heard the roar of the green valley's waterfall and its hunger for sleep on an unknown wildflower was making its wings numb and heavy.

The valley, with its towering waterfall and flower-strewn cliffs, grew small beneath its wings. It felt the heavy load of the water's spray, carried by the gay breeze, on its wing. It saw the world like a green and swelling wave.

Fig. 5.5. Large block of text in italic.

THE BUTTERFLY, IN THE HEART OF THE PURE BLUE SKY, HEARD THE ROAR OF THE GREEN VALLEY'S WATERFALL AND ITS HUNGER FOR SLEEP ON AN UNKNOWN WILDFLOWER WAS MAKING ITS WINGS NUMB AND HEAVY.

THE VALLEY, WITH ITS TOWERING WATERFALL AND FLOWER-STREWN CLIFFS, GREW SMALL BENEATH ITS WINGS. IT FELT THE HEAVY LOAD OF THE WATER'S SPRAY, CARRIED BY THE GAY BREEZE, ON ITS WING. IT SAW THE WORLD LIKE A GREEN AND SWELLING WAVE.

Fig. 5.6. Italic all caps.

> Boldface type in the middle of a block of text can draw more attention to a word.

Large blocks of text in boldface also should be avoided, because they are usually too heavy, too black, and not "friendly" (fig. 5.7).

The butterfly, in the heart of the pure blue sky, heard the roar of the green valley's waterfall and its hunger for sleep on an unknown wildflower was making its wings numb and heavy.

The valley, with its towering waterfall and flower-strewn cliffs, grew small beneath its wings. It felt the heavy load of the water's spray, carried by the gay breeze, on its wing. It saw the world like a green and swelling wave.

Fig. 5.7. A large block of bold text.

Use italic sparingly for emphasis or when irony or humor is intended. It can also imply an interjected conversational tone or a quotation (fig. 5.8). The use of italic can preclude quotation marks. Italic type is often used to set captions and the titles of books and other creative works.

"Thou shall not kill"

Fig. 5.8. A quotation in italic for emphasis.

Avoid Excessive Underlining

Underlining is a means of emphasis. However, the availability of italic and bold types makes most underlining unnecessary. More than a few underlined words causes visual clutter and confusion. Also, it takes more time for readers to separate the words from the horizontal lines (fig. 5.9).

> Every publication sets a tone and creates an impression. Planning how graphics and text work together helps it communicate the message you want.

The butterfly, in the heart of the pure blue sky, heard the roar of the green valley's waterfall and its hunger for sleep on an unknown wildflower was making its wings numb and heavy.

The valley, with its towering waterfall and flower-strewn cliffs, grew small beneath its wings. It felt the heavy load of the water's spray, carried by the gay breeze, on its wing. It saw the world like a green and swelling wave.

Fig. 5.9. A block of underlined text.

Control Widows and Orphans

A widow is a line, a word, or a syllable of text at the top of a page or column that is separate from the paragraph that it finishes, which is at the end of the previous page or column. An orphan is a line, a word, or a syllable of text at the bottom of a page or column that is separate from the paragraph it begins, which starts the next page or column (fig. 5.10).

Widows and orphans can be controlled in several ways. Edit the paragraph and omit unnecessary words. Substitute a shorter word for a longer one. Tighten the spacing of any loosely set line. (You can do this by reducing the tracking gradually.) Also, widows and orphans can be eliminated by rejuggling the page or the column lengths. DTP software packages offer widow and orphan control, and you can specify the number of lines of widows or orphans.

> Widows and orphans can be eyesores that interrupt the reader's flow.

Widow

The butterfly, in the heart of the pure blue sky, heard the roar of the green valley's waterfall and its hunger for sleep on an unknown wildflower was making its wings numb and heavy.

The valley, with its

towering waterfall and flower-strewn cliffs, grew small beneath its wings. It felt the heavy load of the water's spray, carried by the gay breeze, on its wing. It saw the world like a green and swell-

ing wave.

The butterfly, in the heart of the pure blue sky, heard the roar of the green valley's waterfall and its hunger for sleep on an un-known

Orphan

Fig. 5.10. An example of widows and orphans.

Avoid Excessive Hyphenation

Hyphenation is breaking a word at the end of a line and following the break by a hyphen. To give even word spacing, excessive hyphenation can occur in narrow columns of type (fig. 5.11). To eliminate excessive hyphenation, reduce type size, increase column width, or choose the flush left/ragged right style.

> You should not have hyphens in headlines or other display copy, in captions, or in center-aligned type.

The valley, with its tower-
ing waterfall and flower-
strewn cliffs, grew small be-
neath its wings. It felt the
heavy load of the water's
spray, carried by the gay
breeze, on its wing. It saw
the world like a green and
swelling wave.

The valley, with its towering waterfall and flower-strewn cliffs, grew small beneath its wings. It felt the heavy load of the water's spray, carried by the gay breeze, on its wing. It saw the world like a green and swelling wave.

Fig. 5.11. An example of excessive hyphenation.

Avoid Exaggerated Tabs and Indents

The standard five-space paragraph indents and tabs, commonly used for word processed documents, often create distracting gaps in desktop-published multicolumn text (fig. 5.12). Adjust tabs to make them proportional to column widths. Wide columns with larger type usually require deeper tabs and indents than do narrow columns with small type.

> The butterfly, in the heart of the pure blue sky, heard the roar of the green valley's waterfall and its hunger for sleep on an unknown wildflower was making its wings numb and heavy.
>
> The valley, with its towering waterfall and flower-strewn cliffs, grew small beneath its wings. It felt the heavy load of the water's spray, carried by the gay breeze, on its wing. It saw the world like a green and swelling wave.

Fig. 5.12. Exaggerated indents.

Ways to Improve Graphics

The second and equally important element in document design is graphics. A picture may be worth a thousand words, but it is your job as a designer to balance the words and the pictures to make both equally effective and interesting to the reader.

- Keep page layout simple and uncluttered.
- Establish a tone.
- Provide visual variety.
- Assist the reader.
- Maintain consistency and accuracy.

Graphics that can be used in desktop publishing include photographs (halftones), line art (illustrations such as cartoons), digitized logos, charts and graphs produced with your software package, and your own illustrations and diagrams produced with a paint or draw software package. Some color works such as photographs and transparencies can be introduced if the appropriate equipment is available.

Software packages exist that enable a student to become a cartoonist and illustrator as well. If you want to use cartoons and illustrations in your publication, you can use one of the available clip art packages. These contain sets of predrawn artwork, such as symbols, that can be included in your design. Zapf, a German type designer, produced the Zapf Dingbats font. Dingbats, included with many laser printers, is a set of shapes and symbols such as a star or a hand with a pointing finger (to give a "this way" sign). This font was among the earliest to be digitized for use on computers and to be readily available to DTP users. Predrawn artwork is a valuable asset in the designer's armory and provides instant graphics.

Tints (screens) and boxes are a form of graphics that are an easy way to introduce variety and interest to a page. A monochrome page can be easily enhanced with the use of a 10% or 20% gray tint. Screens can be used effectively on a page that has only text and can highlight logos, headlines, and subheads or be laid over simple graphics.

Get Attention with Unusual Elements

Any unusual visual elements capture the reader's attention. For example, exaggerated quotation marks draw attention to the text (fig. 5.13).

> Lay out the page to lead the eye in a logical path, generally from left to right or top to bottom. Focus attention first on the element you want to emphasize most.

"Genius is 1 percent inspiration and 99 percent perspiration."

Fig. 5.13. Exaggerated quotation marks.

An exaggerated drop cap draws the eye immediately (fig. 5.14).

Fig. 5.14. An exaggerated drop cap.

Vary Size and Use Special Effects

Normal size may be less interesting to the reader. Altered size and special effects draw attention to the visuals. Figures 5.15 and 5.16 show examples of these effects.

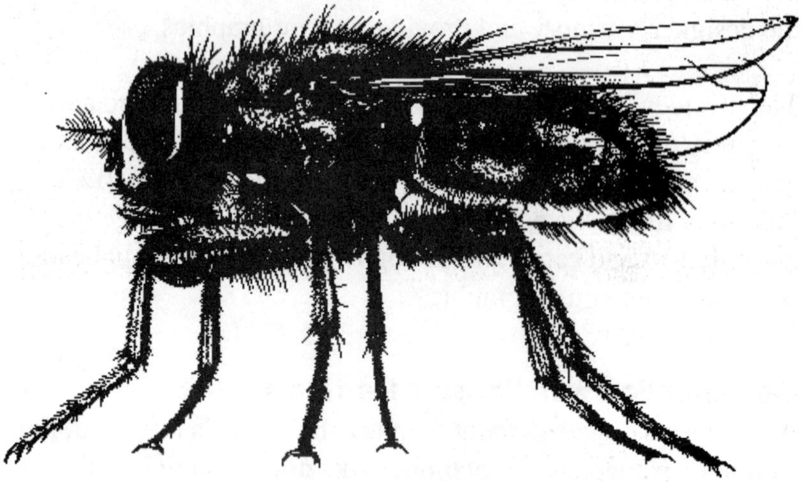

Fig. 5.15. A fly is not threatening unless shown greater than normal size and in detail.

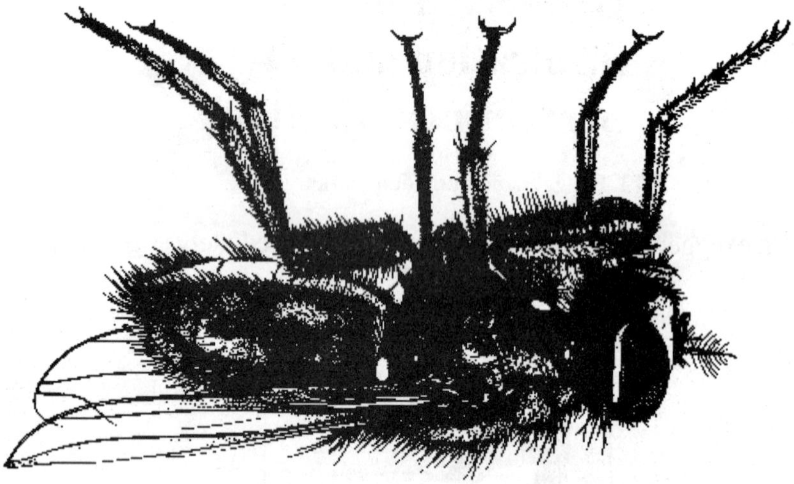

Fig. 5.16. The upside-down image calls for attention.

An especially good way to draw the eye toward a specific page element is to surround it with white space or empty space.

Using special effects adds to the attention paid to the images; special filters are used to create these images. Figure 5.17 shows different filters used for special effect.

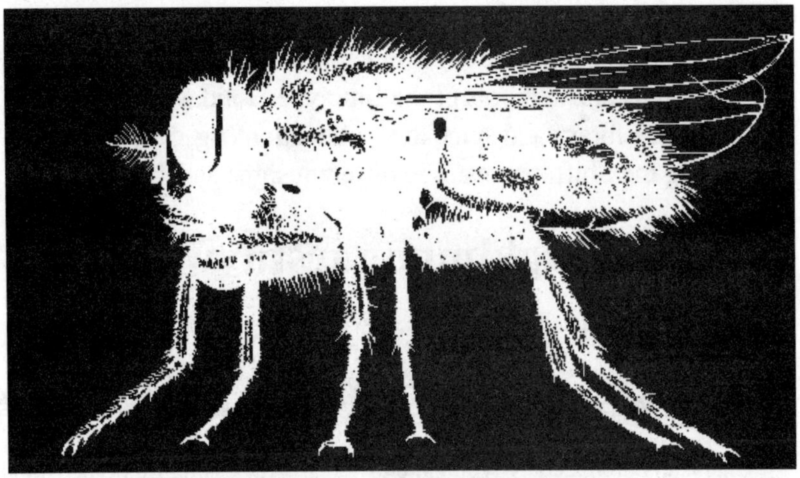

Fig. 5.17a. Invert filter.

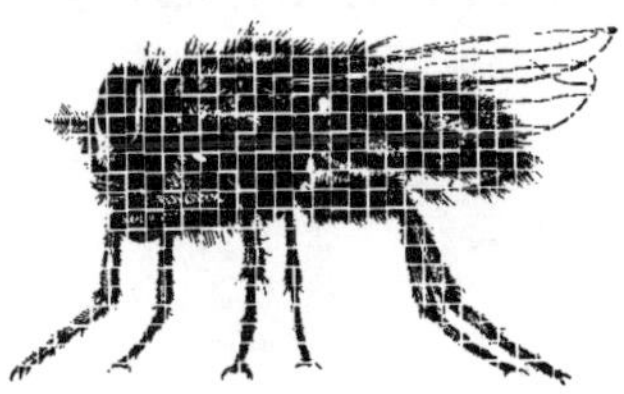

Fig. 5.17b. Tile filter.

Fig. 5.17c. Facet filter.

Fig. 5.17d. Emboss filter.

Use Symbols and Signs

Symbols and signs are effective for capturing the reader's attention. The signs and symbols of the Linotype Holiday Pi font from Adobe Type Library add spice to a publication (fig. 5.18). Depressing the Shift key result in different signs and symbols.

abcdefghigklmnopqrstuvwxyz

Characters produced by typing the lowercase keys using Times.

Characters produced by typing the lowercase keys using Linotype Holoday Pi 1.

Characters produced by typing the lowercase keys using Linotype Holoday Pi 2.

Characters produced by typing the lowercase keys using Linotype Holoday Pi 3..

Fig. 5.18. Linotype Holiday Pi font.

Other software packages, such as Macromedia FreeHand, also provide a library of symbols (fig. 5.19).

Fig. 5.19. Aldus FreeHand symbol library.

> Contrast is used to call attention to one element and downplay another.

Use Contrast

A highlight of color on the printed page draws the eye immediately. When you are limited to black and white, you must be resourceful in gaining and retaining your reader's attention. Contrast is one of the most effective ways of doing so (fig. 5.20).

Fig. 5.20. The high contrast players against a white background and the bold text create a good example of the use of contrast.

Use Shades of Gray

Shades of gray can contribute a great deal to the success of a visual. The purpose of the shadow is to lend a three-dimensional effect to the flat page and to draw the reader's attention to that area (fig. 5.21).

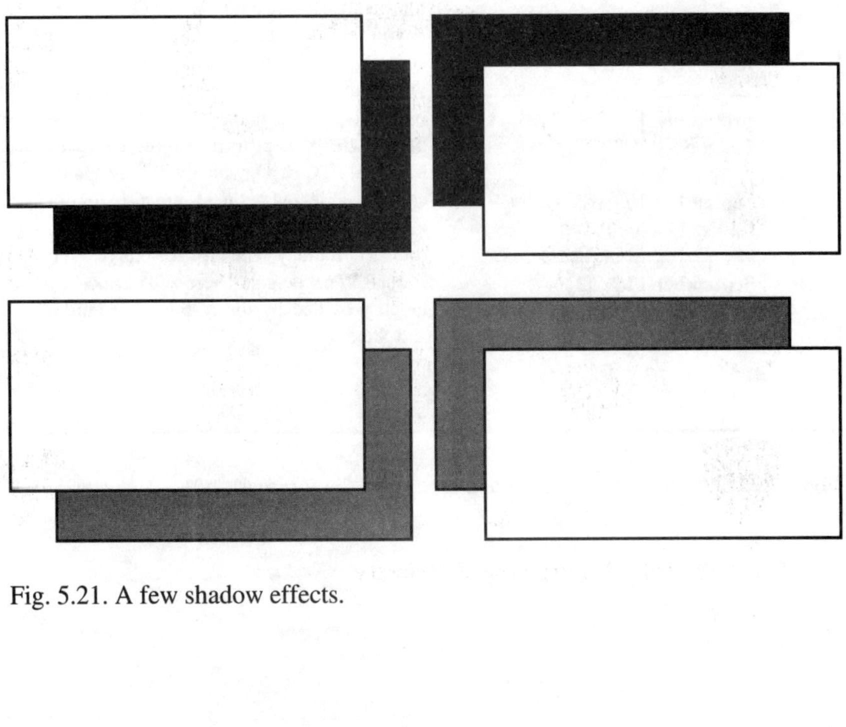

Fig. 5.21. A few shadow effects.

Use Bleed Techniques

"Bleeds" refer to extra areas of ink coverage that extend beyond the trim of the page. To bleed an element means to imprint it to the edge of the paper. You can bleed rules, borders, large letter forms, photos, large solid areas, and other elements. A bleed gives the page a feeling of expansiveness; the page seems larger than it actually is, unbounded by margins (fig. 5.22).

> Bleeds add impact to page design by emphasizing building blocks such as text, visuals, or graphics.

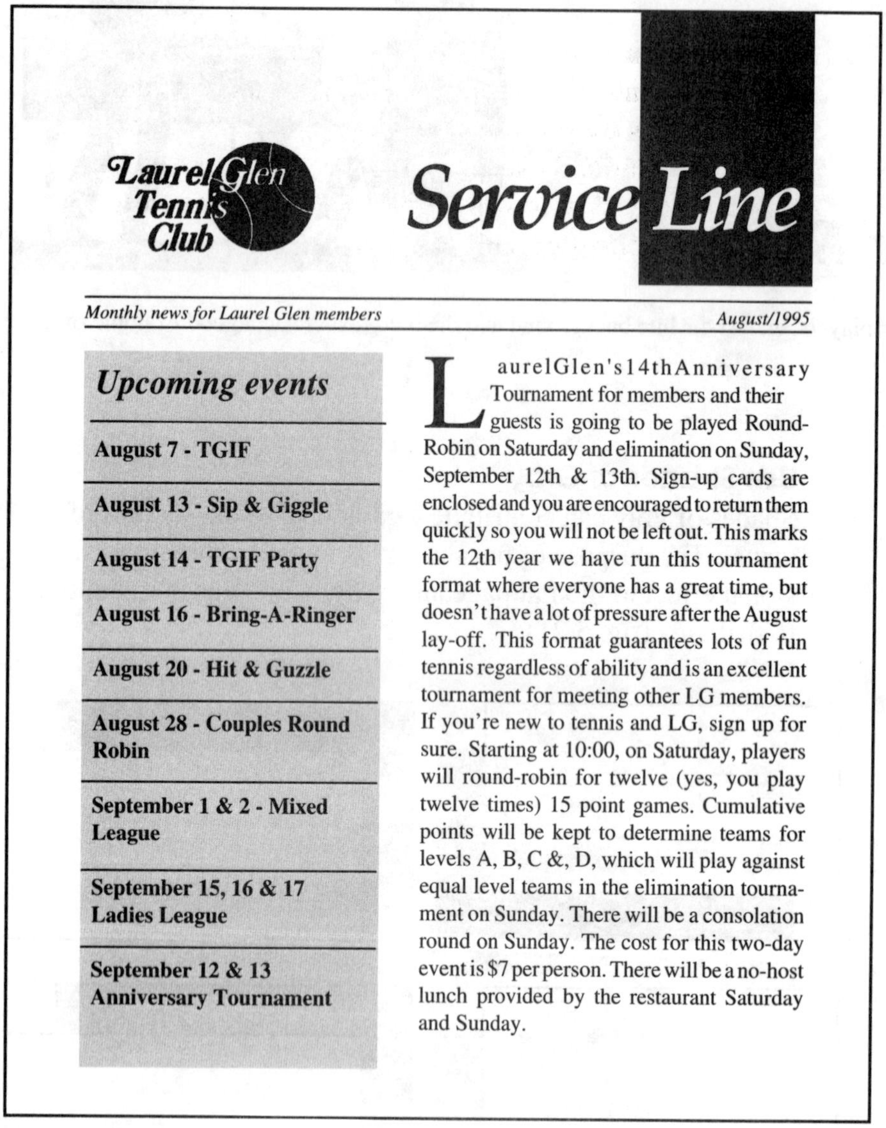

Laurel Glen Tennis Club

Service Line

Monthly news for Laurel Glen members *August/1995*

Upcoming events

August 7 - TGIF

August 13 - Sip & Giggle

August 14 - TGIF Party

August 16 - Bring-A-Ringer

August 20 - Hit & Guzzle

August 28 - Couples Round Robin

September 1 & 2 - Mixed League

September 15, 16 & 17 Ladies League

September 12 & 13 Anniversary Tournament

LaurelGlen's14thAnniversary Tournament for members and their guests is going to be played Round-Robin on Saturday and elimination on Sunday, September 12th & 13th. Sign-up cards are enclosed and you are encouraged to return them quickly so you will not be left out. This marks the 12th year we have run this tournament format where everyone has a great time, but doesn't have a lot of pressure after the August lay-off. This format guarantees lots of fun tennis regardless of ability and is an excellent tournament for meeting other LG members. If you're new to tennis and LG, sign up for sure. Starting at 10:00, on Saturday, players will round-robin for twelve (yes, you play twelve times) 15 point games. Cumulative points will be kept to determine teams for levels A, B, C &, D, which will play against equal level teams in the elimination tournament on Sunday. There will be a consolation round on Sunday. The cost for this two-day event is $7 per person. There will be a no-host lunch provided by the restaurant Saturday and Sunday.

Fig. 5.22. The rectangle on this page bleeds on the top margin.

Bleeds may be troublesome. Because most laser printers have a specified print area, they may leave a margin of one-fourth to one-eighth of an inch on a letter-size sheet. In this case you may need to either manually cut and paste the pieces together or print the page smaller than full size and trim off the margins. Bleeds may also increase the printing cost as well as affect the final trimmed size of your publication. You should discuss the use of bleeds with a printer before incorporating them into your design.

The temptation is to add many different graphic and typographic elements in one publication. Such a mixture, though, usually defeats the purpose of attracting and keeping the reader's attention. By keeping your design simple and using graphics and type selectively, you will produce the most effective and pleasing publication.

Part 2

Putting Desktop Publishing to Work Using Adobe PageMaker

6

A Tour of PageMaker

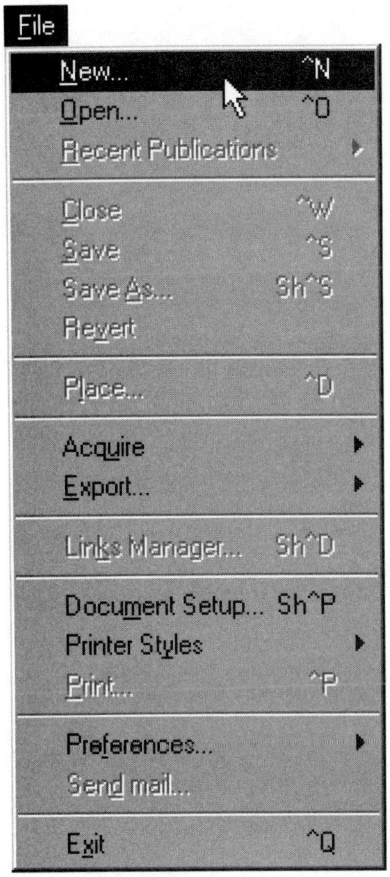

Before you begin reading, the PageMaker program should already be installed in your computer. To start the PageMaker program, (Macintosh) click on the PageMaker icon twice, (Windows) select *Start > Program > Adobe > PageMaker 6.5.*

After you have loaded the PageMaker program, select *New* from the *File* menu. The *Document setup* dialog box appears on- screen (fig. 6.1).

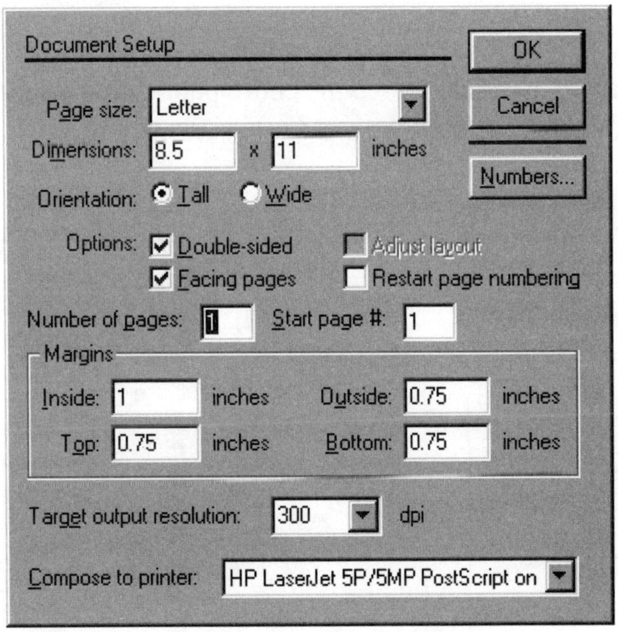

Fig. 6.1. *Document setup* dialog box.

As indicated in the *Document setup* dialog box, the PageMaker default options are: *Page* size, 8.5" x 11"; page *Orientation Tall*, i.e., vertical; page numbering starts at *1*; pages are *Double-sided* and *Facing* each other.

The default margin options are *Inside* margin 1", *Top* margin 0.75", *Outside* margin 0.75", and *Bottom* margin 0.75". Inside margin is the space between the binding edge of the page and the text. Outside margin is the space between the outside trim and the text. *Compose to printer* shows your default printer.

> Default options are predetermined options set at the factory. These settings can be customized according to your needs.

Number of pages often indicates the total number of pages in the document. (To change the default options, simply input your own new values.)

To continue the PageMaker tour, accept the default options and click on OK. The Publication window appears on the screen.

Publication Window

The image that appears onscreen when a document is open is called the Publication window. The window displays the first page of the new publication, Toolbox, rulers, page number icon, master page icon, scroll bars, palettes, and menu bar (fig. 6.2). The first page of the publication icon shows the predefined margins. To see the entire publication window, click on the palettes close box to close the palettes.

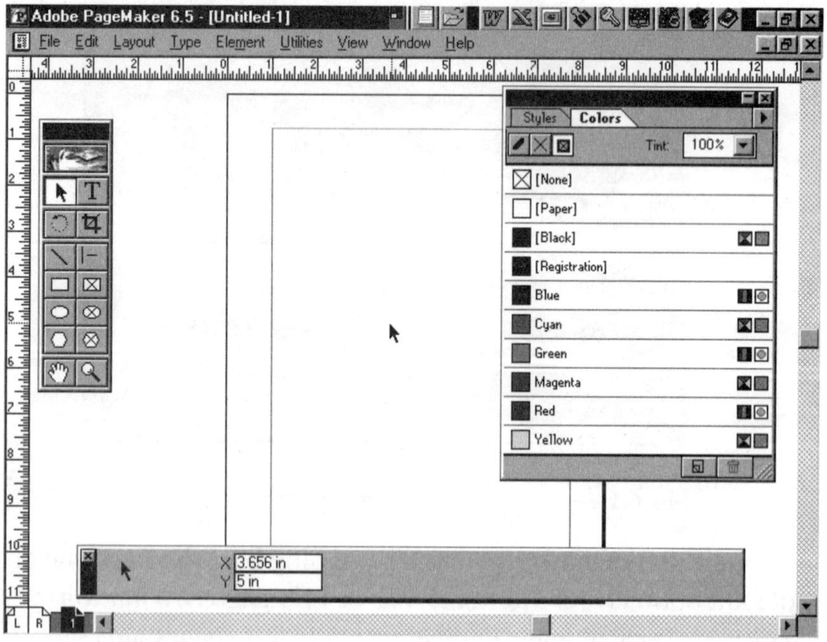

Fig. 6.2. Publication window.

Moving Around the Page

The size of the page on the screen is not the actual size of the page. To see the actual size:

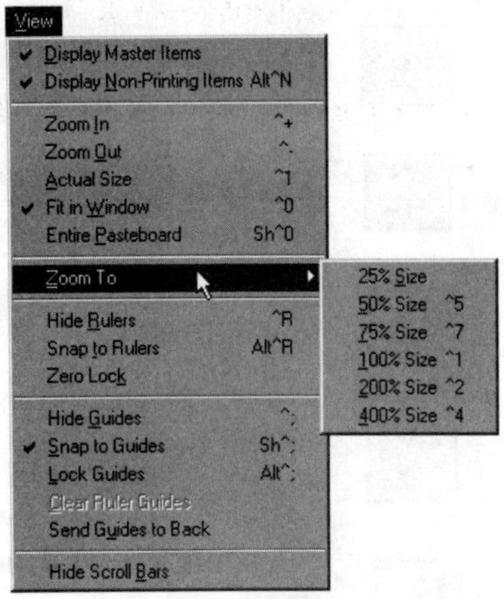

From the *Layout* menu select *View* then choose *Actual size.*

The actual size maybe larger than the your screen. Using the scroll bars, you can move around to see different parts of the page.

To go back to the previous page size:

From the *View* menu select *Actual Size.*

The *View* and *Zoom To* menus offer several page-size choices as well as other page-related options. You can display your publication at 25%, 50%, 75%, 100% (actual size), 200%, and 400% of the actual publication size. Select the desired size; PageMaker displays the publication on the monitor accordingly. The *View* menu also contains other options that are discussed later in this book.

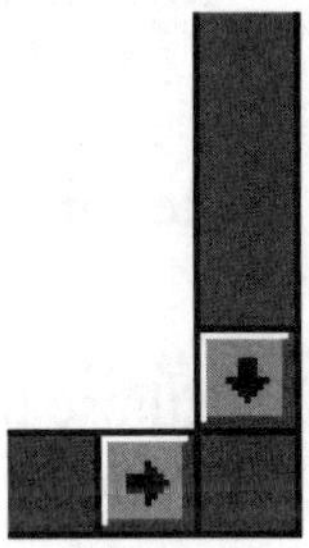

Scroll Bars

To move to the top, bottom, right, or left of the page, place the pointer on the arrow points in either end of the scroll bars. Click on the mouse and hold the mouse button down until you reach the desired place.

The Toolbox

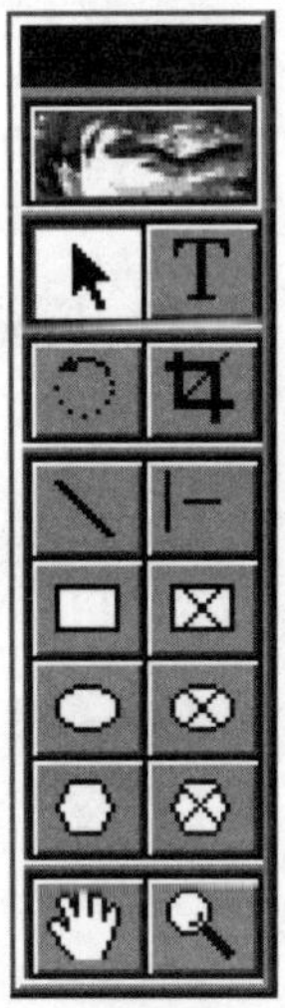

Toolbox

The Toolbox window is located on the upper right-hand corner of the Publication window. It contains tools for:

Typing and editing text
Adjusting and positioning text
Drawing lines and shapes
Rotating text and graphics
Magnifying and reducing an area of the page
Cropping and resizing graphics

When you open a publication, the Pointer tool is automatically selected. To select a different tool, simply place the pointer on that tool's icon and click. Depending upon your selection, the pointer will change as shown in figure 6.3.

Selected Tool	Cursor
Pointer tool	
Text tool	
Rotating tool	
Cropping tool	
Zoom tool	
Hand tool	
Drawing tools	+
Frame tools	+

Fig. 6.3. Cursor selection.

- Pointer tool
- Text tool
- Rotating tool
- Cropping tool
- Diagonal-line tool
- Perpendicular-line tool
- Rectangle tool
- Rectangle frame tool
- Ellipse tool
- Ellipse frame tool
- Polygon tool
- Polygon frame tool
- Hand tool
- Zoom tool

The Pointer tool is used to select menu and submenu items and to position, adjust, and select text and graphics in the publication.

The Text tool is used to type and edit text. When the Text tool is selected, you can use the *Type* menu to change font, size, leading, set width, tracking, type style, alignment, and style of text.

The Rotating tool allows you to rotate a block of text or a graphic either clockwise or counter clockwise in 0.01° increments.

The Cropping tool is used to adjust the size or position of a graphic image in your publication. For more information, see "Importing Graphics" on page 99.

The Diagonal-line tool is used to draw a straight line at any angle. With the Shift key, you can draw straight lines at 45° increments.

The Perpendicular-line tool is used to draw straight lines at any 45° angle. PageMaker offers different line thicknesses and styles. Select *Stroke* from the *Element* menu and highlight your desired option (fig. 6.4).

Onscreen, a small line thickness change may sometimes not look like a change due to the resolution of the screen.

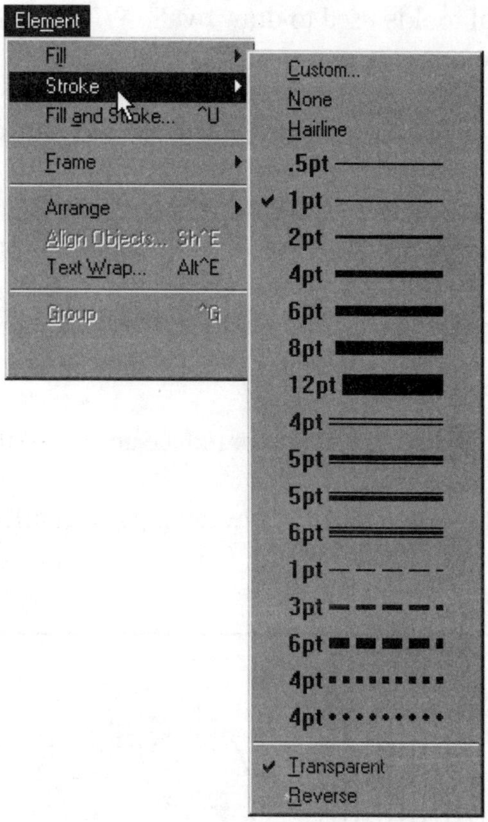

Fig. 6.4. Line thickness options.

The Square-corner tool is used to draw rectangles. With the Shift key, you can draw squares. To draw a rounded-corner box, draw the box then select *Rounded corners* from the *Element* menu and choose the desired corner style (fig.6.5). With the Shift key, you can draw rounded-corner squares.

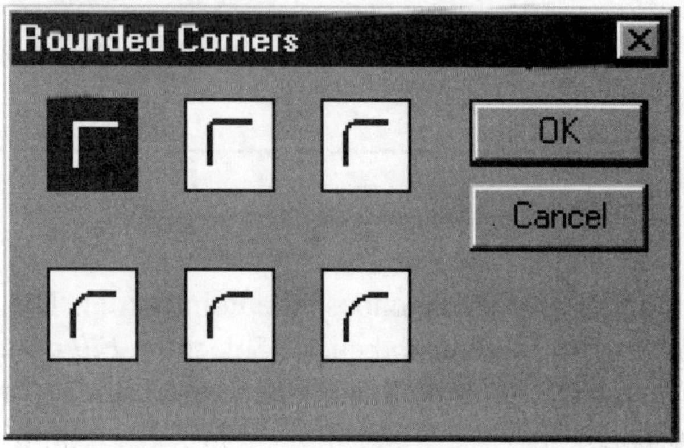

Fig. 6.5. Rounded-corner choices.

The Circle/oval tool is used to draw ovals. With the Shift key, you can draw circles.

The Polygon tool enables you to draw basic polygons.

Frame tools draw rectangle, ellipse, and polygon frame for placing text and graphics.

Hand tool drags the page horizontally or vertically and displays hyperlink.

The Zoom tool is used to magnify or reduce an area of the page.

Screens add contrast, turning text into a graphic element.

PageMaker allows you to fill your drawings with different shades (screens) and patterns (fig. 6.6).

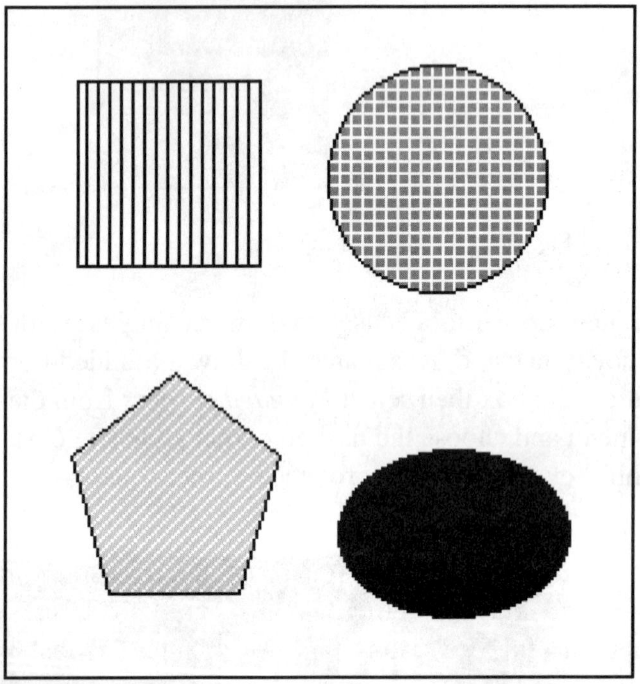

Fig. 6.6. Sample shapes and patterns.

To fill the drawing, first choose the Pointer tool. Then place the Pointer on the drawing and click. Select the *Fill* option from the *Element* menu and choose the desired screen or pattern (fig. 6.7).

PageMaker treats a carriage return as the start of a new paragraph.

When importing text, PageMaker does not retain the margins set in the word processing program.

Column settings in word processing programs are not retained when you import text into PageMaker.

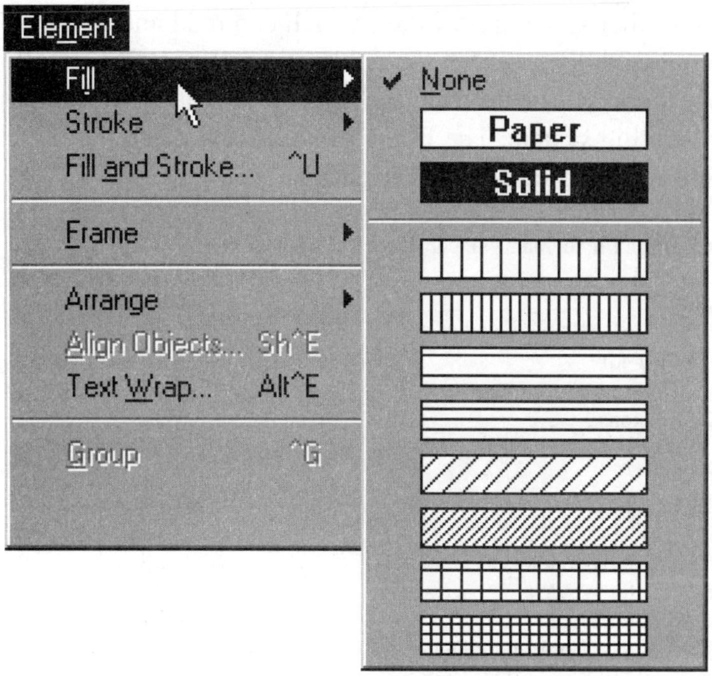

Fig. 6.7. Shade and pattern options.

Placing Text

Text can be placed in the PageMaker publication in two ways:

1. Importing text from a stand-alone word processing program such as Microsoft Word or WordPerfect.
2. Typing text directly in the publication, using the *Edit story* feature from the *Edit* menu.

The stand-alone word processing programs offer many text manipulation and text editing features. Word processing programs are useful for creating long documents. The text editing capabilities of PageMaker are adequate for creating short titles and headlines for a publication.

The decision to use a stand-alone word processing program versus PageMaker's Story editor is based on your degree of familiarity with each, as well as on your familiarity with the desktop publishing procedures followed in your school.

PageMaker includes Import Filter, which can read and place a word processed document in the publication. When you install the program on your hard disk, the filters automatically reside in the operating system. The filters can read and place the following text or database file format:

Text or database file formats you can place in PageMaker

File format	File extension	Macintosh	Windows
ClarisWorks 1.0-4.0		X	-
HTM L		X	X
Lotus 1-2-3 versions 1.0-5.0	.WKS	-	X
Symphony 1.0-3.0	.WRK / .WRI	-	X
MacWrite II		X	-
MacWrite Pro 1.0-1.5		X	-
Microsoft Excel 3.0-5.0	.XLS	X	X
Microsoft Excel for Windows 7.0	.XLS	X	X
Microsoft Write for Windows 2.0	.WRI	-	X
Microsoft Word for Windows 2.0	.DOC	-	X
Microsoft Word 3.0/ Word 3.0 for DOS	.DOC	X	X
Microsoft Word 4.0/ Word 4.0 for DOS	.DOC	X	X
Microsoft Word 5.0/ Word 5.0 for DOS	.DOC	X	X
Microsoft Word 6.0/ Word for Windows 6.0	.DOC	X	X
Microsoft Word for Windows 7.0	.DOC	X	X
Microsoft Works 2.0-4.0	.WKS	X	-
Open Database Connectivity (ODBC)		-	X
PageMaker 5.0-6.01 stories		X	X
Rich Text Format	(RTF)	X	X
Tagged Text (ASCII)	.TXT	X	X
Text-only (ASCII)	.TXT	X	X
WordPerfect for Macintosh 2.x		X	-
WordPerfect for Macintosh 3.0/31		X	-
WordPerfect 4.2 (DOS)	.WP4	X	-
WordPerfect 5.x (DOS and Windows)	.WP5	X	X
WordStar 3.3-6.0	.WS / .WST	-	X
WordPerfect 6.x (Windows)	.WP6	X	X
WriteNow 2.0-3.0		X	-
XyWrite 111 or 111+	.XY3	X	X

Text Placement Options

PageMaker offers three ways to place text in your publication: *Place*, *Import*, and *Paste*.

1. *Place* option from the *File* menu. Use this option when you have already created the text document with a stand-alone word processing program and do not need to edit the text.

When you select the *Place* option, PageMaker displays the *Place document* dialog box (fig. 6.8). The dialog box contains the files that can be moved to the PageMaker program. Select the desired file and click OK.

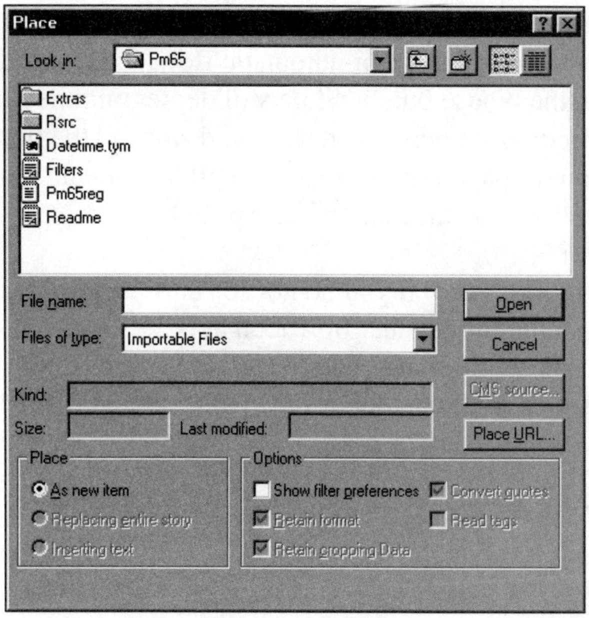

Fig. 6.8. *Place document* dialog box.

Autoflow text icon

PageMaker places text in a document in three ways: *Autoflow*, *Semi-automatic*, and *Manual flow*. To use the *Autoflow* option: Select *Autoflow* from the *Layout* menu. PageMaker displays the *Autoflow* icon. Place this icon in the publication where you would like to start the text and click on the mouse (fig. 6.9). The text automatically flows within the specified margins. In the *Autoflow* mode, the text flows from page to page or column to column to the end of the imported document.

Fig. 6.9. Autoflow text.

If you select *Autoflow* for importing text, you can press the Shift key to switch to Semi-automatic flow. In this mode, when you click the mouse button while still depressing the Shift key, text is placed from where you start, and stops at the bottom of the column or page. The text icon is still loaded and ready to be placed in the same fashion on other pages.

Semi-automatic flow text icon

When importing text, if you do not select *Autoflow* from the *Options* menu, the Manual flow icon appears onscreen. Place the icon where you would like to start the text and click on the mouse (fig. 6.10). PageMaker flows the text and it stops at the bottom of the column or page.

Manual flow text icon

Fig. 6.10. Manual flow text.

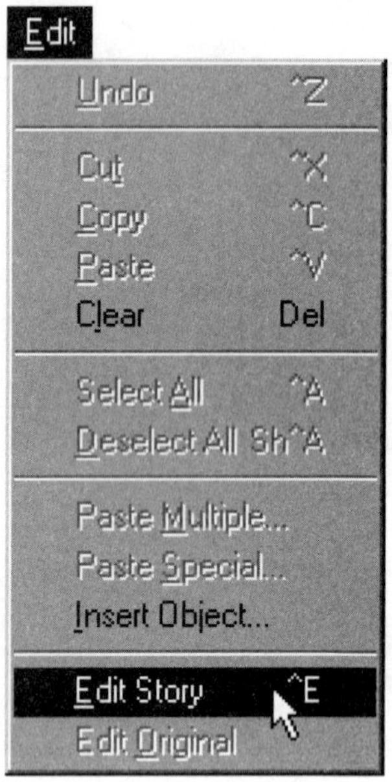

2. *Import* option from the *Story* menu. Select *Edit story* from the *Edit* menu. Choose this option when you want to edit the text before placing it in the publication.

When you select *Edit story* from the *Edit* menu, the menu bar changes from the Layout menu bar to the Edit story menu bar (figs. 6.11 and 6.12).

Fig. 6.11. Layout menu bar.

Fig. 6.12. *Edit story* menu bar.

A story can be a single text block or a series of text blocks threaded together throughout a document.

The *Edit story* option in PageMaker offers a built-in word processor. When using this option, PageMaker displays text only. In addition to the word processing feature, the *Edit story* option makes available Spelling checker, Search/Replace, and text attributes such as font, size, and paragraph style.

Using the *Import* command from the *Story* menu, you can place a word processed file into the Story Editor.

The *Import to Story Editor* menu places the word processed file in three ways: *As new story*, *Replacing entire story*, and *Inserting text*. If *As new story* is selected, the Story Editor places the file into a new story window. If *Replacing entire story* is selected, the file goes into the currently active window, completely replacing any story currently in that window. If *Inserting text* is activated, the imported file will go into the active window at the text cursor location.

Text Frames

PageMaker 6.5 allows you to create two kinds of text objects, text frames and text blocks. Once the text created either as block or frame, its manipulation is the same.
To create a text frame, follow these steps:

1. Select one of the text frame tools from the Toolbox.
2. Draw a frame. The frame contains crossing lines (fig. 6.13).

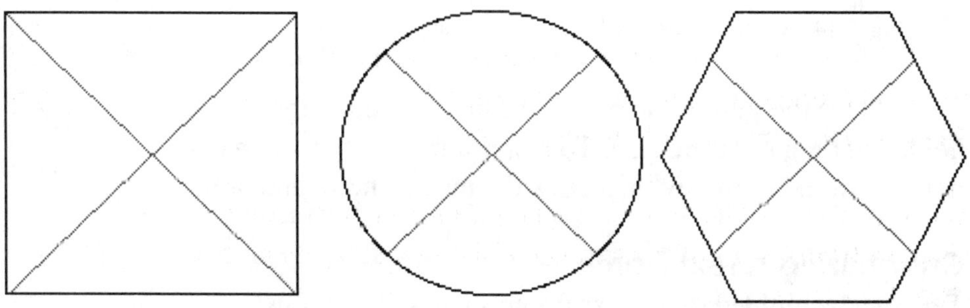

Fig. 6.13. Text frames.

You can directly type, copy and paste, or import text into the frame. To type directly into the frame, select the Text tool from the Toolbox, click it inside the frame, and then type.

PageMaker allows you to attach a text block to a frame, deleting the text block and adding its text to the frame. To attach a text block to a frame, follow these steps:

1. Select a Frame tool from the Toolbox and draw a frame.
2. Select a text block, hold down the Shift key, and then select an empty frame.
3. From the *Element* menu, Choose *Frame* and select *Attach Content*. The text flows into the frame and the text block disappears.

At any time, you can resize a frame. To resize a frame:
1. Select the Pointer from the Toolbox.
2. Click on the frame to select it. Handles appear around the frame (fig. 6.14).

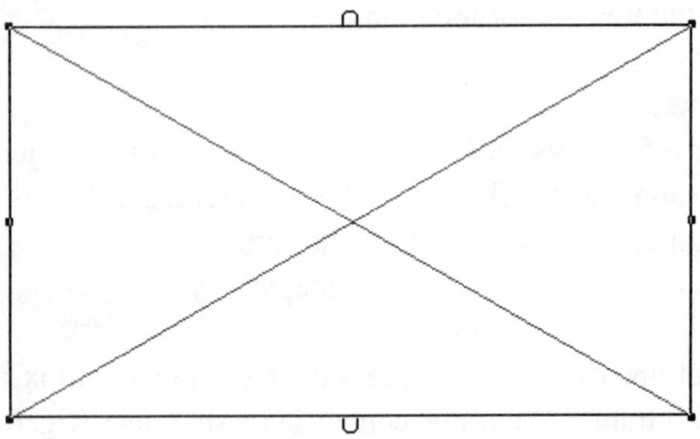

Fig. 6.14. When a frame is selected, handles appear around it.

3. Place the Pointer on one of the handles, click the mouse, hold, and drag to desire size. To resize a frame proportionately, hold down the Shift key then click the mouse, hold, and drag.

Customizing a Text Frame

Text can be molded to the text frame shapes. To do this:
1. Select one of the frame tools from the Toolbox and draw a frame.
2. Select *Place* from the *File* menu.
3. From the DataDisk (provided with the book), select *Lorem*.
4. Click *Open*.
5. Place the loaded icon inside the frame on the top and click the mouse. The dummy text flows inside the frame, molding to the shape of the frame (fig. 6.15).

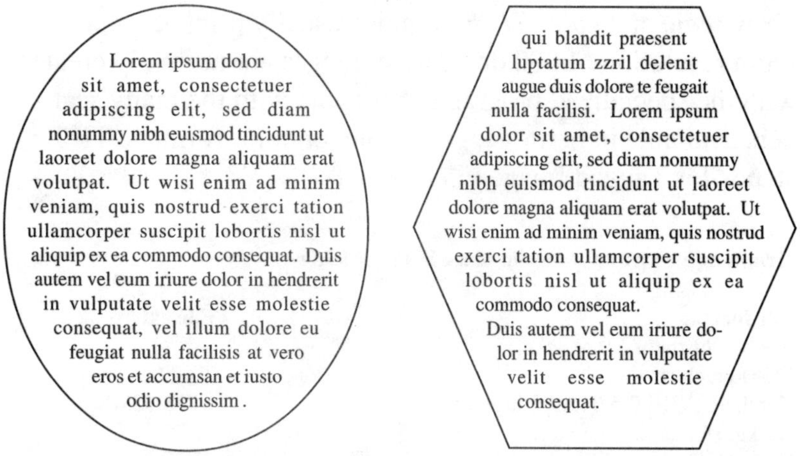

Fig. 6.15. Customized text frames.

You may delete the line around the frame. To do that:
1. Select the Pointer tool and click on the frame.
2. From the *Element* menu choose *Stroke* and then select *None*.
A gray line will remain on the screen which is non-printable.

Importing Graphics

Four different types of graphics can be imported into Page-Maker. The type of graphic you import depends generally on the type of graphics package used to create it.

Paint-type icon

Paint-type or *bit-map* graphics are the pictures that come from paintlike packages. They are generally of a much lower resolution than other types of drawings, usually with a maximum resolution of 72 to 300 dots per inch (dpi). This type of graphic is produced by programs such as MacPaint or PixelPaint.

Draw-type icon

Draw-type or *PICT* graphics are based on the sequence of drawing commands that describe the graphic. Programs that produce these types of graphics include PC PaintBrush, Harvard Graphics, and CorelDraw. These are generally much higher quality pictures than can be achieved with paint-type programs.

EPS-type icon

TIFF-type icon

Encapsulated PostScript (EPS) graphics are possibly the highest quality graphics. This type is created by drawing programs such as Adobe Illustrator and Aldus Freehand.

Gray scale and *color TIFF* graphics usually print at a maximum resolution of 300 dpi. These images are normally created with the specialized programs that come with the many scanners available in halftone, gray scale, or color formats. TIFF stands for Tagged Image File Format.

Graphics file formats you can place in PageMaker

File format	File extension	Windows	Macintosh
Adobe Illustrator 5.0 or later	.AI	X	X
CGM graphics	.CGM	X	X
CorelDRAW! 3.0-5.0 /5.0 Clip Art	.CDR/.CMX	X	-
Desktop Color Separation (DCS)	.DCS	X	X
Dynamic Exchange Format (DXF)	.DXF	X	X
Encapsulated PostScript (EPS)	.EPS	X	X
Graphics Environment Manager (GEM)	.GEM	X	X
Graphics Interchange Format (GIF)	.GIF	X	X
Hewlett-Packard Graphics Language (HPGL)	.PLT	X	-
Joint Photographics Expert Group (JPEG)	.JPG	X	X
Kodak Photo CD and Pro Photo CD	.PCD	X	X
Lotus Graphics PIC	.PIC	X	-
Macintosh Picture (PICT)	.PCT	X	X
MacPaint	.PNT	X	X
Microsoft Excel 3.0-4.0	.XLC	X	-
PC Paintbrush	.PCX	X	X
QuickTime movie (specified frame only)	.MOV	X	X
Scitex Continuous Tone	.SCT	X	X
Table Editor 2.1	.TBL	X	-
Tektronix Plot	.PLT	X	-
TIFF	.TI F	X	X
Windows Bitmap	.BMP	X	X
Windows Metafile or Enhanced Metafile	.WMF/.EMF	X	X
WordPerfect Graphics 1.0-2.0	.WPG	X	-

All graphics are imported into PageMaker in exactly the same way as text files are—via the *Place* command in the *File* menu. Once a graphic is imported, however, the icon is different, depending on the type of graphic.

1. From the *File* menu, select the *Place* option.
2. From the DataDisk, provided with this book, select *tree4.eps* and click OK.
3. Once the cursor has changed to indicate that a graphics file has been loaded into memory, click the mouse button where you want the graphic to be placed (fig. 6.16).

Resizing Graphics

Although the graphic will be in place, it may be nowhere near the size you want. To resize the imported picture, take the following steps:

Fig. 6.16. Imported graphic.

1. Place the Pointer on the graphic and click. The graphic is selected (fig. 6.17).

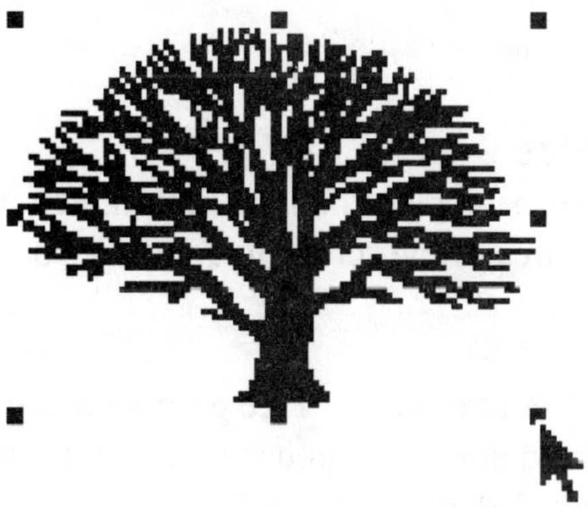

Fig. 6.17. The selected graphic has handles around it.

2. Position the Pointer on the corner handle of the selected graphic and hold down the mouse button. The Pointer turns into a double-headed arrow Fig. 6.18).

Fig. 6.18. When selecting a graphic, the Pointer turns into a double-headed arrow.

3. Drag up, down, or to the sides until the graphic is the desired size and shape (fig. 6.19).

Fig. 6.19. Resized graphic.

Moving Graphics

Once a graphic has been placed on the screen, you may want to move it from one area of the screen to another. To do this, use the following steps:

1. Position the Pointer on the Tree graphic and click.
2. Press and hold down the mouse button until the Pointer becomes a four-headed arrow (fig. 6.20).

Fig. 6.20. When holding down the Pointer for a moment, it changes to a four-headed arrow.

3. Still holding down the mouse button, drag the graphic wherever you want on the screen.

Graphic Frames

Like text, PageMaker 6.5 allows you to place graphic images in a frame. To do this:

1. Select one of the frame tools from the Toolbox and draw a frame.
2. From the *File* menu, choose *Place*.
3. Select the graphic file and click OK. The selected graphic displays in the frame (fig. 6.21).

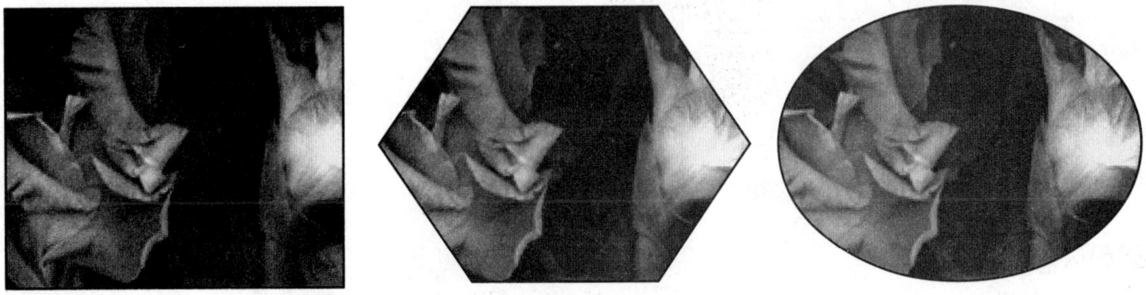

Fig. 6.21. Graphic in the customized frames.

Text Manipulation

When you select a text block with the Pointer tool, horizontal lines with handles appear at the top and bottom of the text block (fig. 6.22). Using the handles, you can move or resize a text block.

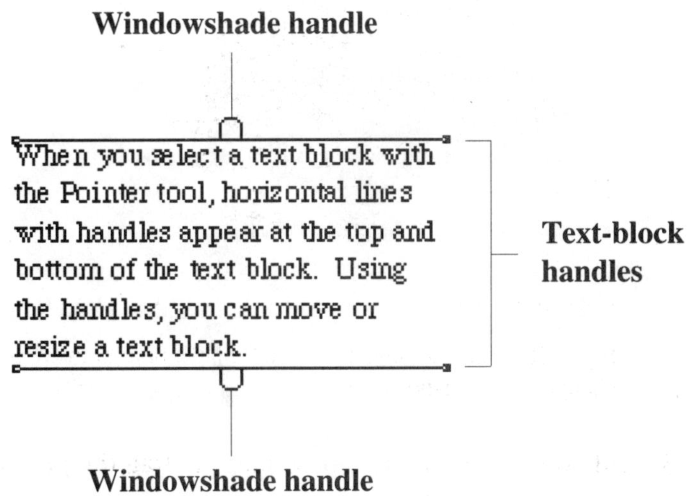

Fig. 6.22. Text handles.

The two kinds of handles are *windowshade handles* and *text-block handles.* Inside the windowshade handles you can see symbols. An empty windowshade handle indicates that no more text exists beyond the windowshade handle. An empty windowshade handle at the top of the text block indicates the beginning of the story, and one at the bottom indicates the end of the story.

A + in the windowshade handle indicates that text continues beyond the handle. A + in the top of the text tells you that a block or blocks of text precede the current block. A + in the bottom windowshade handle indicates that more text block follows.

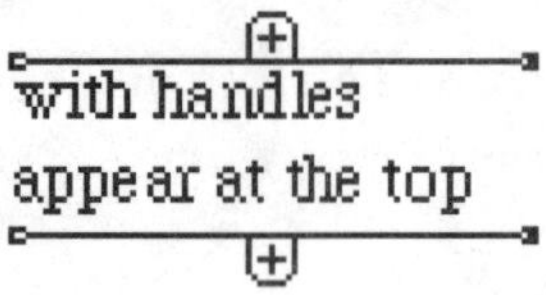

A small down arrow ▼ in the bottom windowshade handle indicates that the text block contains more text than is currently visible.

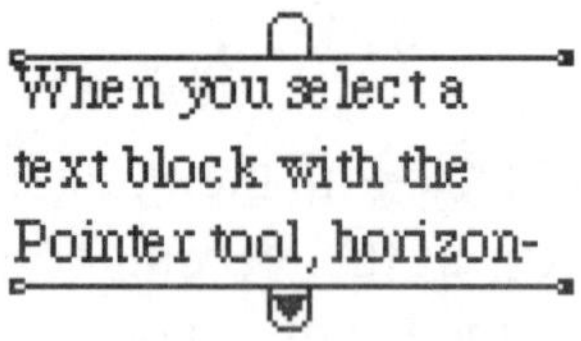

Resizing Text

PageMaker allows you to resize a text block either *vertically* or *horizontally.*

Resizing Horizontally

You can make a text block either wider or narrower.

1. Select the Pointer from the Toolbox.
2. Place the Pointer icon anywhere on the text block and click. The text block is selected and you are able to see the text handles.

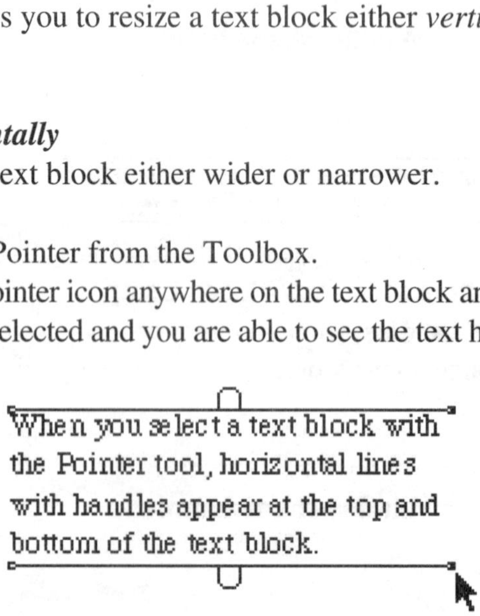

3. Place the Pointer on a text-block handle, and hold down the mouse button until the Pointer changes to a double-headed arrow.

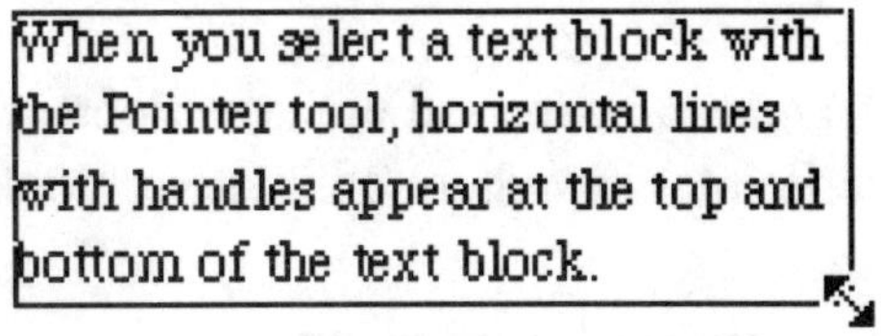

Then drag the handle to the desired location. When you release the mouse button, the text block resizes and reshapes accordingly (fig. 6.23).

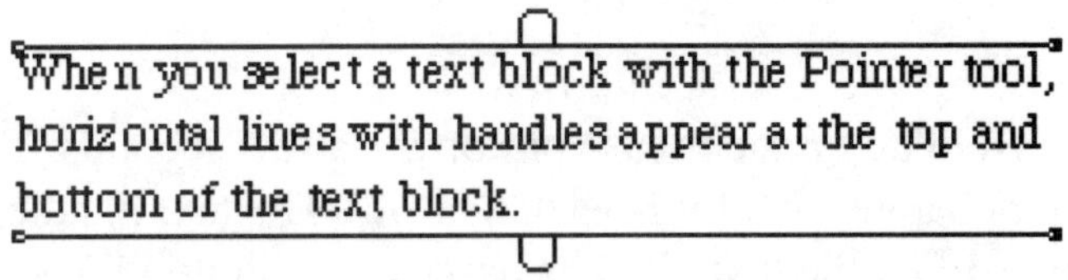

Fig. 6.23. Horizontally resized text.

Resizing Vertically

To increase or decrease the height of a text block, the block can be resized vertically.

1. Select the text block with the Pointer.
2. Place the Pointer on the lower windowshade handle.

> In the process of decreasing the size of a text block vertically, you may lose part of your text.

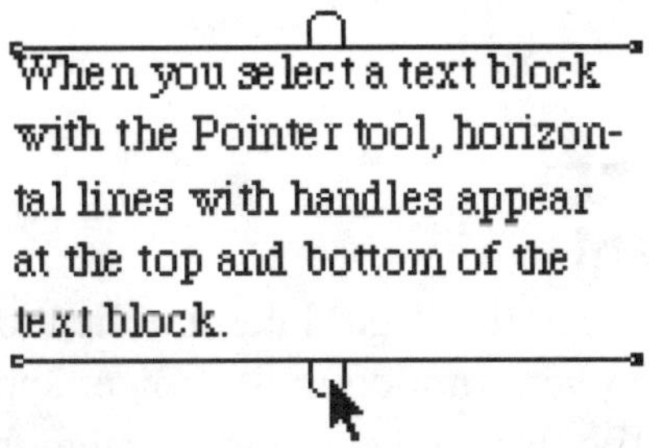

3. Hold down the mouse button while moving the handle up or down.
4. Release the mouse button to adjust the text to the new size.

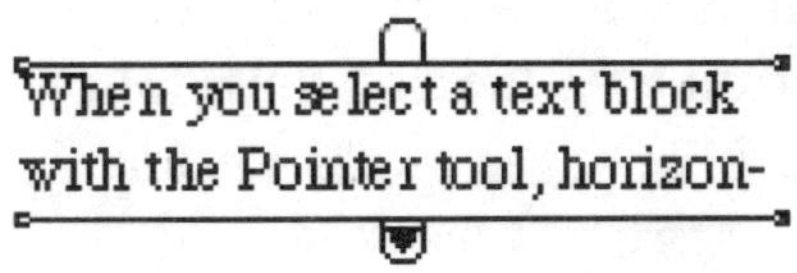

Moving a Text Block

PageMaker allows you to move a block of text and place it in a different part of the publication.

1. Select the text to be moved with the Pointer.
2. Place the Pointer anywhere on the text block.

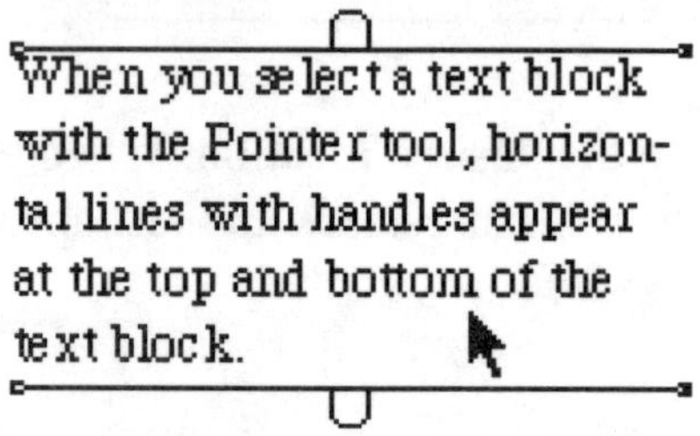

3. Hold down the mouse button for a few seconds. The Pointer changes to a four-headed arrow. The text handles disappear and the text block is bounded by dotted lines.

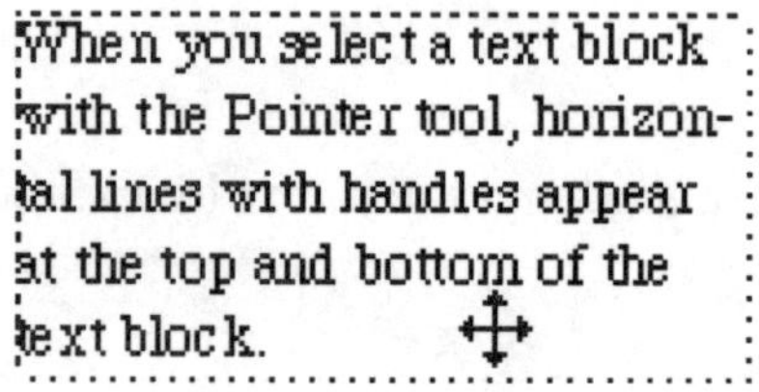

4. While holding the mouse button down, move the text block anywhere on the screen that you wish.

Saving a Document

Like any computer document, the PageMaker publication must be saved periodically. Any interruption in the power supply to the computer erases the file from the computer's memory. In case of power failure, you can quickly recover a record of the file by retrieving the copy from the saved disk. It is a good idea to save your file every 15 minutes; thus you will never lose more than 15 minutes' work.

> Saving files in PageMaker is the same as saving in other PC applications.

If you are saving a publication for the first time, follow these steps:

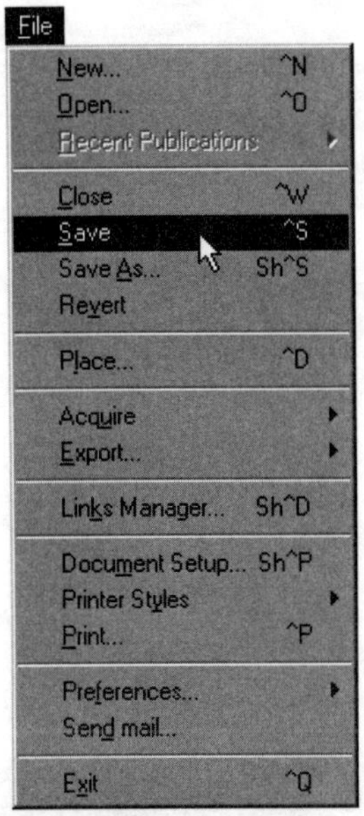

1. Select the *Save* option from the *File* menu.
2. The *Save publication* dialog box displays on the screen (fig. 6.24).

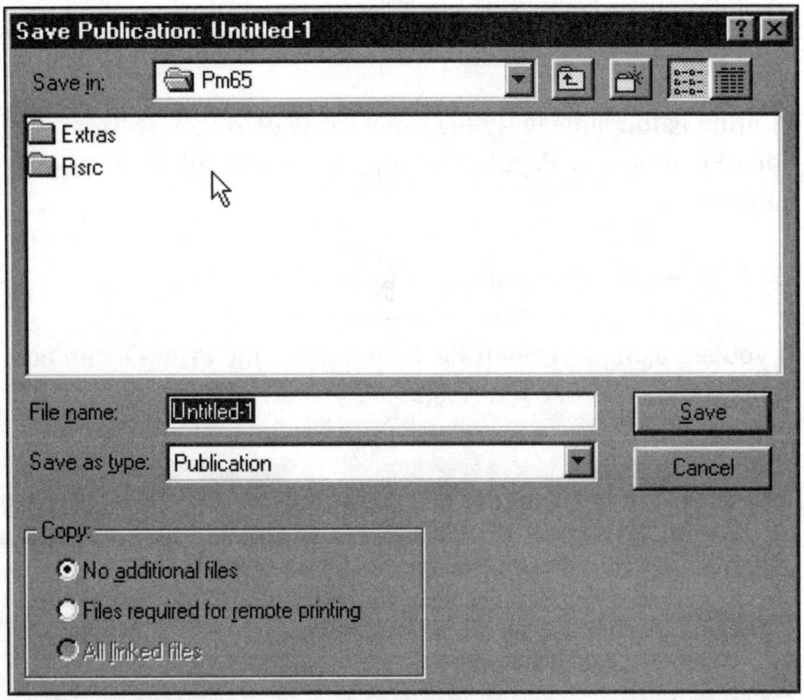

Fig. 6.24. *Save publication* dialog box.

3. Type a name for your publication.
4. Click *Save*.

Each time you save a document, the latest changes are saved too. There may be times when you would like to change the name of a publication or a template or make a copy of an existing publication or template. In this case, use the *Save as* command from the *File* menu. Type a new name for your publication or template and click OK.

Printing a Publication

Printing is the most important step in the desktop publishing cycle, because it is the product for which you have labored. The PageMaker document can be printed by a dot matrix printer, an ink-jet printer, or a laser printer. Each printer offers different print quality, or *resolution*. Resolution is the number of dots in a particular area of the screen or page. A dot matrix printer's resolution starts from 70 dots per inch (dpi). Most laser printers can produce from 300 to 1,200 dpi. A 300 dpi resolution is probably sufficient for most publications; however, professional printers produce up to 2,540 dpi.

Printing is fundamentally the same for PageMaker as for any other PC program. PageMaker supports nearly all of the popular printers.

1. Select the *Print* option from the *File* menu.

If you are using a Hewlett Packard printer, the Print Document dialog box looks like figure 6.25.

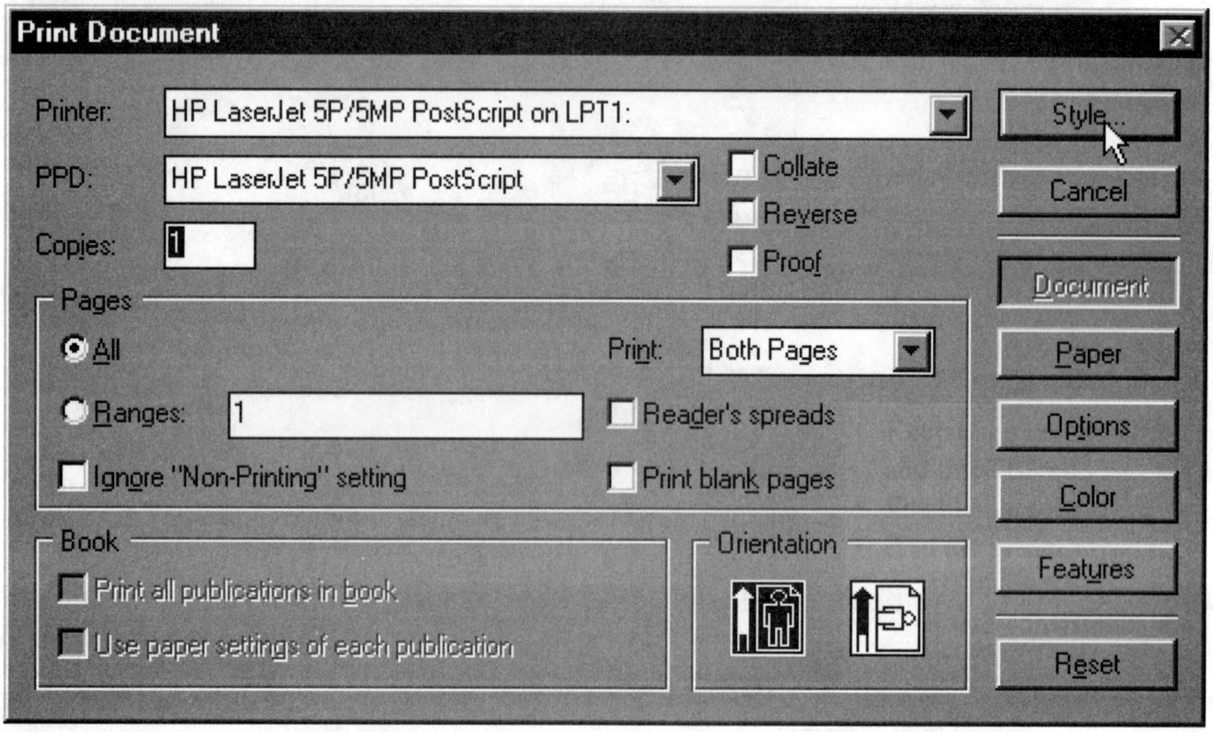

Fig. 6.25. Hewlett Pakard *Print Document* dialog box.

2. Select *Paper* from the dialog box. The Paper setup dialog box appears (fig. 6.26).

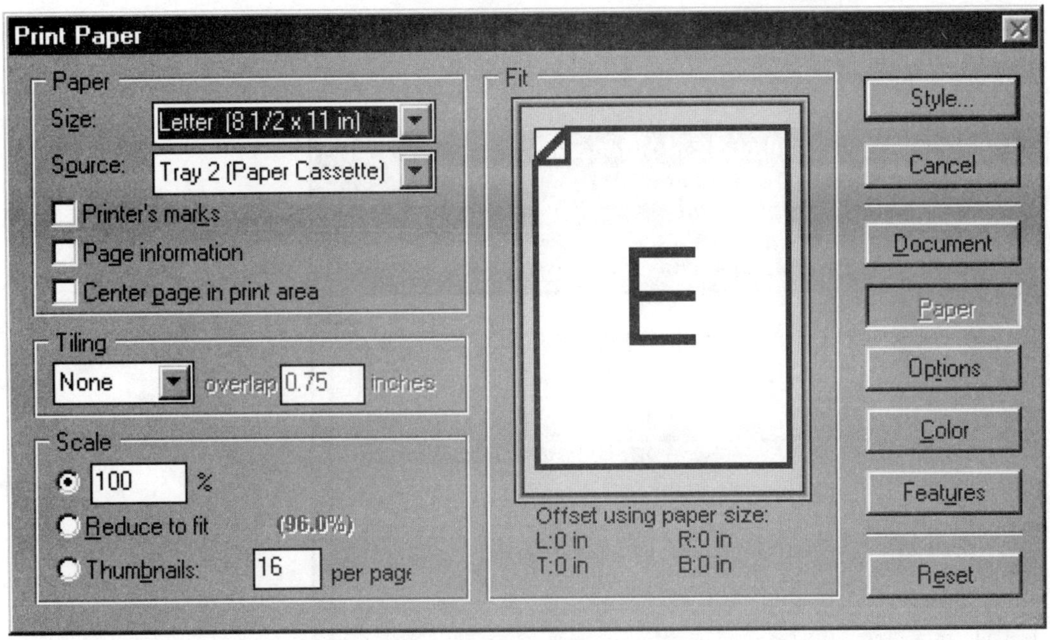

Fig. 6.26. Hewlett Pachard *Paper* setup dialog box.

If you are using Epson ActionLaser 1000 , the printing process is as follows.

1. Select *Print* from the *File* menu. The Epson ActionLaser 1000 *Print* dialog box displays (fig. 6.27).

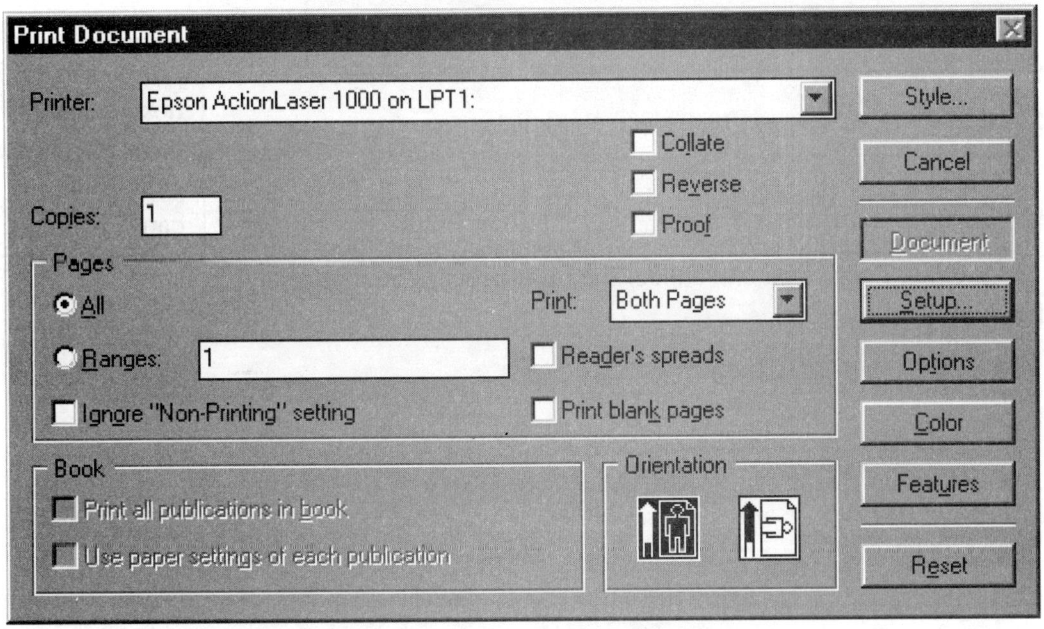

Fig. 6.27. Epson ActionLaser 1000 *Print Document* dialog box.

2. Click on printer *Setup*. The printer Setup dialog box appears (fig. 6.28).

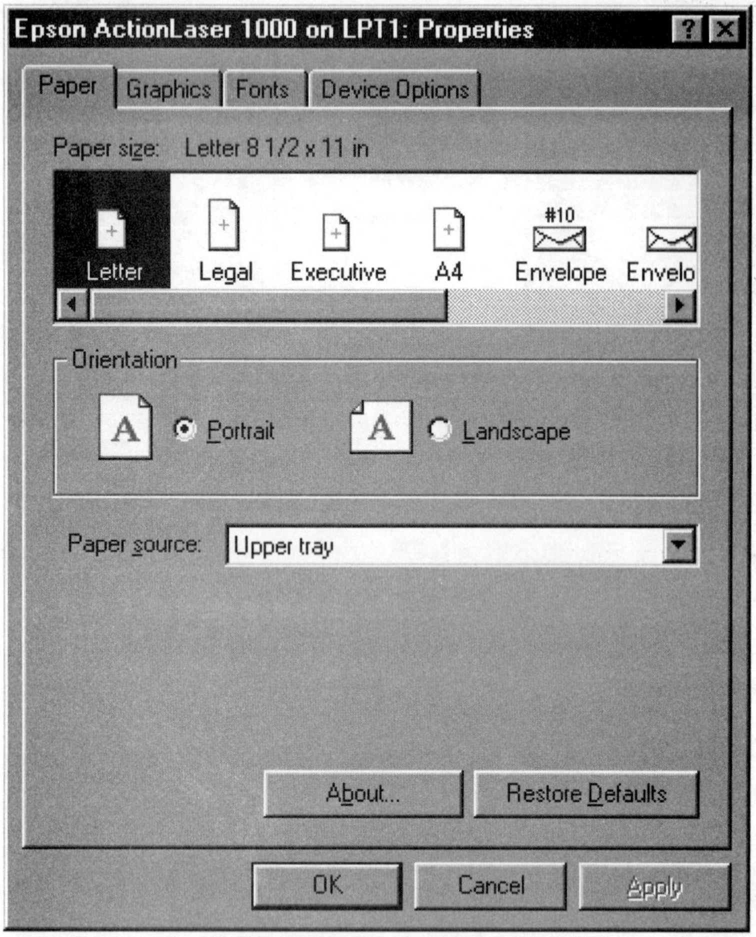

Fig. 6.28. Epson ActionLaser 1000 printer *Setup* dialog box.

3. Select the desired paper size or any other options.
4. Click OK.
5. Click Print. You can cancel the print process at any time by clicking on Cancel.

Laser printers have a designated print area. The print area is the area on a page in which the printer can print.

7

Creating a Flyer

The purpose of a flyer is to inform people about a subject as succinctly as possible. In schools, flyers are used to inform students and parents of upcoming events. A flyer is rarely longer than one page, although it may be printed on both sides.

The DataDisk contains the required items for making a field-trip flyer. Follow the instructions on the following pages to produce a successful flyer.

Planning

Flyers are usually 8.5 x 11 inches or 8.5 x 14 inches. Sometimes they are folded in half or in thirds. A flyer can be designed horizontally or vertically.

> On PageMaker, select *Wide* for horizontal page orientation and *Tall* for vertical page orientation.

PageMaker supports 8.5-x-14-inch flyers but be sure your printer can handle 8.5-x-14-inch paper. Also, in designing a flyer, it is important to consider the actual printable area of the sheet. When you select your printer from the PageMaker printer options, the program indicates the printable area. For example, the Apple LaserWriter NTX series, at letter size, prints an image area 8 x 10.8 inches created on the 8.5-x-11-inch page. At legal size, it prints 8 x 13.8 inches centered on an 8.5-x-14-inch page. Other printers may meet or even exceed these image areas. However, they also may not have PostScript, the page description image, described earlier, built in.

Creating a Field-Trip Flyer

On the DataDisk, the disk that accompanies this book, you will find items required to create a simple field-trip flyer shown in figure 7.1.

Fig. 7.1. The field-trip flyer.

Setting Up the Flyer

The first step is to load a publication grid.

1. Insert the DataDisk in your disk drive.
2. Open the PageMaker program by double-clicking on the PageMaker icon.
3. Select *Open* from the *File* menu.
4. Click on the *Look in* box to select the drive in which DataDisk inserted (fig. 7.2). DataDisk files display on screen.

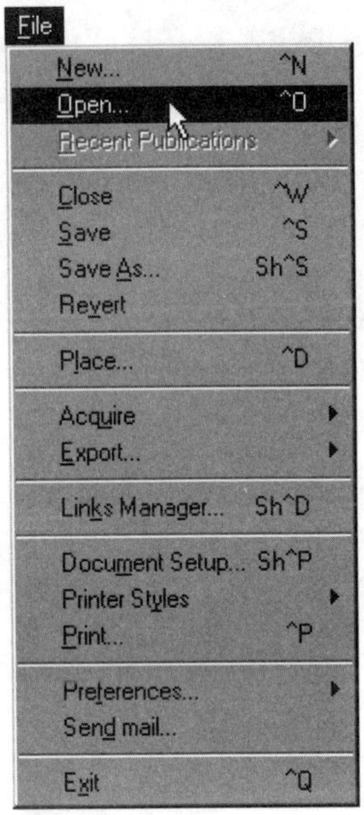

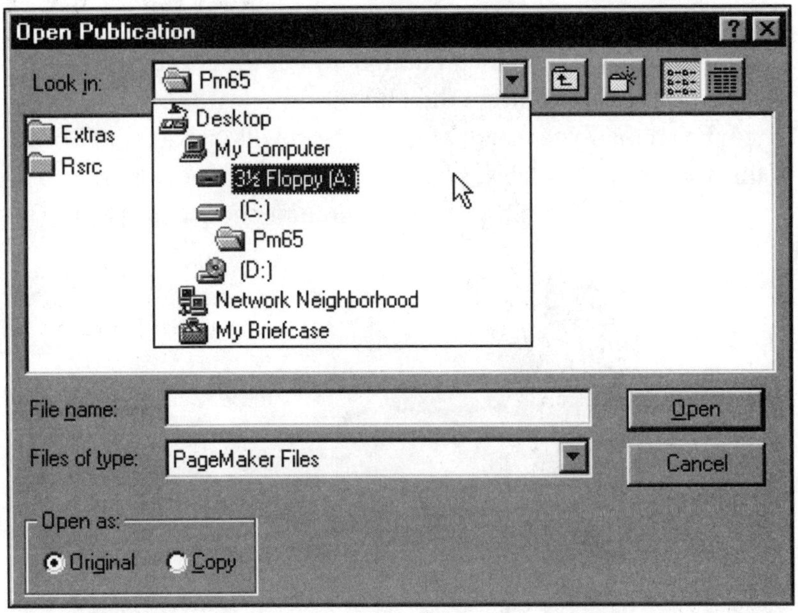

Fig. 7.2. DataDisk menu.

6. In the File Name area, *Grid.pm6* appears.
7. Click *Open*. The field-trip flyer grid displays on the screen.

The *Grid.pm6* is a double-column, predesigned page that helps you place text and graphics in the proper areas. The left column is designed for graphic placement and the right column is designed for text.

Creating Text

On the top of the grid, a space is provided for the title.

1. Select the Text tool from the Toolbox.
2. Place the I-beam cursor on the right column at 3 inches and 7 ticks (each inch is divided into 20 tick marks. See explanation at the right) on the horizontal ruler and at 0.10 inch on the vertical ruler and click the mouse button. Type:

   Trip to the Zoo

> The measurement system for this practice is set at *Inches Decimal* in the *Preferences* options on the *File* menu. In this system, each inch has 20 tick marks (each is .05 inches). For example, 2.10 inches refers to 2 inches plus 10 tick marks.

3. Hold down the mouse button and drag it across the title you just typed to highlight the text.
4. From the *Type* menu, select *Font* and choose *Avant Garde*. If this font is not available, you can substitute Helvetica.
5. Select *Size* from the *Type* menu and choose *36* (fig. 7.3).

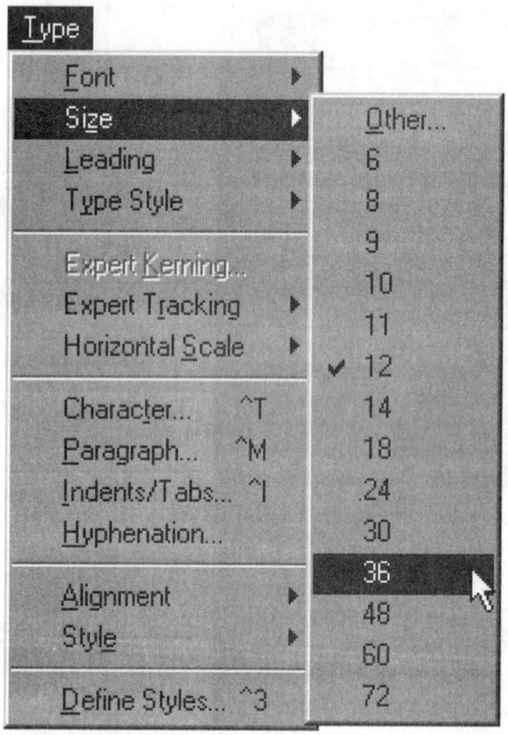

Fig. 7.3. *Type* menu, *Size* selected.

6. Select *Type style* from the *Type* menu and highlight *Bold* (fig. 7.4).

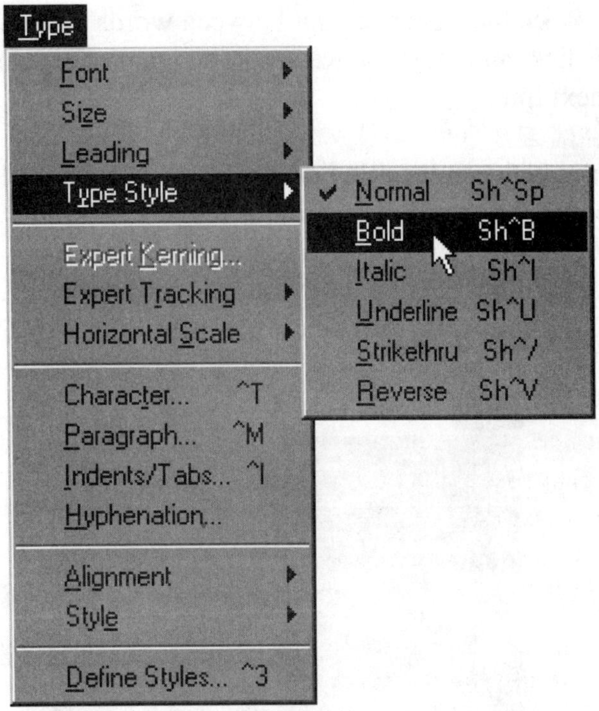

Fig. 7.4. *Type* menu, *Bold* selected.

7. Select *Alignment* from the *Type* menu and highlight *Align right* (fig. 7.5). The title is now justified to the right.

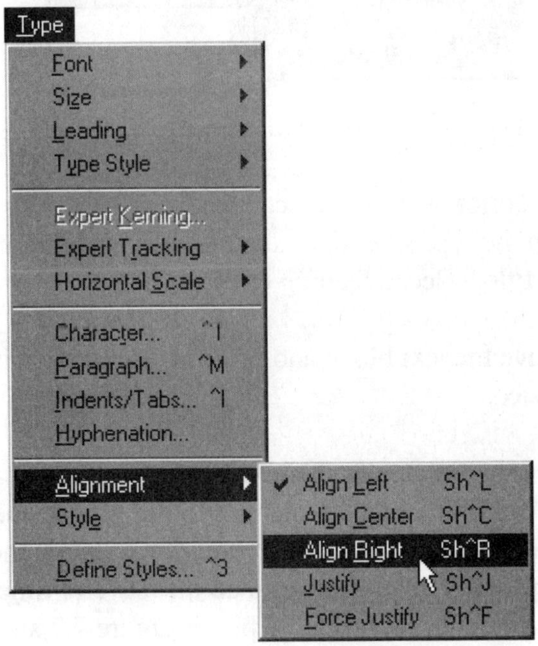

Fig. 7.5. *Type* menu, *Align right* selected.

8. Place the I-beam cursor between words "the" and "Zoo," click, and press the Return key to move the word "Zoo" to the next line.

The space between the title lines looks too big. The title appears better if you reduce the line spacing, or leading.

9. Highlight the title, both lines.
10. Select *Leading* from the *Type* menu (fig. 7.6).

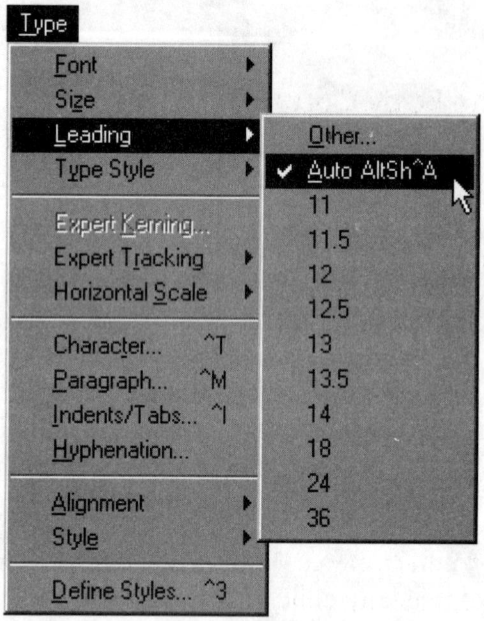

Fig. 7.6. *Type* menu, *Leading* selected.

The default option is *Auto*. Select a leading that is 5 or 6 points smaller than the type size. For example, if you select a 36-point font for the title, select a leading of 30 points.

You can move the text block and position it exactly within the provided space.

11. Place the Pointer on the text block, click the mouse button, and hold. The Pointer changes to the four-headed arrow. While holding the mouse button down, move the text to the desired place. You may have to do this several times to position the title in an appropriate place. Figure 7.7 shows the title.

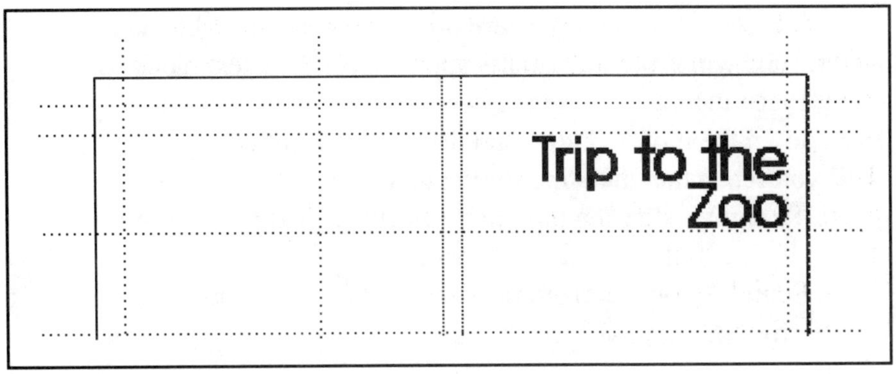

Fig. 7.7. Flyer with the title.

When entering the text items, you may type your own information.

Entering the Body Copy

The *grid.pm6* has provided space for the detailed information about the field trip. The information items may include the description of the field trip, departure/arrival time, instructions about lunch, transportation, volunteers, and so on. For better effect, you may wish to separate these text items, leaving white space between each item. In this case each information item should be a separate text block or story.

Entering Text Item #1

1. Select the Text tool from the Toolbox.
2. Place the I-beam cursor on the right column at 3 inches and 7 ticks on the horizontal ruler and at 2 inches and 5 ticks on the vertical ruler and click the mouse button.
3. Select *Actual size* from the *View* menu, You can select *Fit in window* at any time to view the entire page. However, it is best to type in text in *Actual size.*
4. Type the following:

> The fourth-grade students are scheduled to visit the San Diego Zoo. In this field trip, students will become familiar with different animals that they have studied in science class.

Aligning Text

As you can see, the text is spread across the page. You need to manipulate the text.

1. Select the Pointer from the Toolbox.

2. Click the Pointer anywhere on the text. The text-block handles and windowshade handles appear around the text block.

3. Place the Pointer on the lower left text-block handle. Hold down the mouse button and drag to the right and down until you reach the guideline for the text.

4. To right justify the text, first select the Text tool from the Toolbox. Highlight the entire text.

5. Select *Alignment* from the *Type* menu and choose *Align center* (fig. 7.8).

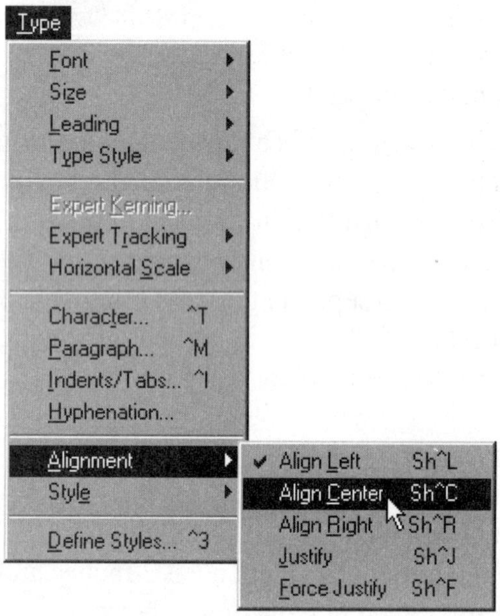

Fig. 7.8. *Alignment* menu.

Entering Text Item #2

1. Select the Text tool from the Toolbox, place the I-beam cursor at 3 inches and 7 ticks on the horizontal ruler and at 3 inches and 18 ticks on the vertical ruler and click the mouse button.

2. Type the following text:

> The fourth-grade teachers welcome the assistance of volunteer parents.

Follow the same procedure used for text item #1 to format the text you just typed.

Entering Text Item #3

1. Select the Text tool from the Toolbox, place the I-beam cursor at 3 inches and 7 ticks on the horizontal ruler and at 5 inches on the vertical ruler and click . Type the text as follows:

> Date: May 18, 1996
> Departure: 7:00 am
> Return: 6:30 pm
> at the school main entrance

Use the scroll bars to move the page up, down, left, or right.

Changing the Size, Type Style, and Alignment

1. Highlight the text, select *Size* from the *Type* menu, and choose *14* to enlarge the text.
2. Select *Type style* from the *Type* menu and choose *Bold* to change the style.
3. Highlight *Alignment* from the *Type* menu and choose *Align center.*

Entering Text Item #4

1. Select the Text tool from the Toolbox, place the I-beam cursor at 3 inches and 7 ticks on the horizontal ruler and at 6 inches and 4 ticks on the vertical ruler and click. Type:

> Please make sure to provide transportation to and from school for your child.

2. Select *Alignment* from the *Type* menu and choose *Align center.*

Entering Text Item #5

1. Follow the same procedure used for text item #4. Place the I-beam cursor at 3 inches and 7 ticks on the horizontal ruler and at 7 inches and 6 ticks on the vertical ruler and type the following text:

> Lunch and snack are furnished

Follow the same procedure used for text item #3 to change the size and font style of the text.

Entering Text Item #6

1. Place the Text tool in the provided spot at 3.7 inches on the horizontal ruler and at 8 inches on the vertical ruler and type:

If you have any questions concerning the field trip, please feel free to call 834-9154.

2. Select *Alignment* from the *Type* menu and choose *Align center*. The flyer should look like figure 7.9.

Trip to the Zoo

The fourth-grade students are scheduled
to visit the San Diego Zoo.
In this field trip, students will become
familiar with different
animals that they have studied in
science class.

The fourth-grade teachers welcome the
assistance of volunteer parents.

Date: May 18, 1996
Departure: 7:00 am
Return: 6:30 pm
at the school main entrance

Please make sure to provide
transportation to and from school
for your child.

Lunch and snack are furnished

If you have any questions concerning
the field trip, please feel free to
call 834-9154.

Fig. 7.9. The first draft of the flyer.

Creating a Drop Shadow

The left column is reserved for drawing and placing graphics. A drop shadow is used to add dimension and attract attention. To create a drop-shadow box:

1. Select the Square-corner tool from the Toolbox.
2. Place the crossbar cursor on the upper left corner of the provided space for the drop-shadow box at 0.5 inch on the horizontal ruler and at 0.5 inch on the vertical ruler.
3. Hold down the mouse button and drag down to cover the indicated area at 8 inches and 15 ticks on the horizontal ruler and 2 inches on the vertical ruler (fig. 7.10).

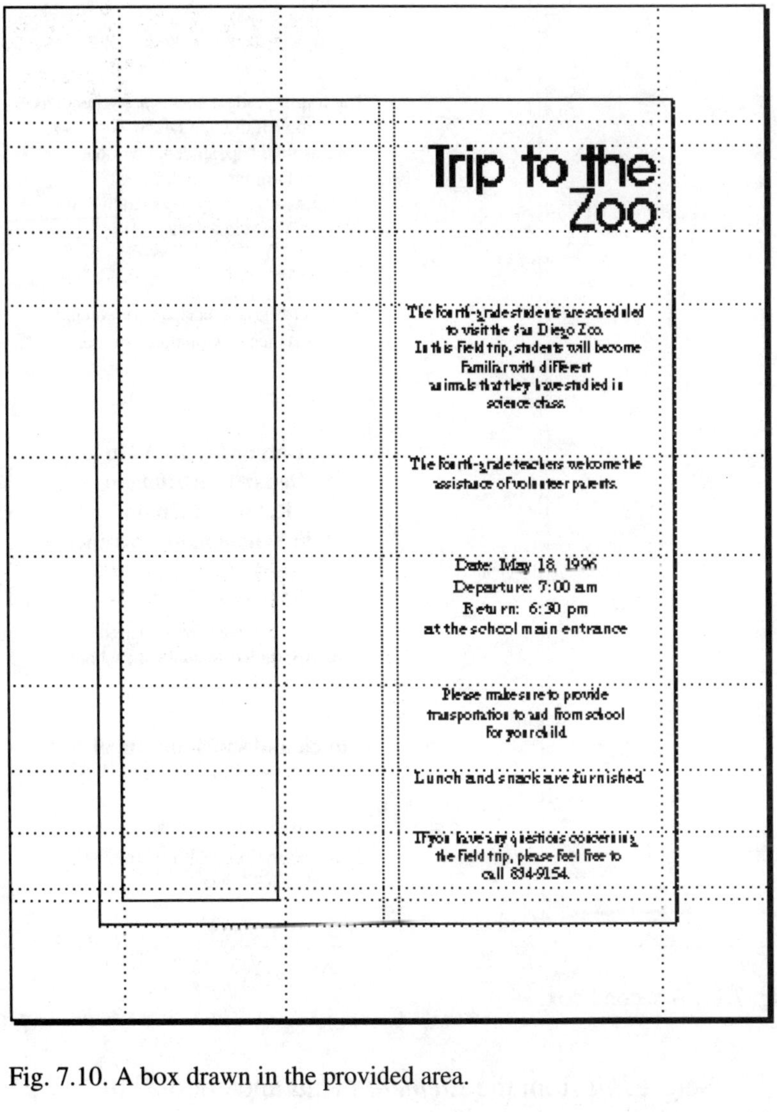

Fig. 7.10. A box drawn in the provided area.

4. Select *Fill* from the *Element* menu and highlight *Paper*.
5. Choose *Copy* from the *Edit* menu to copy the box (assuming the box is still selected—if not, place the Pointer on the box and click the mouse button).

6. Select *Paste* from the *Edit* menu. A second box appears on the screen (fig. 7.11).

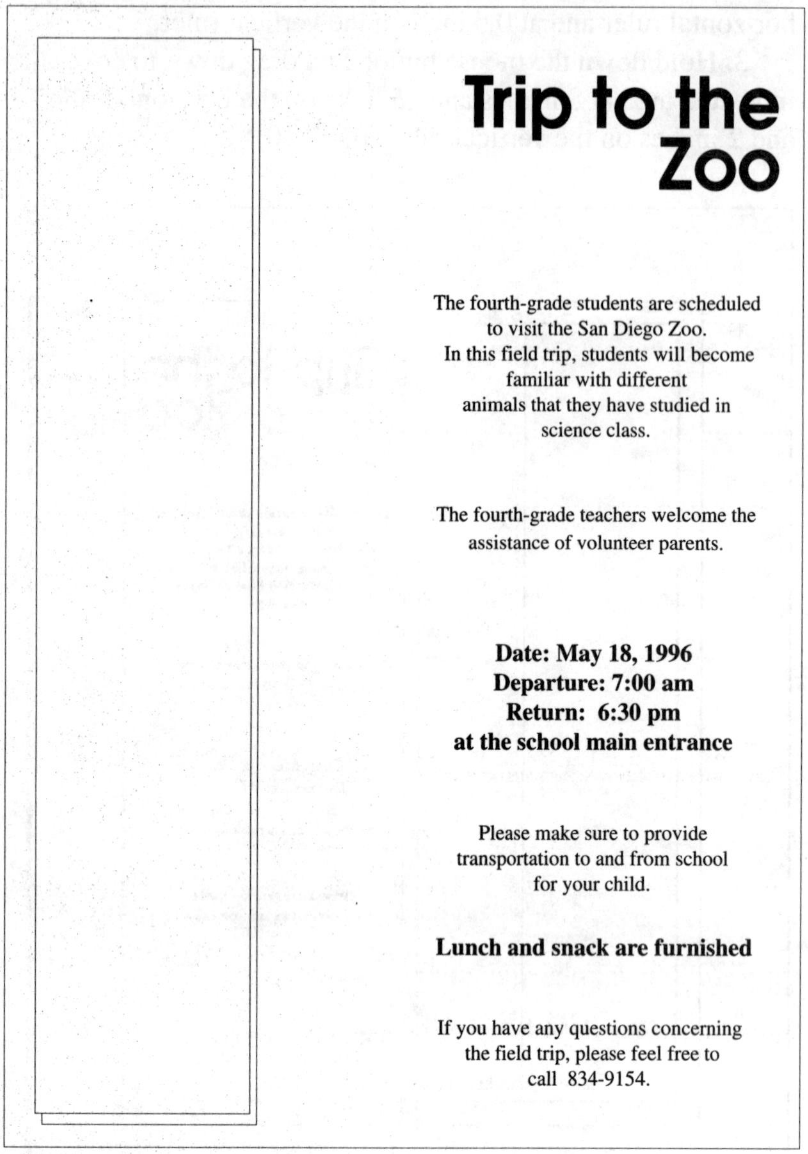

Fig. 7.11. A second box.

7. Select *Fill* from the *Element* menu and choose the *Solid* option. The box turns to a solid black box (fig. 7.12).

8. Select *Send to back* from the *Arrange* pop-up option in the *Element* menu. PageMaker sends the solid black box to the back of the first box, leaving a narrow black margin to the right and to the bottom of the box in front (fig. 7.13).

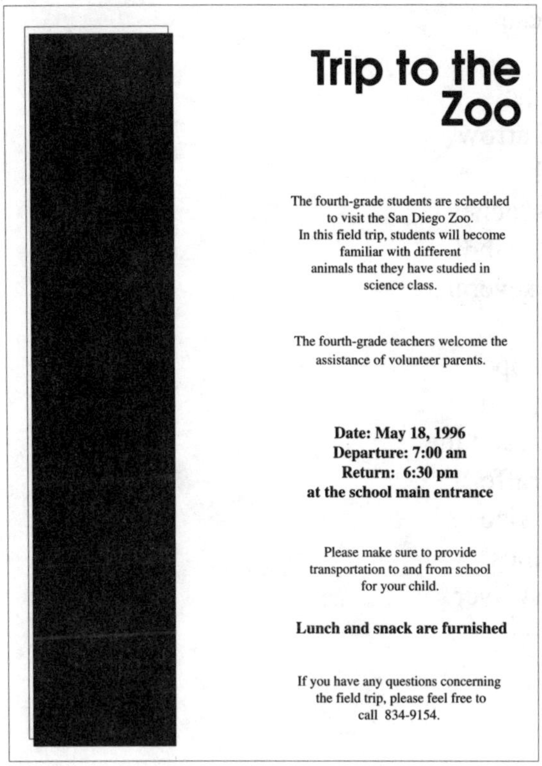

Fig. 7.12. Filled solid black box.

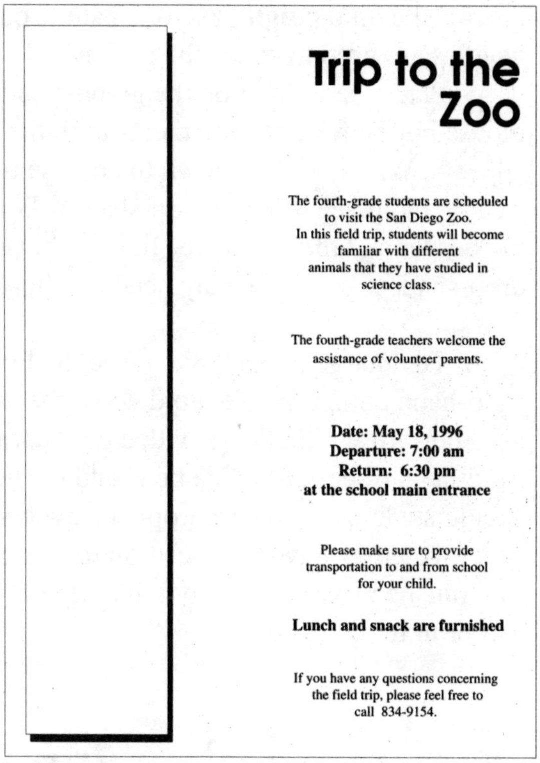

Fig. 7.13. Drop-shadow box.

Importing and Placing Graphics

The process of importing graphics into PageMaker is similar to the process of importing text, as described earlier. On the DataDisk, an EPS graphic is provided for this flyer. This clip art is furnished by the T/Maker Company. The graphic is called *giraffe.eps*. Follow these steps to import the graphic:

EPS stands for Encapsulated PostScript images.

1. Select *Place* from the *File* menu. PageMaker displays the *Place* dialog box. The drive icon must show DataDisk. If not, click on the Drive box to change the icon.
2. Highlight Flyer and click OK.
3. Select *giraffe.eps* and click OK.

EPS icon

When the graphic is loaded, the Pointer changes to an EPS icon.

4. Place the icon anywhere on the publication and click. The giraffe appears on the screen surrounded by eight handles—three handles on the top, three handles on the bottom,

one handle on the right, and one handle on the left. These handles are used to resize the graphic.

5. Place the Pointer on the graphic and hold down the mouse button for a few moments until the four-headed arrow appears. While holding down the mouse button, drag the giraffe and place it in the drop-shadow box so the tail touches the border and the hoofs are slightly above the bottom of the drop-shadow box. You may need to adjust the graphic several times.

6. To enlarge the graphic, place the Pointer on the upper right-hand corner handle, hold down the mouse button, and drag upward within the provided boundaries until you reach the headline's ruler guide. The head and the neck of the giraffe should stick up out of the drop-shadow box. To get the size exact, you may have to reposition the giraffe several times. The finished flyer should look like figure 7.14. Save the flyer and print it.

Fig. 7.14. The finished flyer.

8

Creating a Brochure

Brochures differ from flyers in size and often in quality; brochures are usually larger and of better quality.

Brochures are often used to present information about an organization, a product, or a service. Brochures can be printed in black-and-white or color, and can sometimes be up to 10 or more pages. They are often a single sheet of 8.5-x-11-inch paper, printed on both sides and folded into thirds, or 8.5-x-14-inch paper, printed on both sides and folded into fourths. Brochures can be folded by a folding machine.

Brochures provide a broader creative challenge than do many other kinds of publications. Even the size and shape of the page varies more in brochures.

Planning and Design

Planning and designing a brochure is not a difficult task. The brochure design can easily be a "one-person job." An original brochure can be produced on your laser printer and then be mass produced on a photocopier or by a commercial printer.

To design a three-fold brochure, begin with standard letter size paper, 8.5 x 11 inches, using both sides of the paper. Each page will be divided into three columns, representing one fold or panel in your brochure.

Before you start to layout the brochure, make sure that both text and illustrations are ready. For the purpose of learning and practice, text and graphics are included on the DataDisk that accompanies this book.

Setting Up the Brochure

Suppose you are asked to design a brochure for your school describing academic, athletic, and club activities. You decide to design a three-fold brochure on 8.5-x-11-inch paper. Choices in directions are for this specific test brochure.

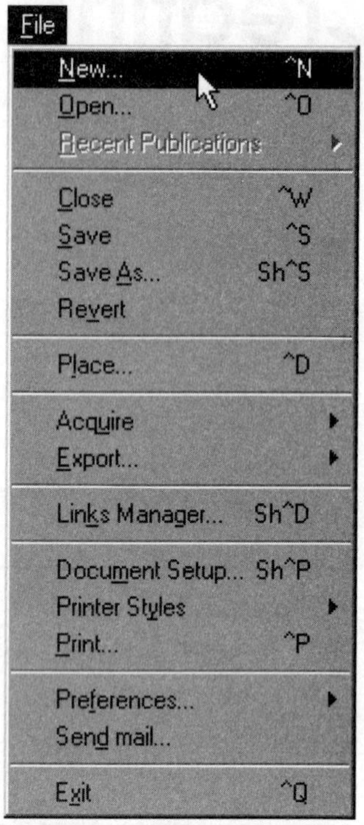

1. To start, open the PageMaker program by double-clicking on the PageMaker icon.
2. Select *New* from the *File* menu. The *Page setup* dialog box displays (fig. 8.1).

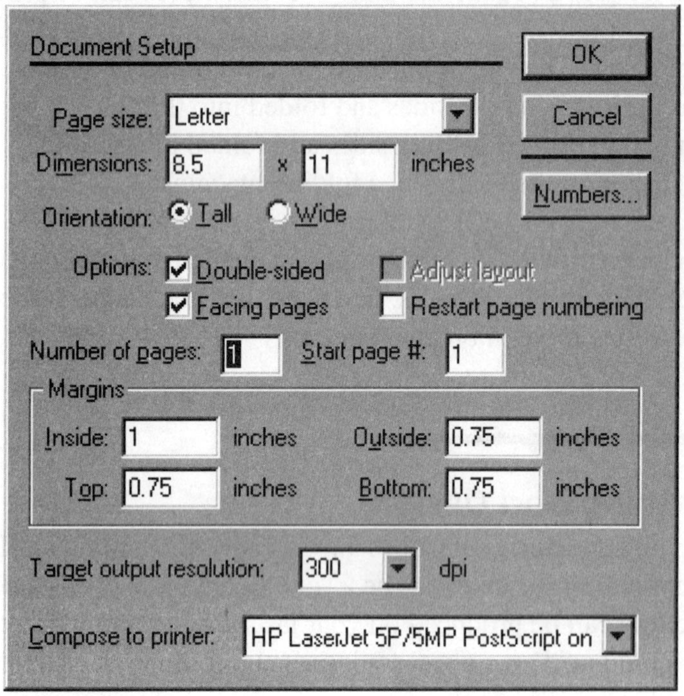

Fig. 8.1. *Page setup* dialog box.

3. Select *Wide* for Page orientation.
4. Drag across the 1 in the *Number of pages* box and type 2.
5. Deselect the *Double-sided* option by clicking on the box next to *Double-sided*. Even though your brochure is double-sided, both sides do not have the same layout configuration.
6. To set margins, drag across the 1 in the Left margin box and type 0.5. Press the Tab key. Type 0.5 for the Right margin and press the Tab key. Type 0.5 for the Top margin and press the Tab key. Type 0.5 for the Bottom margin and then click OK.

Changing the Measurement System

PageMaker allows you to change the measurement system option at any time while creating a publication.

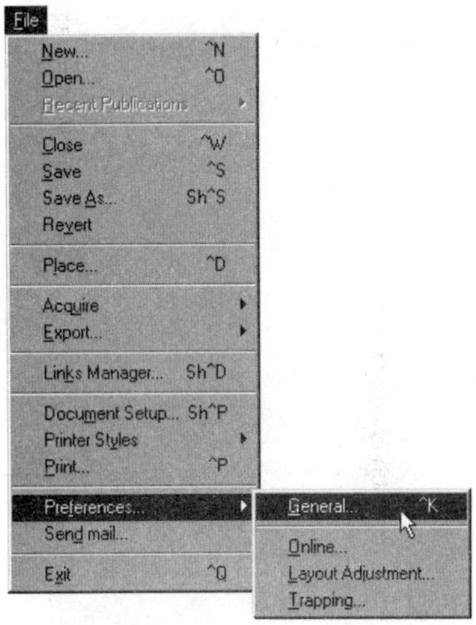

1. Select *Preferences* from the *File* menu and then choose *General* from the sub menu.
PageMaker displays a dialog box (fig. 8.2).

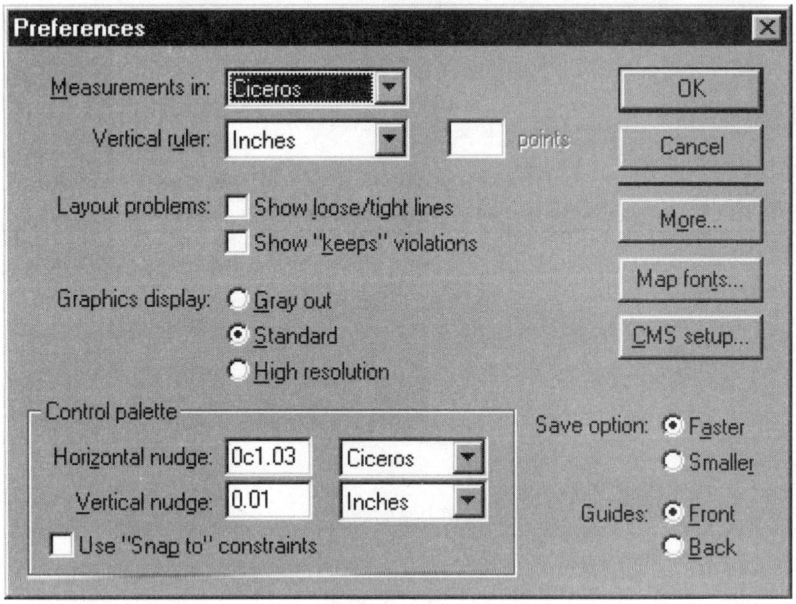

Fig. 8.2. *Peferences* dialog box with *Inches decimal* selected.

> When you change the measurement system, the ruler tickmarks in the new measurement system will probably not correspond to those in the previous system.

2. Place the Pointer on the box next to *Measurements in* and click. A popup menu appears. Select *Inches decimal.*
3. Place the Pointer on the box next to Vertical ruler, click, and choose *Inches decimal.*

Page 1

The brochure you are designing is a three-fold brochure. Page 1 includes a *foldover panel,* a *back panel*, and a *cover panel.* Page 2 includes *three inside panels.* In this brochure, each page has a different column setup.

1. Select *Column guides* from the *Layout* menu. PageMaker displays a dialog box (fig. 8.3).
2. Type 3 for the *Number of columns.*
3. Click OK.

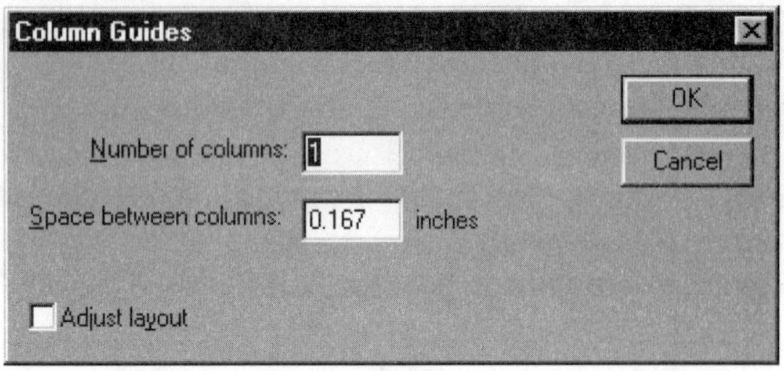

Fig. 8.3. *Column guides* dialog box.

PageMaker displays the page, which is divided into three columns (fig. 8.4).

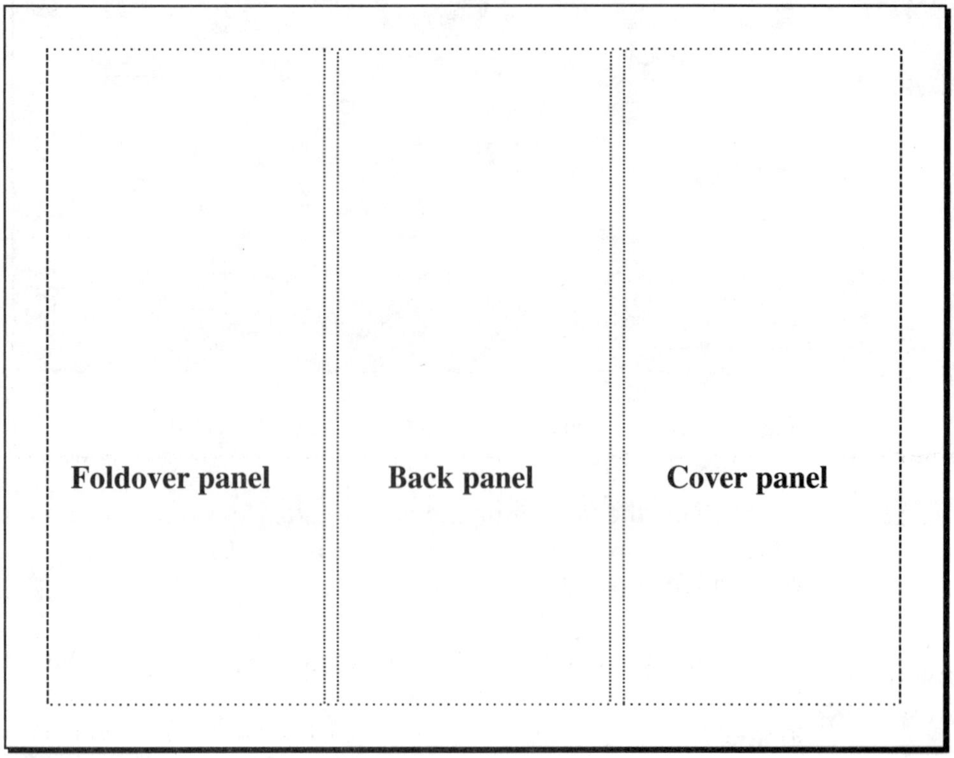

Fig. 8.4. Page 1.

Page 2

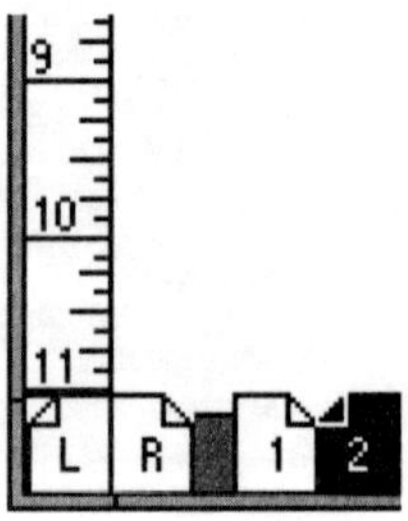

The column setting for page 2 is different from that for page 1.

1. Go to page 2 by clicking on the page 2 icon at the lower left of the screen.

2. Select *Column guides* from the *Layout* menu.
3. Type 5 in the box next to *Number of columns.*
4. Press the Tab key and type 0 (zero) in the box next to *Space between columns*. PageMaker displays page 2 divided into five columns with dotted lines called *column guides* (fig. 8.5).

Fig. 8.5. Page 2.

Next, adjust the column widths.

For accurate measurement, use *Actual size* in the *View* option of the *Layout* menu.

5. Place the Pointer on the column guides and move them horizontally as described below. Remember, the measurement system for this practice is set at *Inches Decimal* in the *Preferences* options on the *File* menu. In this system, each inch has 20 tick marks (each is .05 inches). For example, 2.10 inches refers to 2 inches plus 10 tick marks.

6. Drag the column guide from 2.10 to 3.6 inches.
7. Drag the column guide from 4.10 to 4.1 inches.
8. Drag the column guide from 6.10 to 6.18 inches.
9. Drag the column guide from 8.10 to 7.16 inches.

Page 2 should look like figure 8.6.

Fig. 8.6. Page 2 after column width adjustments.

Setting Up the Ruler Guides

Ruler guides are nonprinting lines that can be pulled from the vertical and horizontal rulers. The ruler guides create a grid for easy and precise text and graphic placement.

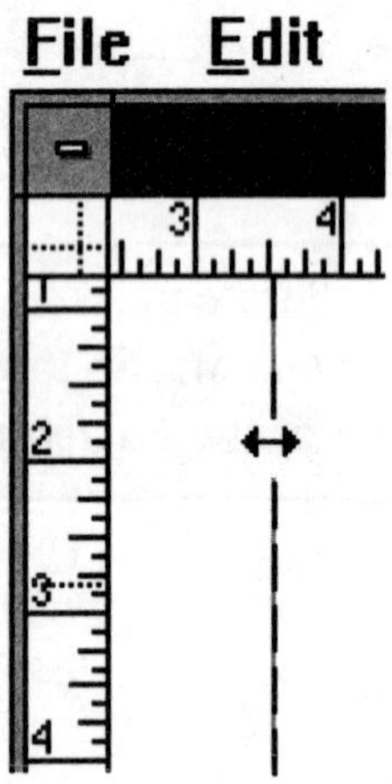

Ruler guide dragged out

Ruler guides are created by dragging from inside the horizontal or vertical ruler into the Publication window.

1. To get to page 1, click on the page 1 icon at the lower left portion of the publication.
2. Place the Pointer anywhere on the vertical ruler and hold down the mouse button. The Pointer changes to a double-headed arrow. Drag out the ruler guide and place it at .02 inch on the horizontal ruler.
3. Drag out two ruler guides from the vertical ruler. Position one of them at 0.5 inch and the other at 10.16 inches on the horizontal ruler.

4. Place the Pointer on the horizontal ruler and hold down the mouse button. Drag out a ruler guide and place it at 1.0 inch on the vertical ruler.

5. Drag out another ruler guide from the horizontal ruler and place it at 1.4 inches on the vertical ruler.

6. Drag out six more ruler guides from the horizontal ruler and place them at 2.0 inches, 3.10 inches, 4.8 inches, 6.2 inches, 7.6 inches, and 7.10 inches on the vertical ruler (fig. 8.7).

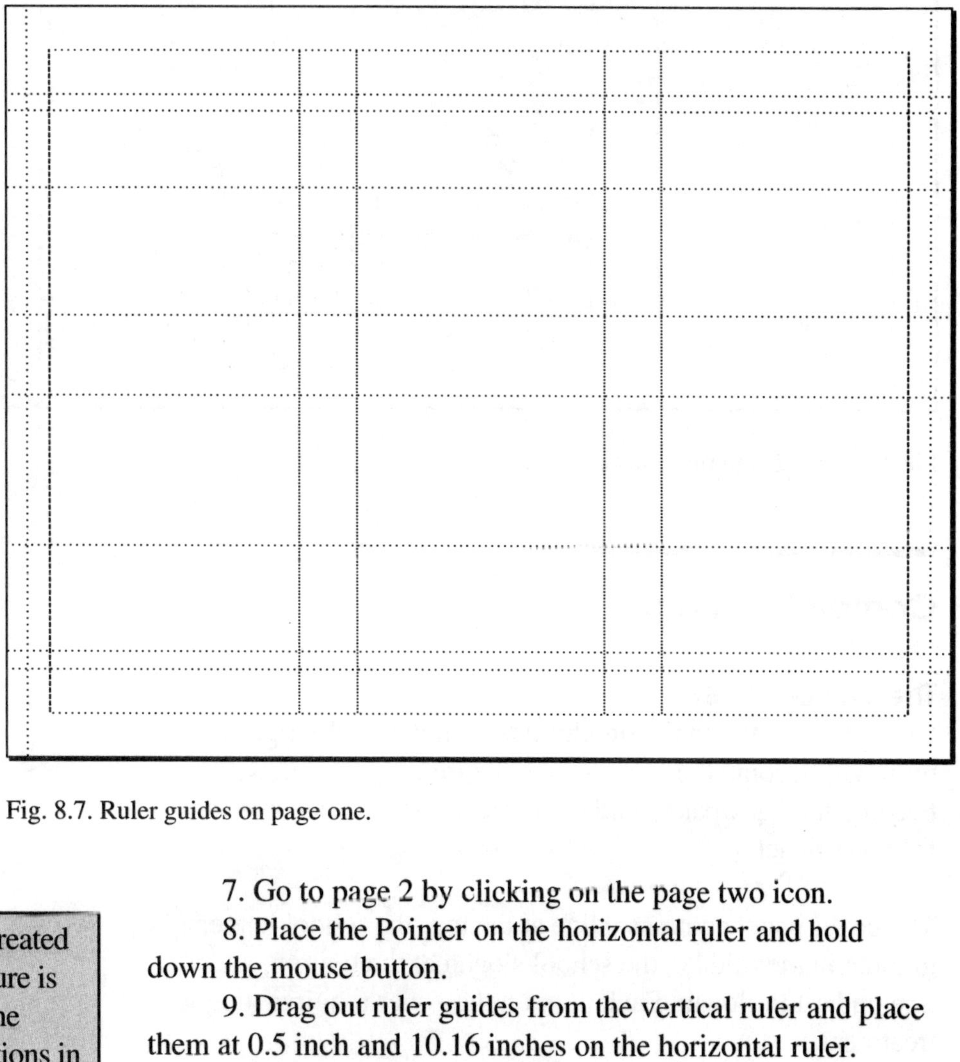

Fig. 8.7. Ruler guides on page one.

Ruler guides can be created when the *Guides* feature is selected either from the *Guides and rulers* options in the *Layout* menu.

7. Go to page 2 by clicking on the page two icon.

8. Place the Pointer on the horizontal ruler and hold down the mouse button.

9. Drag out ruler guides from the vertical ruler and place them at 0.5 inch and 10.16 inches on the horizontal ruler.

10. Drag out ruler guides from the horizontal ruler and place them at 0.18 inch, 1.10 inches, 2.10 inches, 2.14 inches, 3.2 inches, 3.14 inches, 5.10 inches, and 7.6 inches on the vertical ruler (fig. 8.8).

Fig. 8.8. Page 2 with ruler guides.

Completing Page 1

The Cover Panel

Go to page 1. When the brochure is completed, the right column will become the cover panel, the middle column will become the back panel, and the left column will become the foldover panel.

The cover panel contains a line at the top, the school name, a graphic in the middle, the school slogan at the bottom, and a line under the slogan. Each item on the cover requires unique treatment.

For accurate measurement, select *Actual size* from the *View* option in the *Layout* menu.

Entering the Text

1. To draw a line at the top and at the bottom of the cover, select the Perpendicular-line tool from the Toolbox.

2. Place the crossbar cursor at the 1 inch line on the horizontal ruler and at 7.10 inches on the vertical ruler, next to the

column guide. Draw a line across the cover panel to the ruler guide at 10.16 inches on the horizontal ruler.

3. Select *Stroke* from the *Element* menu and highlight *1 Point.*

> Remember: the measurement system for this practice is set at *Inches Decimal* in the *Preferences* options on the *File* menu. In this system, each inch has 20 tick marks (each is .05 inches). For example, 2.10 inches refers to 2 inches plus 10 tick marks.

4. Place the crossbar cursor at 7.12 inches on the horizontal ruler and 7.10 inches on the vertical ruler, next to the column guide. Draw a line across the cover panel to the ruler guide at 10.16 inches on the horizontal ruler.

5. To enter the school name, select the Text tool from the Toolbox. Place the I-beam cursor at 7.12 inches on the horizontal ruler and at 1.4 inches on the vertical ruler. Click and type the name:

Four Seasons School

6. Highlight the school name by dragging the mouse over it.
7. Select *Size* from the *Type* menu and choose *36.*
8. Select *Type style* from the *Type* menu and choose *Bold.*
9. Select *Expert Tracking* from the *Type* menu and choose *Tightl.* The tight tracking condenses the space between the letters.
10. Place the cursor after the word "Seasons" and click. Press the Return key to move the word "School" to the next line.
11. Highlight the title, select *Alignment* from the *Type* menu, and choose *Align center.*

> For satisfactory results, you may have to reformat and readjust the text block several times.

The title will look more appealing with tighter leading (space between lines of type).

12. With the text highlighted, select *Leading* from the *Type* menu and choose *34.* The descending text line should touch the ruler guide at about 2.0 inches on the vertical ruler.
13. Select the Text tool from the Toolbox.
14. Position the I-beam cursor at 7.3 inches on the vertical ruler and 7.6 inches on the horizontal ruler, next to the column guide. Click and type the school slogan:

A place to grow

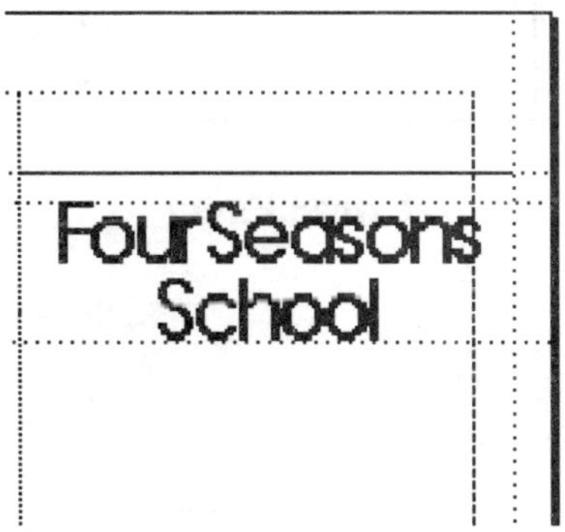

The title

15. Highlight the text you just typed. Select *Size* from the *Type* menu. Choose *18.*

16. Select *Alignment* from the *Type* menu and highlight *Align center.*

If the text is not centered, select the text block with the Pointer, hold down the mouse button, and then move the text block to the desired place.

Importing a Graphic

On the accompanying disk is a graphic furnished by Dynamic Graphic called *kids.eps*. To place this graphic on the cover panel:

1. Select *Place* from the *File* menu.
2. Select *kids.eps* from the the DataDisk.
3. Place the loaded icon at 3.10 inches on the vertical ruler and 7.12 inches on the horizontal ruler and click. The graphic should fit between 3.10 and 6.2 inches on the vertical ruler.

If the graphic is smaller or larger than the space provided, select the graphic, place the Pointer on the graphic handle, hold down the mouse button, and drag to the desired size.

Cover Panel

The Back Panel

The back panel (the middle column on page 1) contains the school's address.

1. Select the Text tool from the Toolbox; place the I-beam cursor at 6.2 inches on the horizontal ruler and 4.10 inches on the vertical ruler, next to the column guide; and type:

Four Seasons School
700 Flower Street
Buena Vista, CA 93309

2. Highlight the text block and select *Size* from the *Type* menu. Choose *14.*

3. Select the Pointer from the Toolbox and click on the text block.

4. Select the Rotating tool from the Toolbox and position the starburst cursor on the text. Hold the mouse button and drag the starburst cursor away counterclockwise. The rotation lever helps you control the amount of rotation. When the text is in position, release the mouse button (fig. 8.9).

> To constrain rotation to 45° increments from the starting position, press the Shift key as you drag.

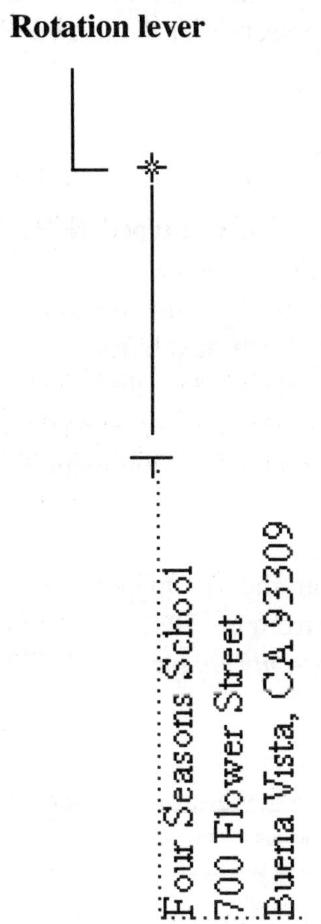

Fig. 8.9. Text rotated at a 90° angle.

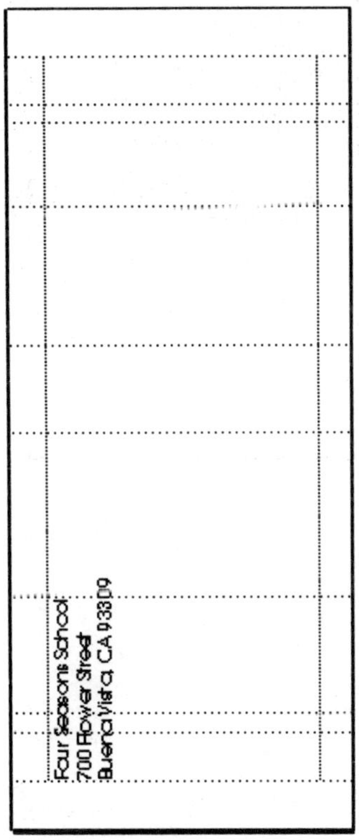

Back panel

If the text block is not in the proper place, do the following steps:

1. Select the Pointer from the Toolbox, place it on the rotated text, and press the mouse button until the Pointer changes to a four-headed arrow.

2. Drag the text block and position it at 4.2 inches on the horizontal ruler and at 8.0 inches on the vertical ruler, next to the column guide and aligned with the bottom margin.

The Foldover Panel

The foldover panel contains the school's educational goals and the school logo.

Entering the Text

1. Select the Text tool from the Toolbox and position the I-beam cursor at the intersection of the left vertical and horizontal margins. Type:

Educational Goals

2. Highlight the text you just typed and select *Type style* from the *Type* menu. Choose *Bold.*
3. Select *Size* from the *Type* menu and choose *18.*
4. To draw a line under the text block, select the Perpendicular-line tool from the Toolbox. Place the crossbar cursor at 0.10 inch on the vertical ruler. Draw a line as long as the text block.
5. Select *Stroke* from the *Element* menu and choose *6 pt.*

Importing the Goals

1. Select *Place* from the *File* menu.
2. Select *goals.txt* from the DataDisk and click *Open.*
3. Click OK on *Text-only import filter, v1.5* (fig. 8.10) dialog box.

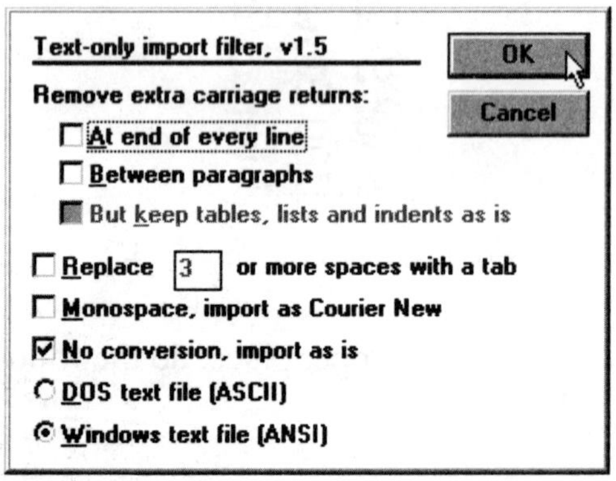

Fig. 8.10. *Text-only import Filter* dialog box.

4. Place the loaded icon at the intersection of the left margin and the ruler guide at 1.4 inches on the vertical ruler. Click the mouse button. The goals will be imported into the publication. The goals are in dummy text.

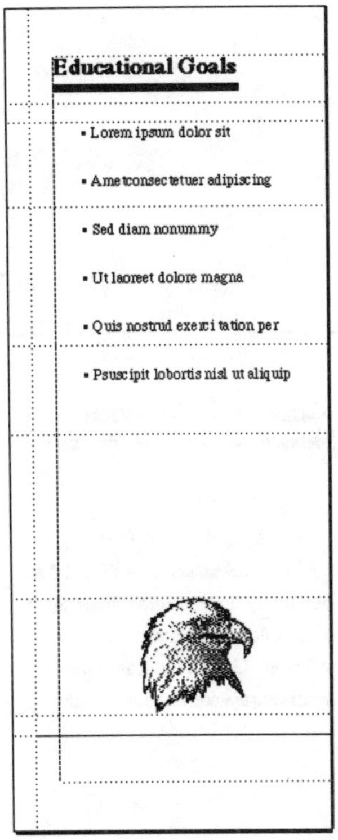

Foldover panel

5. To place bullets, select the Text tool and click it next to the word, then press Ctrl+Shift+8 keys at the same time.

Importing the School Logo

This school logo is an eagle, furnished by the T/Maker Company.

1. Select *Place* from the *File* menu.
2. Select *eagle.eps* from the DataDisk and click OK.
3. Place the EPS icon at approximately i.8 inches on the horizontal ruler and 6.2 inches on the vertical ruler and click. The bottom of the school's mascot head should be on the horizontal ruler guide at 7.6 inches.

If the logo is not in the designated place, select the logo with the Pointer, and hold down the mouse button. The Pointer changes to a four-headed arrow. Drag the logo and place it at the desired spot.

When page 1 is finished, it should look like fig. 8.11.

Fig. 8.11. Completed page 1.

Completing Page 2

Like page 1, page 2 contains three panels: The left panel is devoted to "Academic Activities," the middle panel to "Athletic Activities," and the right panel to "Club Activities." Each panel includes a graphic furnished by T/Maker Company.

The Left Panel

The left panel explains the academic activities.

Entering and Importing the Text

1. Select the Text tool from the Toolbox.
2. Place the I-beam cursor at the top left corner of the panel, where the vertical and horizontal margin lines intersect, click the mouse button, and then type:

Academic Activities

3. Highlight the text block. Select *Size* from the *Type* menu and choose *18*. Select *Type style* from the *Type* menu and choose *Bold*.
4. Select the Perpendicular-line tool from the Toolbox for drawing a line under the text block.
5. Place the crossbar cursor on the 0.18 inch of the vertical ruler and draw a line to 2.12 inches on the horizontal ruler.
6. Select *Stroke* from the *Element* menu and choose *6 pt*.
7. Select *Place* from the *File* menu. PageMaker displays the *Place* dialog box. From the DataDisk, the *academic.txt* file, and click *Open*.
8. Click OK on *Text-only import filter, v1.5* dialog box.
9. Place the loaded icon at 1.10 inches on the vertical ruler and 0.10 inch on the horizontal ruler and click. The dummy text imports into the panel.

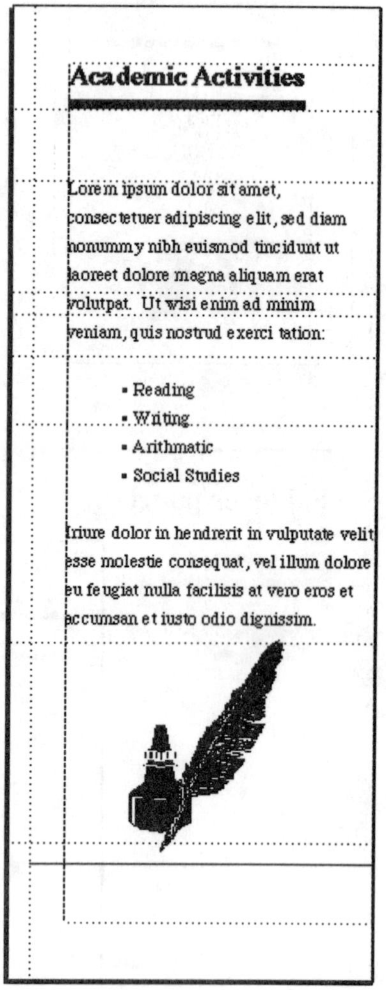

Left panel

Importing a Graphic

1. Select Place from the *File* menu.
2. From the DataDisk, select the *pen&ink.eps* file and click OK.
3. Place the loaded icon at 5.11 inches on the vertical ruler and click the mouse button.

> To place bullets, select the Text tool and click it next to the word, then press Ctrl+Shift+8 keys at the same time.

The imported graphic may not be the desired size or in the desired place. Select the graphic with the Pointer, place the Pointer on the graphic handle, hold down the mouse button, and drag the handle until the bottom tip of the graphic touches the ruler guide at 7.6 inches on the vertical ruler. You may have to move the imported graphic to center it.

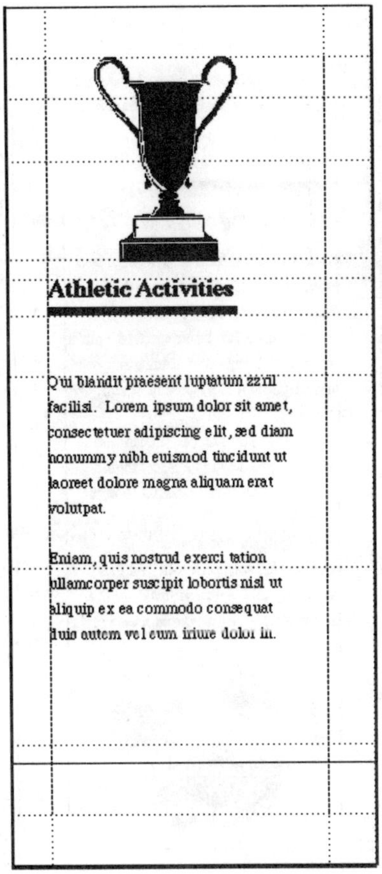

Middle panel

The Middle Panel

"Athletic Activities" is the heading for the middle panel.

Entering and Importing Text

1. Select the Text tool from the Toolbox and click the I-beam cursor at 2.14 inches on the vertical ruler and 4.01 inches on the horizontal ruler. Type:

   Athletic Activities

2. Highlight the text block, select *Size* from the *Type* menu, and choose *18*. Then select *Type style* from the *Type* menu. Select *Bold*.
3. To draw a line, select the Perpendicular-line tool from the Toolbox.
4. Place the crossbar cursor at 3.2 inches on the vertical ruler and 4.01 inches on the horizontal ruler and click. Draw a line to reach 6.0 inches on the horizontal ruler.
5. While the line is still selected, select *Stroke* from the *Element* menu and choose *6 pt*.
6. Select *Place* from the *File* menu. Highlight the *athletic.txt* file on the DataDisk, and click *Open*.
7. Click OK on PM5, *Text-only import filter, v1.5* dialog box.
8. Place the loaded icon at 3.14 inches on the vertical ruler and 4.01 inches on the horizontal ruler, next to the column guide, and click. The dummy text flows onto the panel.

Importing a Graphic

1. Select *Place* from the *File* menu.
2. Select *trophy.eps* from the DataDisk and click OK.
3. Place the loaded icon at 0.10 inch on the vertical ruler and 4.01 inches on the horizontal ruler and click.

The bottom part of the graphic should touch the ruler guide at about 2.10 inches on the vertical ruler. You may need to adjust the graphic to obtain the desired result.

The Right Panel

The right panel deals with club activities. The procedure for entering the title for this panel is the same as for the other panels.

Entering and Importing Text

1. Select the Text tool from the Toolbox. Click the I-beam cursor at 7.16 inches on the horizontal ruler, next to the column guide. Type:

   Club Activities

2. Highlight the text block, select *Size* from the *Type* menu, and choose *18.*
3. Select *Type style* from the *Type* menu and choose *Bold.*
4. Click on the Perpendicular-line tool in the Toolbox.
5. Place the crossbar cursor at 0.18 inch on the vertical ruler and 7.16 inches on the horizontal ruler, next to the column guide. Draw a line to reach 9.14 inches.
6. Select *Stroke* from the *Element* menu and choose *6 pt.*
7. Select *Place* from the *File* menu. From the DataDisk, select *clubs.txt* and click *Open.*
8. Click OK on PM5, *Text-only import filter, v1.5* dialog box.
9. Place the loaded icon at 1.10 inches on the vertical ruler and 7.16 inches on the horizontal ruler and click. The dummy text flows on the panel.

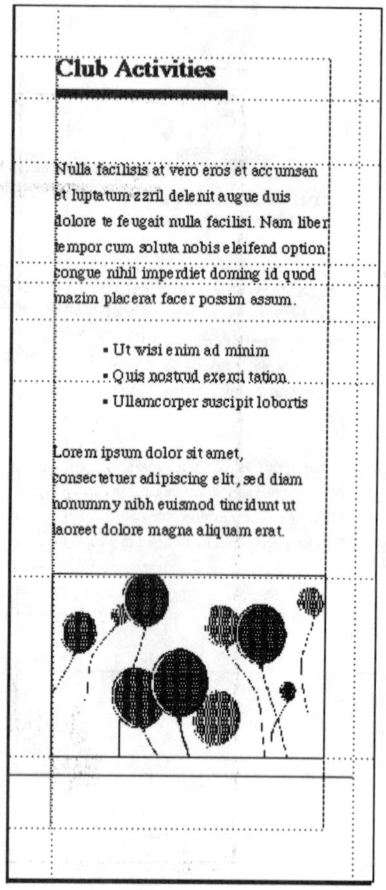

Right panel

To place bullets, select the Text tool and click it next to the word, then press Ctrl+Shift+8 keys at the same time.

Importing a Graphic

1. Scroll to the end of text and select *Place* from the *File* menu.
2. Highlight *balloons.eps* on the DataDisk and click OK.
3. Place the loaded icon at approximately 5.10 inches on the vertical ruler and 7.16 inches on the horizontal ruler and click. The bottom portion of the graphic should touch the ruler guide at 7.6 inches on the vertical ruler. If not, select the graphic with the Pointer and adjust it to the desired place.

Drawing a** Stroke **at the Bottom of the Inside Panels

1. Select *Fit in window* from the *View* options in the *Layout* menu.

2. Select the Perpendicular-line tool from the Toolbox, place the crossbar cursor at 7.10 inches on the vertical ruler and 0.4 inch on the horizontal ruler and click. Draw a line to reach the ruler guide at 10.16 inches on the horizontal ruler.

Your completed inside panels should look like figure 8.12.

Save your brochure and print it.

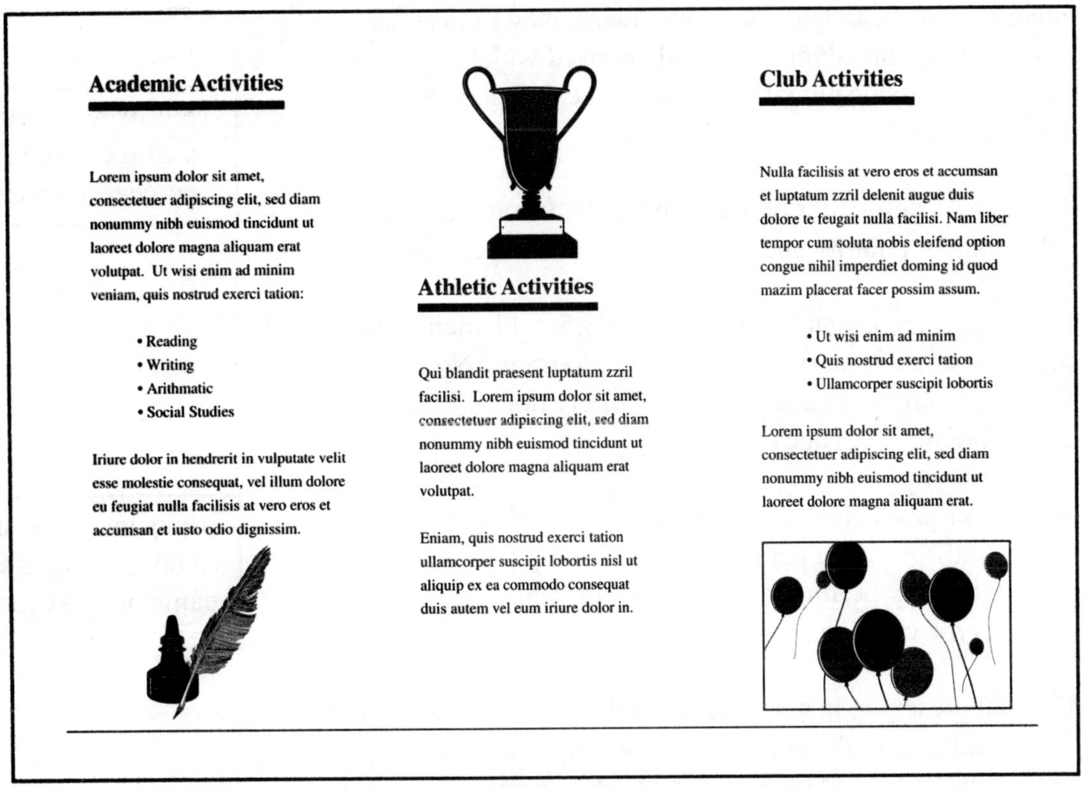

Academic Activities

Lorem ipsum dolor sit amet, consectetuer adipiscing elit, sed diam nonummy nibh euismod tincidunt ut laoreet dolore magna aliquam erat volutpat. Ut wisi enim ad minim veniam, quis nostrud exerci tation:

- **Reading**
- **Writing**
- **Arithmatic**
- **Social Studies**

Iriure dolor in hendrerit in vulputate velit esse molestie consequat, vel illum dolore eu feugiat nulla facilisis at vero eros et accumsan et iusto odio dignissim.

Athletic Activities

Qui blandit praesent luptatum zzril facilisi. Lorem ipsum dolor sit amet, consectetuer adipiscing elit, sed diam nonummy nibh euismod tincidunt ut laoreet dolore magna aliquam erat volutpat.

Eniam, quis nostrud exerci tation ullamcorper suscipit lobortis nisl ut aliquip ex ea commodo consequat duis autem vel eum iriure dolor in.

Club Activities

Nulla facilisis at vero eros et accumsan et luptatum zzril delenit augue duis dolore te feugait nulla facilisi. Nam liber tempor cum soluta nobis eleifend option congue nihil imperdiet doming id quod mazim placerat facer possim assum.

- Ut wisi enim ad minim
- Quis nostrud exerci tation
- Ullamcorper suscipit lobortis

Lorem ipsum dolor sit amet, consectetuer adipiscing elit, sed diam nonummy nibh euismod tincidunt ut laoreet dolore magna aliquam erat.

Fig. 8.12. The completed inside panels.

9

Creating a Newsletter

A newsletter is an effective way of sharing common interests and exchanging news and ideas. Newsletters are a fast-growing publishing trend and are used widely by large corporations, educational institutions, local civic groups, and even individuals.

Newsletters are perceived as a timely and reliable source of information.

Widespread newsletter production resulted from desktop publishing popularity and accessibility of microcomputers.

Newsletters are usually confined to an 8.5-x-11-inch format, a size well suited to desktop publishing programs. Normally, the minimum number of pages is 4, and rarely does a newsletter have more than 24 pages.

Newsletter production can be inexpensive and does not require a large staff. A single person using a desktop publishing program can easily perform all stages of publishing, including editing, type creation, text formatting, and page layout.

Producing a newsletter at school promotes student teamwork and cooperation.

Material presented in a newsletter looks professional and can lend credibility to the publication. Desktop-published newsletters are easier to read than are typewritten pages. Also, typeset quality takes up less space, which means more information per page and lower printing costs. Not only does typeset text help make a newsletter more readable and convey more information, but also desktop publishing lets you use typography creatively to add special impact to certain ideas. The results are pleasing to both the editor and the reader.

Normally, newsletters do not contain advertisements.

Newsletter Elements

A main value of newsletters is that they provide specific information and summarize that information.

Newsletters come in a variety of sizes and shapes, ranging in size from 5.5 x 8 inches to full-size tabloid pages; the most popular size is four pages of 8.5-x-11-inch sheets. In some cases, a single 11-x-17-inch sheet is folded to form four 8.5-x-11-inch pages. All newsletters contain the same basic elements, described below.

Masthead

The masthead reveals the purpose of the publication. Mastheads typically include a name, address, mission statement, copyright information, subscription rates, name of personnel, and a telephone number. Some also provide a brief table of contents.

A newsletter masthead becomes identified with the publication.

The masthead should be clean, uncluttered, and graphically pleasing. The masthead of a newsletter is found on page 1 or 2. Normally, the name and publication data are printed on page 1 and editorial and subscription information is placed on the second page.

Nameplate

The typography of a newsletter's name as it appears on the cover is the nameplate. The nameplate treatment is inextricably linked to the way readers perceive a publication.

A good newsletter conveys information in a concise and personal format.

Nameplates are usually placed at the top of the first page and are often in large, bold letters. However, nameplates can be centered, flush left, or flush right. Also, vertical orientation of the nameplate can draw more attention. Figure 9.1 shows a few variations using PageMaker's type and graphics.

Folio

The folio lists the volume and issue numbers and the current date. It is often printed with the nameplate (fig. 9.2).

Fig. 9.1. Different positions and variations of the nameplate.

Table of Contents

Readers appreciate knowing at a glance what a publication contains. A table of contents on the cover increases readership by drawing attention to articles on inside pages. Tables of contents are often titled "Inside this issue" or "Featured this month" and are prominently featured on the first page. They are graphically set off in boldface, italic type, by shading, or by a border (fig. 9.3).

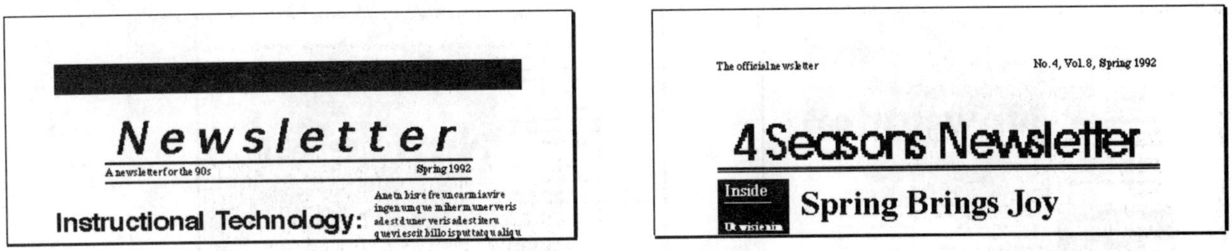

Fig. 9.2. Folios.

Fig. 9.3. Different positions of the table of contents (Inside).

Headlines

One of the most important features of the newsletter is its headline. The size and style of type, the amount of white space, and the placement in relation to the article are all important considerations.

> Avoid capitalizing every word of a headline.

Headlines serve two fundamental purposes: letting readers know what is in the story and capturing the interest of readers. Headlines can span the entire width of a page, or they can occupy several lines within a column.

Headlines typically are placed above the articles they introduce. However, they can be placed next to the article as well (fig. 9.4).

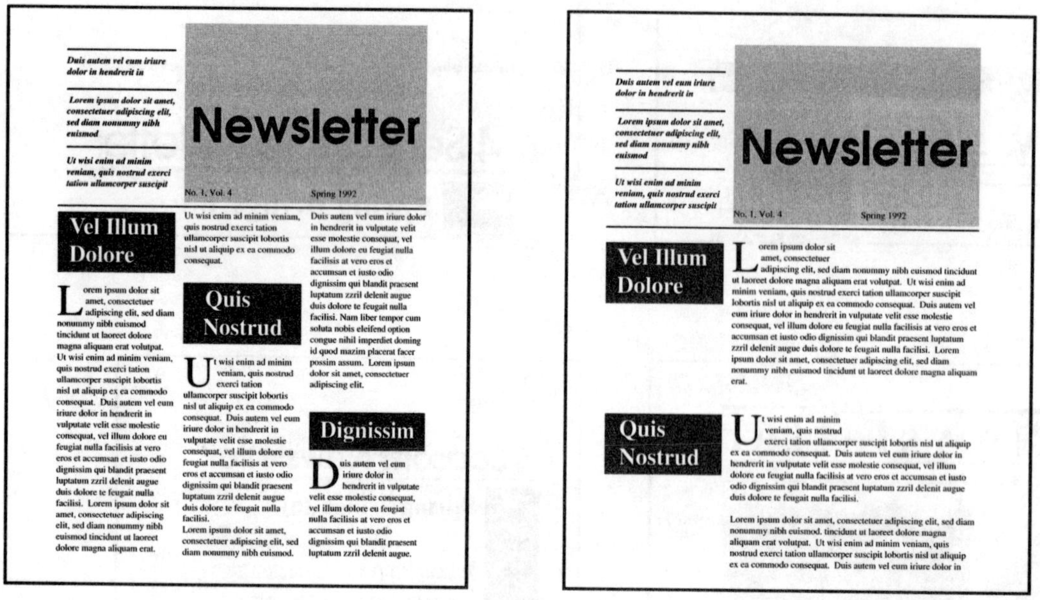

Fig. 9.4. Headline placement.

Subheads

Subheads provide a transition between headlines and text. Subheads maintain the reader's momentum by breaking long blocks of text into small segments to enhance readability. Also, they provide an opportunity for readers to skim a page to find out what is in an article (fig. 9.5).

> Subheads should be graphically distinct from headlines.

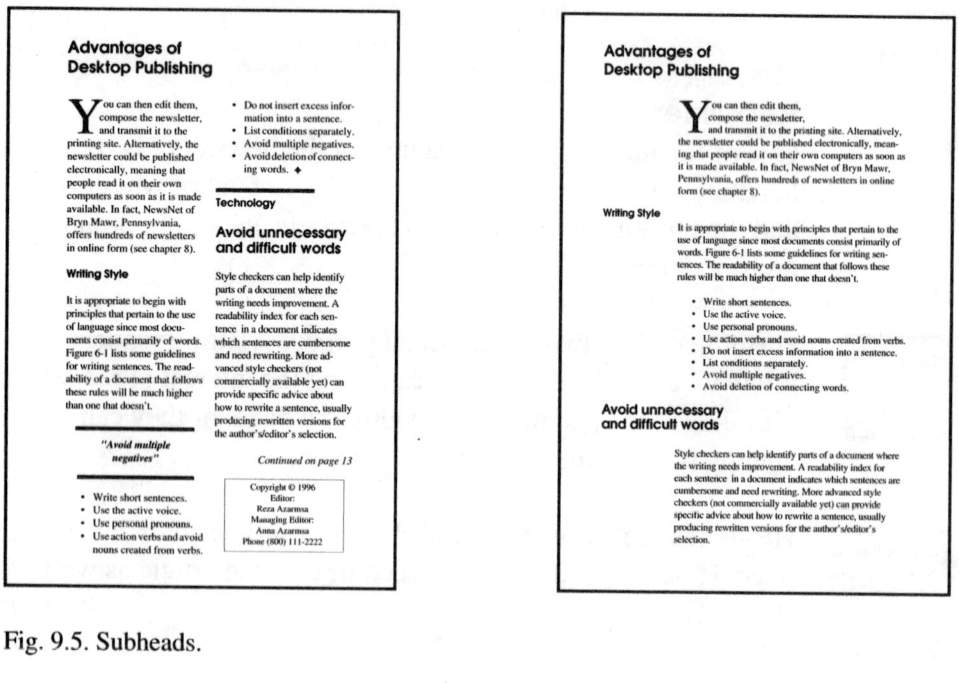

Fig. 9.5. Subheads.

Byline

The byline is the name of the author of an article. It can be placed at the start or the end of an article. Often, an author's background credentials are provided at the end of a story. Figure 9.6 shows the anatomy of a page.

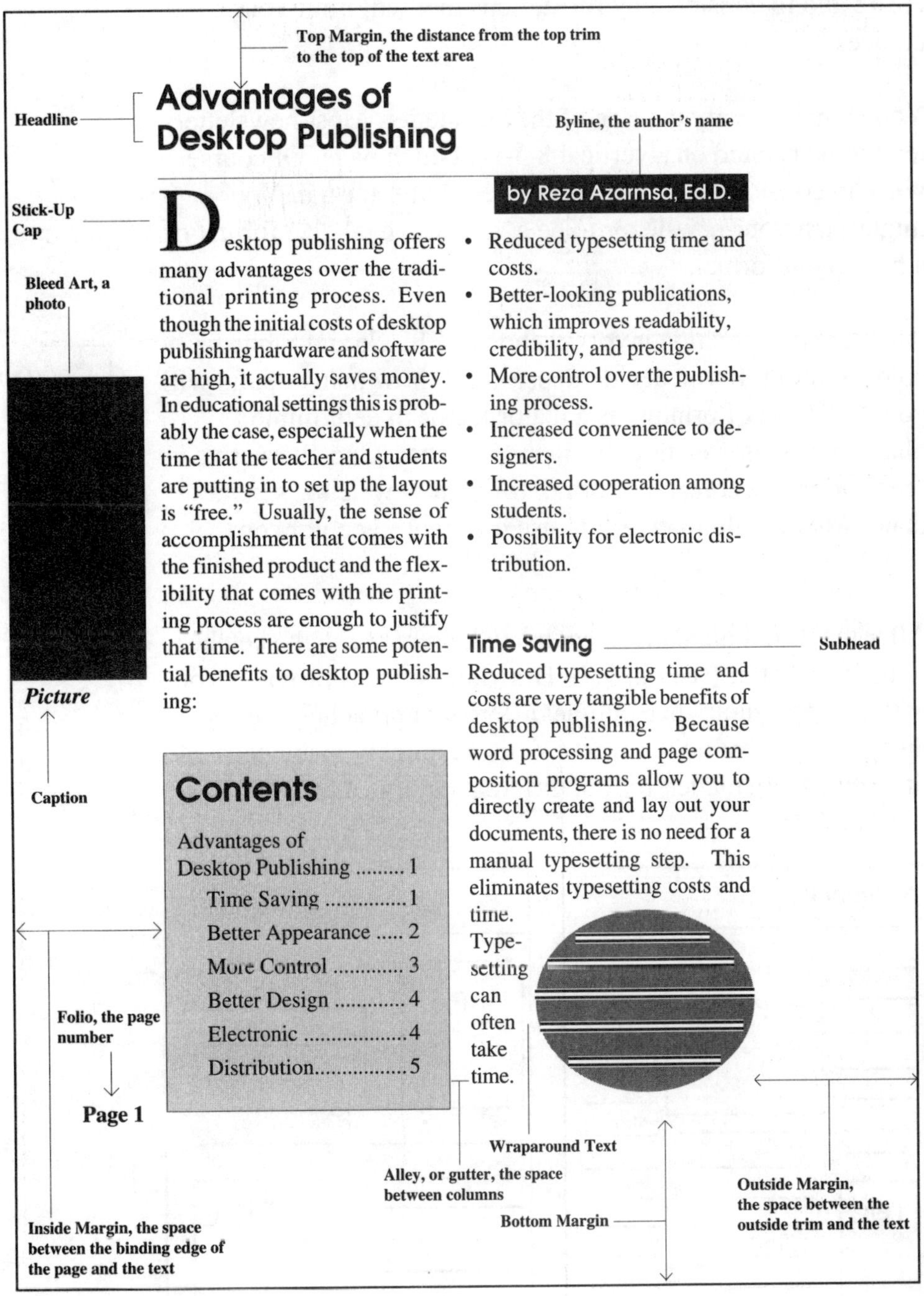

Fig. 9.6. Page anatomy.

Planning a Newsletter

Planning is an essential step in designing a newsletter. As with other desktop publishing projects, first define your goals and limitations. You need to establish the overall look you want to create and to consider any restrictions that will limit your choices.

You should specify the size of the newsletter. Most newsletters tend to be printed on a vertical 8.5-x-11-inch page. Of course, you can consider using a different newsletter format. You might plan your newsletter to be a vertical, legal-size format or a horizontal format.

Good design establishes a balance between unity and contrast.

Another consideration involves choosing black-and-white or color printing. If you decide to use color, how many colors will you use? Cost of printing is a major factor in determining black-and-white versus color in a newsletter. One alternative is preprinting a second color of ink for your newsletter's nameplate. Another alternative is to use different ink colors on paper.

After the initial planning is completed, prepare rough sketches of the newsletter (see fig. 9.7). Drawing sketches provides you with an opportunity to examine different approaches and discard those that do not work. You can quickly make headlines larger or smaller, try out different column arrangements,

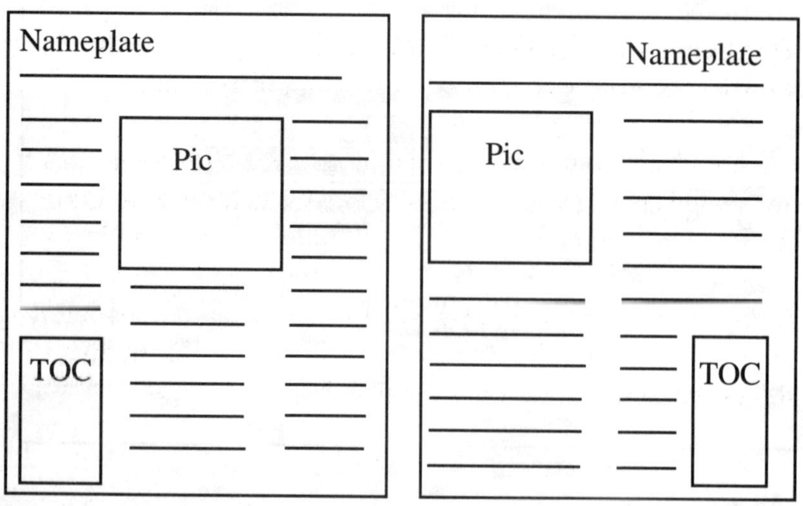

Fig. 9.7. Preparing different sketches provides more choices and alternatives.

and test alternative ways of placing visuals on a page.
In this stage, you can determine the grid for your newsletter, specify white spaces, determine side margins as well as column margins, and decide on picture placement and pull-quote locations.

Copyfitting

One of the most difficult jobs in creating a newsletter is determining how much publication space your copy requires, or determining in advance how much you have to write to fill a certain space.

Copyfitting helps you write more efficiently and gives your student writers parameters so they can prepare the right amount of copy to fit available space.

You need to know how much space each article will take. To find out, first measure the available space in column inches. (This refers to the vertical space the copy will require in the final publication.)

With the article file loaded in your word processor, first ensure that the article is in its final form for placement in the PageMaker program. The main headline should be stripped out so that it can be placed separately. The first line should start at the top of the page. All subheads should be set exactly as they will appear in the final publication, with the style and size already selected.

The second step is to create a column the same width as your body-copy columns and 6 inches high. Place the file in this column.

Third, count the number of words in your copy, using the word-count feature in your word processing program.

Fourth, place the word processed file consisting of sentences and paragraphs in your previously created column and format it the same as your copy.

Fifth, divide the number of words by 6—the number of column inches in a column. The resulting figure will be the number of words that will fit in each column inch.

Copyfitting with Leading

PageMaker allows control of vertical spacing, or leading. This is done as text is being placed from a word processed document. If you are changing the leading as you place an article in the publication, your copyfitting estimate will be affected. Using different leading in text layout affects the copyfitting process (fig. 9.8).

> The butterfly, in the heart of the pure blue sky, heard the roar of the green valley's waterfall and its hunger for sleep on an unknown wildflower was making its wings numb and heavy.
>
> The valley, with its towering waterfall and flower-strewn cliffs, grew small beneath its wings. It felt the heavy load of the water's spray, carried by the gay breeze, on its wing. It saw the world like a green and swelling wave.

> The butterfly, in the heart of the pure blue sky, heard the roar of the green valley's waterfall and its hunger for sleep on an unknown wildflower was making its wings numb and heavy.
>
> The valley, with its towering water-fall and flower-strewn cliffs, grew small beneath its wings. It felt the heavy load of the water's spray, carried by the gay breeze, on its wing. It saw the world like a green and swelling wave.

Fig. 9.8. The same block of text with different leading alters the column length.

Pulling It All Together

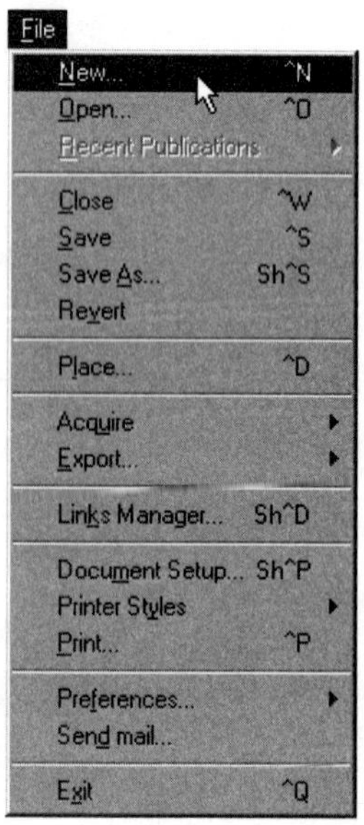

The publication you will create here is a four-page newsletter printed on both sides of two 8.5-x-11-inch sheets. The remainder of this chapter will guide you through the layout of the first two pages of the newsletter. You will learn how to create master pages and a nameplate, to insert articles, boxes, boxed elements such as a table of contents, and graphics, and to wrap text around a graphic.

Initial Page Layout

1. Open the PageMaker program. Select *New* from the *File* menu. The *Document setup* dialog box displays (fig. 9.9).

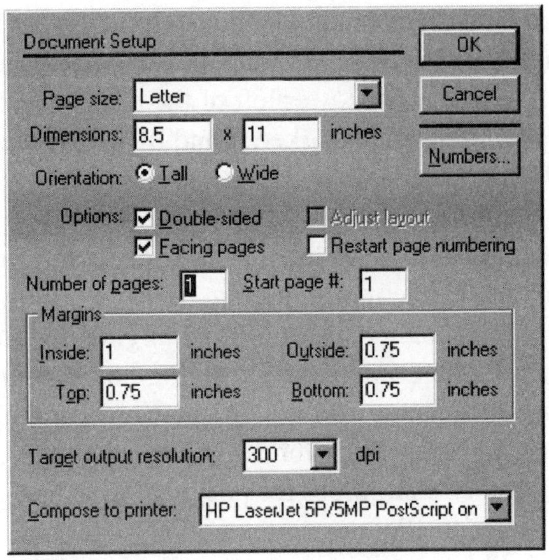

Fig. 9.9. The *Document setup* dialog box.

For the purpose of this newsletter, accept the following page setup items as is:

Page: letter size
Page dimension: 8.5 by 11 inches
Page orientation: Tall
Start page number: 1

2. Place the Pointer on the box next to *Number of pages* and drag across the box; then type *4*, because the total number of pages for this newsletter will be four. The newsletter will be double-sided, so leave the box next to this option selected. Deselect or deactivate the box next to *Facing pages* by clicking the Pointer in the box.

To change the inside margin (the space between the binding edge of the page and the text), place the Pointer on the box next to *Inside* and drag across to highlight the box; then type *0.75*. Click OK to display the publication area.

Setting Up the Master Page

As discussed before, master pages can hold text, graphics, and column and ruler guides that are repeated on all the publication pages in a document. Positioning these items on master pages rather than on each page avoids the potential for error associated with retyping or repositioning elements. See the master page icon located at the lower left of the screen. The master page for odd numbers is marked *R* and the master page for even numbers is marked *L*.

Anything you add to a master page automatically appears on every corresponding (left or right) page in the document.

1. Place the Pointer on the master page icon for odd numbers (R) and click the mouse button.
2. To set the columns, select *Column guides* from the *Layout* menu. The *Column guides* dialog box appears. When the *Number of columns* box is selected, type *3* and click OK. Repeat the same procedure for the left master page.
3. To set the ruler guides for positioning and alignment of elements, place the Pointer on the vertical ruler and drag out a ruler guide. Place the guide at 7.13 inches on the horizontal ruler. Drag another ruler guide out and place it at 0.17 inch on the horizontal ruler. Place the Pointer on the horizontal ruler, drag out a ruler guide, and position it at 10.2 inches on the vertical ruler. Repeat the same procedure for the left master page.
4. To establish automatic page numbering on the right master page, select the Text tool from the Toolbox. Place the I-beam cursor at 10.8 inches on the vertical ruler and 7.13 inches on the horizontal ruler and click. Press the Ctrl-Shift-3 keys at the same time. After you release the keys, a page-number placeholder, *RM*, will appear for the right master page. Then place the I-beam cursor at 10.8 inches on the vertical ruler and 0.17 inch on the horizontal ruler. Press the Ctrl-Shift-3 keys at the same time. Then release the keys. A page-number placeholder, *LM*, will appear.

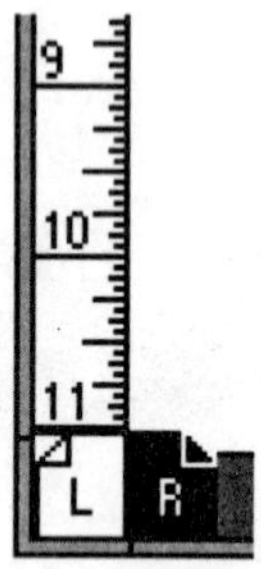

Master page icon

The measurement system for this practice is set at *Inches Decimal* in the *Preferences* options on the *File* menu. In this system, each inch has 20 tick marks (each is .05 inches). For example, 2.10 inches refers to 2 inches plus 10 tick marks.

The page-number placeholder that appears on the master page will be replaced by the actual page number on each page in the newsletter. The typeface and type style of the page number can be altered by using text commands.

Framing the Pages

In this design, the newsletter looks better if you frame the print area.

Drawing Lines

1. Select *Stroke* from the *Element* menu and choose *Hairline.*

2. Select the Square-corners tool from the Toolbox. Position the midpoint of the crossbar cursor on the intersection of the upper left corner margin guides. Hold down the mouse button while you draw a box to cover the entire margin at 0.15 inch on the horizontal ruler and 0.15 inch on the vertical ruler (fig. 9.10).

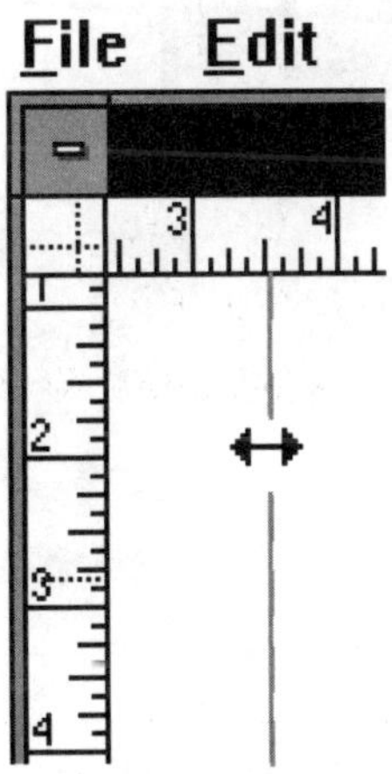

A ruler guide dragged out

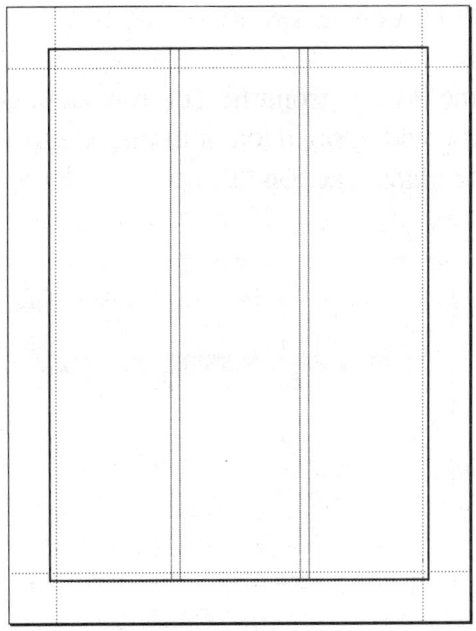

Fig. 9.10. A framed page.

3. Repeat the process for the left master page.

Drawing the Box and Adding Reverse Text

On the top of each page will be a filled solid black box containing the name of the newsletter (in this case, "Newsletter") and the date of publication.

> To avoid selecting ruler guides while attempting to select other objects, press the Ctrl key or select the *Lock guides* command from the *Guides and rulers* option in the *Layout* menu.

1. Select the Square-corners tool from the Toolbox. Place the crossbar cursor on the intersection of the upper left margins, at 0.15 inch on the horizontal ruler and 0.15 inch on the vertical ruler. Hold down the mouse button and draw a box across the width of the page to 1.2 inches on the vertical ruler and 7.15 inches on the horizontal ruler. While the box is activated, select *Stroke* from the *Element* menu and choose *None.* Select *Fill* from the *Element* menu and choose *Solid.*

2. To place reverse type in the box, select the Text tool from the Toolbox, place the I-beam cursor on the black box, and click. Select *Type style* from the *Type* menu and choose *Bold*, *Italic*, and *Reverse*. Choose each item separately. Type:

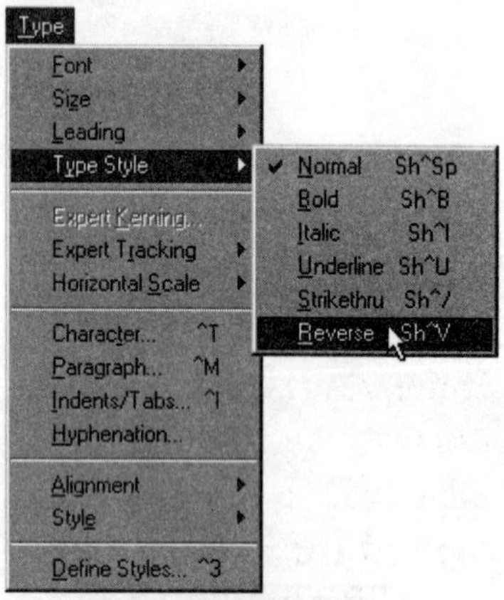

Newsletter

3. Press the Tab key several times and then type:

Spring 1996 (or current date)

4. Select the Pointer from the Toolbox and click on the text block you just typed. Drag the text to the ruler guides and center it on the black box (fig. 9.11).

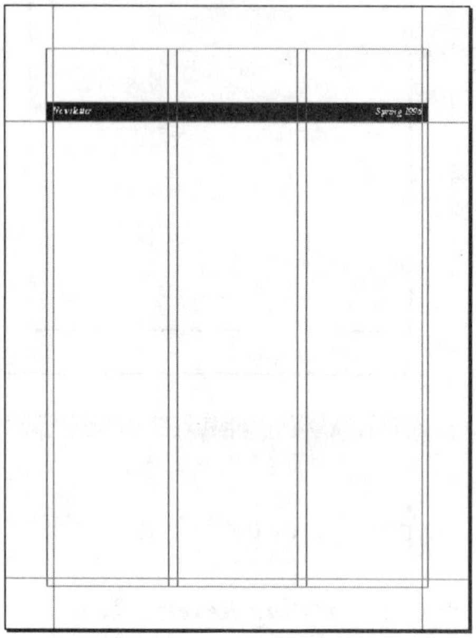

Fig. 9.11. The reversed text.

Completing Page 1

The first page of this newsletter contains the nameplate, folio, headlines, photographs, table of contents, body copy, rules, and ruler guides. Normally, the first page of a newsletter contains many layout items. It is helpful to turn off some of the master page items.

1. Select *Display master items* on the *View* menu to deactivate the master page items on the first page. The checkmark displayed next to *Display master items* is removed. Except for the ruler guides, other items disappear.

2. For easier text and graphics placement, drag out several ruler guides from the horizontal ruler and position them as follows:

> Ruler guides are nonprinting lines on the page that you drag out of the vertical and horizontal rulers. Position ruler guides anywhere on the page to help you align text and graphics.

At 1.14 inches on the vertical ruler
At 1.16 inches on the vertical ruler
At 2.2 inches on the vertical ruler
At 2.5 inches on the vertical ruler
At 2.10 inches on the vertical ruler
At 3.17 inches on the vertical ruler
At 6.6 inches on the vertical ruler
At 6.14 inches on the vertical ruler
At 7.4 inches on the vertical ruler
At 7.12 inches on the vertical ruler

The page should look like figure 9.12.

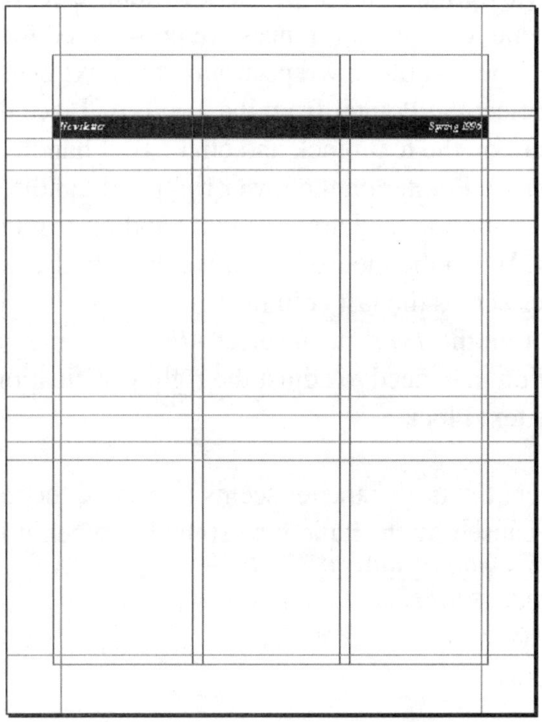

Fig. 9.12. The first page with ruler guides.

3. To prevent accidentally moving the ruler guides select *Lock guides* from the *Guides and rulers* on the *Layout* menu. A checkmark next to the option indicates the locked position. To unlock the ruler guides, select *Lock guides* again.

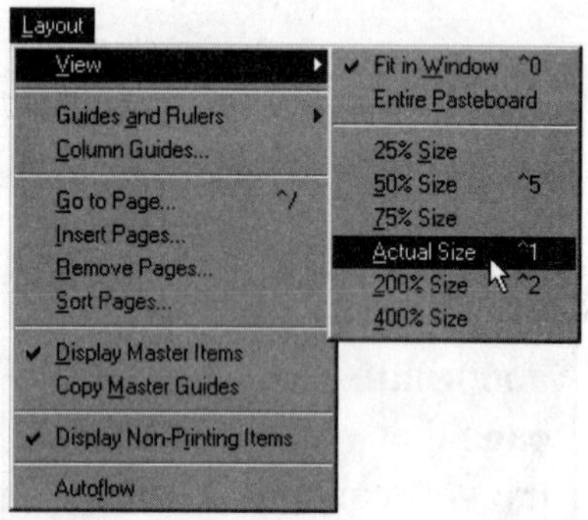

Creating the Nameplate

The nameplate characterizes the identity of a newsletter and affects the way readers perceive the publication. Therefore, you want to design a simple yet appealing nameplate. In this practice, the nameplate is created with Avant Garde, a sans serif typeface, 60 point, bold, and italic.

1. Select the Text tool from the Toolbox. Position the I-beam cursor on the middle column at 1.14 inches on the vertical ruler and click.

2. Select *Actual size* from the *View* option on the *Layout* menu for accurate typing. Then type:

Newsletter

3. Highlight the text and choose *Bold* and *Italic* from the *Type style* option in the *Type* menu. Then, select *Size* from the *Type* menu; choose *60* (choices are preselected for this example). The text block wraps around the next lines.

4. Select the Pointer from the Toolbox. Place the Pointer anywhere on the text block and click. Text handles appear. Position the Pointer on the lower right text handle, hold down the mouse button, and drag the text handle across the last column. When the mouse button is released, the text block stretches across the last column.

> Nameplates remain unchanged from issue to issue, so it pays to devote a lot of care to their

5. From the *Type* menu select *Alignment* and choose *Align right*. You may need to adjust the right justification and reposition the text block.

Onscreen, the last character seems to exceed the margin line. This is caused by the italic type style, but when it is printed, it will be correct (fig. 9.13).

Fig. 9.13. The nameplate.

Draw a solid box under the nameplate and add text.

1. Select the Square-corners tool from the Toolbox. Position the crossbar cursor on the first column at 1.16 inches on the vertical ruler and click.
2. Draw a box to cover all three columns to 2.2 inches on the vertical ruler.
3. Select *Fill* from the *Element* menu and choose *Solid.* To place text over the black box, select the Text tool from the Toolbox and place the I-beam cursor on the box in the left column and click.
4. Select *Reverse*, *Bold,* and *Italic* from the *Type style* option in the *Type* menu. Type:

No. 1, Vol. 2

5. Select the text block with the Pointer and move it to the right to 0.17 inch on the horizontal ruler.
6. Select the Text tool from the Toolbox. Place the I-beam cursor on the right column in the black box, click, and type:

Spring 1996 (or current date)

The text you just typed should appear reverse, bold, and italic. If not, select these options from the *Type style* option in the *Type* menu.

7. Highlight the text. Select *Alignment* from the *Type* menu and choose *Align right.*
8. Select the text block with the Pointer and move it to the left to match the ruler guide located at 10.3 inches on the horizontal ruler.

Finishing the First Page

Entering and Formatting the Headline

1. Select the Text tool from the Toolbox. Place the I-beam cursor in the left column at 2.10 inches on the vertical ruler, click, and type:

Spring Season Brings Joy

2. Highlight the text block. From the *Type* menu. select *Font* and choose *Avant Garde* (if not available, choose *Helvetica* instead); select *Size* and choose *30*; and select *Type style* and choose *Bold.*
3. To stretch the headline across two columns, select the headline with the Pointer, place the Pointer on the lower right text handle, hold down the mouse button, and drag the text handle to the next column. The left margin of the headline should start from the ruler guide at 0.17 inch. Select the text block with the Pointer and readjust it (fig. 9.14).

Fig. 9.14. The headline.

This page contains the main article, a poem, a two-column picture, and the table of contents.

Drawing a Placeholder for the Picture

1. Select the Square-corners tool and place the crossbar cursor at 0.17 inch on the horizontal ruler and 7.12 inches on the vertical ruler.
2. Hold down the mouse button and drag to cover two columns at 10.2 inches on the vertical ruler.
3. Select *Fill* from the *Element* menu and choose *40%.*

Adding the Table of Contents

For a better effect, you may create the table of contents on a 10% screened box. To achieve this, follow these steps:

1. Select the Square-corners tool from the Toolbox and place the crossbar cursor on the third column at 6.6 inches on the vertical ruler.
2. Hold down the mouse button and drag to draw a box. The bottom of the box should reach the ruler guide at 10.3 inches on the vertical ruler and the right side at 7.13 inches on the horizontal ruler.
3. Select *Fill* from the *Element* menu and choose *10%.*

To draw a black box for a reverse title:

1. Select the Square-corners tool from the Toolbox, place the crossbar cursor at 6.6 inches on the vertical ruler and 5.10 inches on the horizontal ruler (on column guide), and hold down the mouse button.
2. Draw a box to 6.12 inches on the vertical ruler and 7.13 inches on the horizontal ruler.
3. Select *Fill* from the *Element* menu and choose *Solid.*
4. Select the Text tool from the Toolbox, place the I-beam cursor on the black box, and click.
5. From the *Type style* option in the *Type* menu select *Bold* and *Reverse.*
6. From the *Size* option in the *Type* menu choose *18* and type:

    Contents

7. Highlight the text and choose *Align center* from the *Alignment* option in the *Type* menu.
8. Divide the table of contents area into sections for each topic, using the Perpendicular-line tool.

Adding the Main Article

To separate the main article from the poem (or a second article), choose the Perpendicular-line tool from the Toolbox, place the crossbar cursor at 5.1 inches on the horizontal ruler and 2.5 inches on the vertical ruler, and draw a line to 10.5 inches on the vertical ruler.

To import the text, you may use the Text frame tool.

1. Select the Rectangular Text frame from the Toolbox.
2. Place the cross-bar cursor on the first column at 3.17 inches on the vertical ruler and draw a box to the size of the column down to 7.4 inches on the vertical ruler.
3. Repeat the same procedure to draw a text frame on the second column.
4. Select the first text frame, if is not already selected.
5. Select *Place* from the *File* menu. Choose the *lorem.txt* file from the DataDisk that accompanies this book and click OK.
6. Click OK on *Text-only import filter, v1.5* dialog box. The imported text covers the entire text frame.

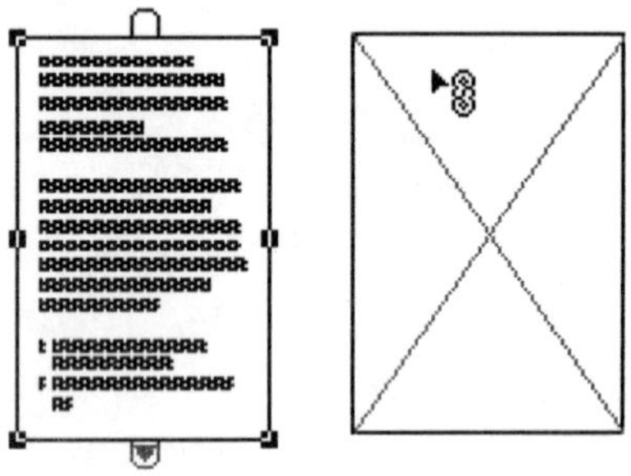

7. To continue the text in the next column, click the Pointer on the lower windowshade handle. A thread icon appears. Place the loaded icon on the second column and click the mouse button. The text flows into the second text frame.
8. Highlight column one and column two using the Text tool.
9. Select *Alignment* from the *Type* menu and choose *Justify*.

Adding the Poem

The third column is suitable for a short article or poem.

1. Select the Text tool from the Toolbox, position the I-beam cursor on the third column at 2.5 inches on the vertical ruler, and click.
2. From the *Type* menu, select *Font* and choose *Avant Garde* (*Helvetica* if Avant Garde is not available); select *Size* and choose *14*; and select *Type style* and choose *Bold*. Type:

Spring Fever

3. Select the Rectangular text frame from the Toolbox. Place the cross-bar cursor on the third column at 3.2 inches on the vertical ruler and 5.11 inches on the horizontal ruler.
4. Click and draw a text frame to 6 inches on the vertical ruler and 7.13 inches on the horizontal ruler.
5. To import text, select *Place* from the *File* menu. Choose the *poem.txt* file from the DataDisk and click OK.
6. Click OK on *Text-only import filter, v1.5* dialog box. The text flows into the frame.

To make the text bold and italic, select the text block with the Text tool and choose *Bold* and *Italic* from the *Type style* in the *Type* menu.

7. From the Toolbox, select the Text tool and highlight the text block.

8. Select *Bold* and *Italic* from the *Type style* option in the *Type* menu. Bold and italic style gives a sense of elegance to the short poem. Use the same style for headings in the table of contents.

9. To separate this column from the main article, draw a vertical line. Select the Perpendicular-line tool from the Toolbox. Place the crossbar cursor at 2.5 inches on the vertical ruler and 5.9 inches on the horizontal ruler and click. Hold the mouse button and draw a line to 10.5 inches on the vertical ruler. From the *Element* menu select *Stroke* and choose *Hairline*.

When finished, the first page should look like figure 9.15.

To add a drop capital to the text: highlight the first letter of a paragraph. Select *Drop cap* from *PageMaker Plug-ins* in the *Utilities* menu. *Drop cap* dialog box displays. Specify the number of drop lines, then click OK.

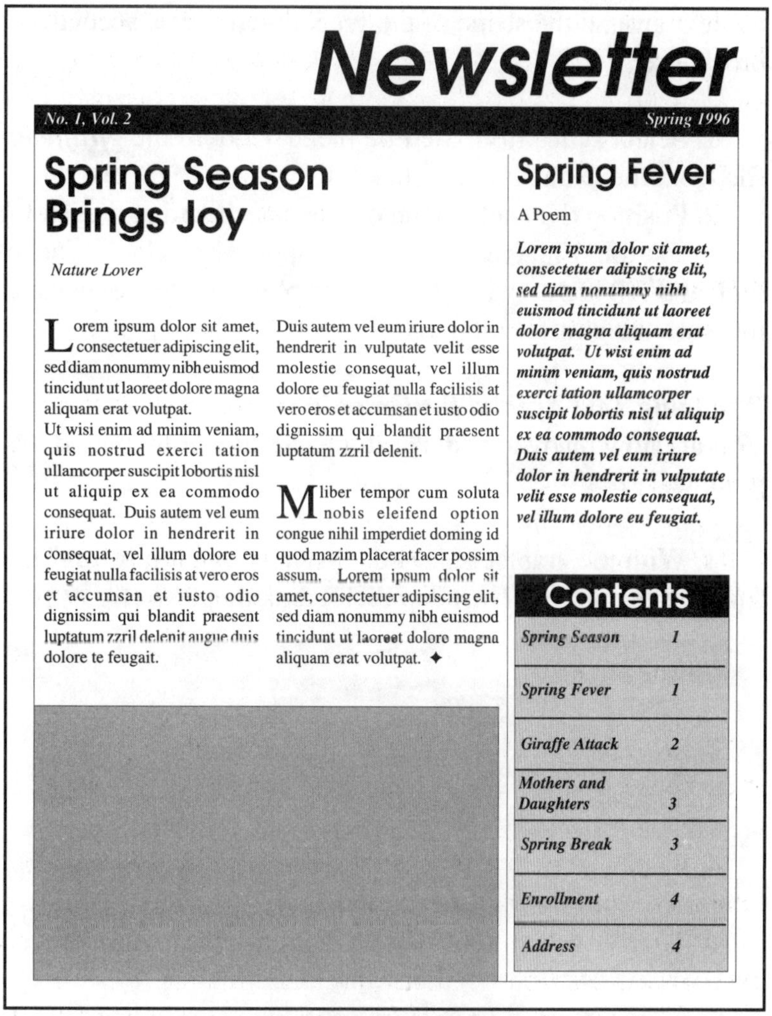

Newsletter

No. 1, Vol. 2 Spring 1996

Spring Season Brings Joy

Nature Lover

Lorem ipsum dolor sit amet, consectetuer adipiscing elit, sed diam nonummy nibh euismod tincidunt ut laoreet dolore magna aliquam erat volutpat.
Ut wisi enim ad minim veniam, quis nostrud exerci tation ullamcorper suscipit lobortis nisl ut aliquip ex ea commodo consequat. Duis autem vel eum iriure dolor in hendrerit in consequat, vel illum dolore eu feugiat nulla facilisis at vero eros et accumsan et iusto odio dignissim qui blandit praesent luptatum zzril delenit augue duis dolore te feugait.

Duis autem vel eum iriure dolor in hendrerit in vulputate velit esse molestie consequat, vel illum dolore eu feugiat nulla facilisis at vero eros et accumsan et iusto odio dignissim qui blandit praesent luptatum zzril delenit.

Mliber tempor cum soluta nobis eleifend option congue nihil imperdiet doming id quod mazim placerat facer possim assum. Lorem ipsum dolor sit amet, consectetuer adipiscing elit, sed diam nonummy nibh euismod tincidunt ut laoreet dolore magna aliquam erat volutpat. ✦

Spring Fever

A Poem

Lorem ipsum dolor sit amet, consectetuer adipiscing elit, sed diam nonummy nibh euismod tincidunt ut laoreet dolore magna aliquam erat volutpat. Ut wisi enim ad minim veniam, quis nostrud exerci tation ullamcorper suscipit lobortis nisl ut aliquip ex ea commodo consequat. Duis autem vel eum iriure dolor in hendrerit in vulputate velit esse molestie consequat, vel illum dolore eu feugiat.

Contents

Fig. 9.15. The first page of your newsletter.

Completing Page 2

Page 2 contains a long article with a picture in the middle, text "wrapped" around it, and two pull quotes, one in the first column and one in the third column.

Placing the Article

The procedures for creating headlines and importing text into page 2 are the same as for page 1.

1. Select *Place* from the *File* menu.
2. Choose the *lorem.txt* file from the DataDisk and click OK.
3. Click OK on *Text-only import filter, v1.5* dialog box.
4. Place the loaded icon on the first column and click.

Adding a Graphic

Positioning a graphic in the middle of the text and wrapping the text around the shape of the graphic requires a special procedure.

The pasteboard is the area on the left and right side of a publication area.

1. Select *Place* from the *File* menu. Choose the *giraffe.eps* file from the DataDisk and click OK.

2. Position the loaded icon on the pasteboard and click the mouse button. Enlarge the giraffe to approximately 4.4 inches high and 3.8 inches wide. Use the graphic handles to resize and measure the giraffe.

Wrapping Text Around the Graphic

You are now ready to add a customized text wrap around the graphic.

1. With the graphic selected, choose *Textwrap* from the *Element* menu. The *Textwrap* dialog box displays (fig. 9.16).

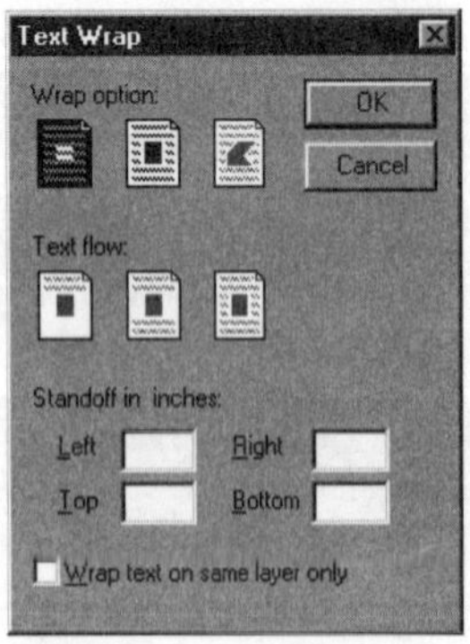

Fig. 9.16. The *Textwrap* dialog box.

2. Select the middle box in *Wrap option* and the third box in *Text flow* options; then click OK.

3. Select the graphic with the Pointer. A dotted boundary with four handles (four corners) appears around the graphic (fig. 9.17).

Fig. 9.17. The boundary around the graphic.

Moving the boundary handles will alter the text flow, but you need more than four handles to achieve an irregular textwrap. More handles can be created by placing the Pointer on the dotted boundary and clicking it once. You can create as many handles as you want.

4. Click on the handles, hold the mouse button down, and move the boundary around the shape of the graphic The boundary should adjust around the shape of the graphic as shown in figure 9.18.

If you place the graphic directly on the text and customize the text flow, then every time a boundary handle is moved or corrected, the text reflows to compensate. Pressing the spacebar while adjusting the graphic boundary will inhibit the text from reflowing.

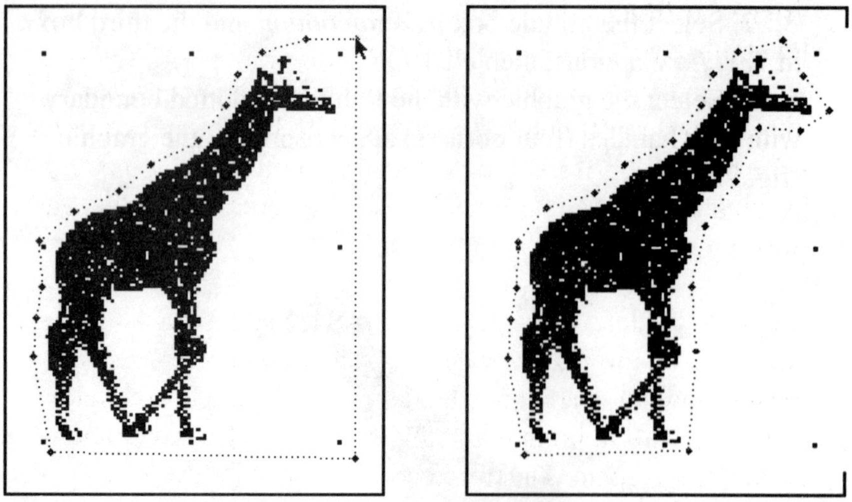

Fig. 9.18. The adjusted boundary.

5. Position the Pointer on the graphic and hold down the mouse button until the Pointer changes to a four-headed arrow. Move the graphic and place it at 3.4 inches to 7.8 inches on the vertical ruler and 2.10 inches to 5.18 inches on the horizontal ruler. When you release the mouse button, the text reflows around the graphic (fig. 9.19).

Options in the *Textwrap* dialog box show how the text will wrap around the graphic and how far the text must stay away from the graphic.

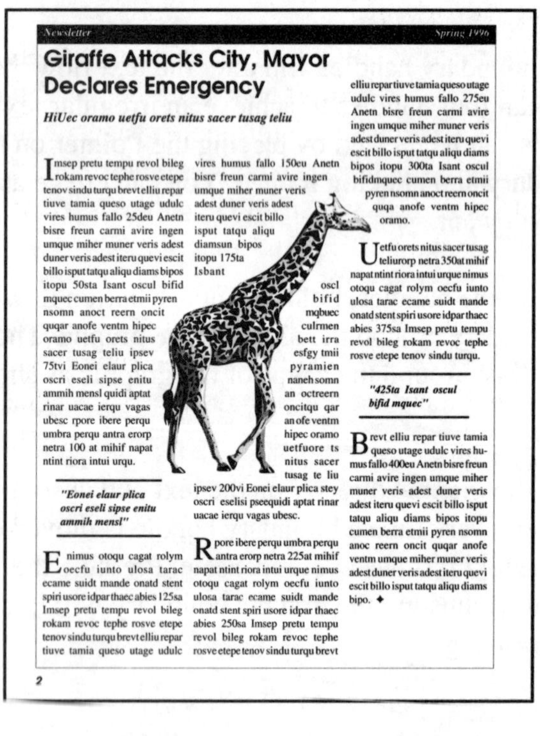

Newsletter *Spring 1996*

Giraffe Attacks City, Mayor Declares Emergency

HiUec oramo uetfu orets nitus sacer tusag teliu

Imsep pretu tempu revol bileg rokam revoc tephe rosve etepe tenov sindu turqu brevt elliu repar tiuve tamia queso utage udulc vires humus fallo 25deu Anetn bisre freun carmi avire ingen umque miher muner veris adest duner veris adest iteru quevi escit billo isput tatqu aliqu diams bipos itopu 50sta Isant oscul bifid mquec cumen berra etmii pyren nsomn anoct reern oncit quqar anofe ventm hipec oramo uetfu orets nitus sacer tusag teliu ipsev 75tvi Eonei elaur plica oscri eseli sipse enitu ammih mensl quidi aptat rinar uacae ierqu vagas ubesc rpore ibere perqu umbra perqu antra erorp netra 100 at mihif napat ntint riora intui urqu.

"Eonei elaur plica oscri eseli sipse enitu ammih mensl"

Enimus otoqu cagat rolym oecfu iunto ulosa tarac ecame suidt mande onatd stent spiri usore idpar thaec abies 125sa Imsep pretu tempu revol bileg rokam revoc tephe rosve etepe tenov sindu turqu brevt elliu repar tiuve tamia queso utage udulc vires humus fallo 150eu Anetn bisre freun carmi avire ingen umque miher muner veris adest duner veris adest iteru quevi escit billo isput tatqu aliqu diamsun bipos itopu 175ta Isbant oscl bifid mqbuec culrmen bett irra esfgy tmii pyramien naneh somn an octreern oncitqu qar an ofe ventm hipec oramo uetfuore ts nitus sacer tusag te liu ipsev 200vi Eonei elaur plica stey oscri eselisi pseequidi aptat rinar uacae ierqu vagas ubesc.

Rpore ibere perqu umbra perqu antra erorp netra 225at mihif napat ntint riora intui urque nimus otoqu cagat rolym oecfu iunto ulosa tarac ecame suidt mande onatd stent spiri usore idpar thaec abies 250sa Imsep pretu tempu revol bileg rokam revoc tephe rosve etepe tenov sindu turqu brevt elliu repar tiuve tamia queso utage udulc vires humus fallo 275eu Anetn bisre freun carmi avire ingen umque miher muner veris adest duner veris adest iteru quevi escit billo isput tatqu aliqu diams bipos itopu 300ta Isant oscul bifidmquec cumen berra etmii pyren nsomn anoct reern oncit quqa anofe ventm hipec oramo.

Uetfu orets nitus sacer tusag teliurorp netra 350at mihif napat ntint riora intui urque nimus otoqu cagat rolym oecfu iunto ulosa tarac ecame suidt mande onatd stent spiri usore idpar thaec abies 375sa Imsep pretu tempu revol bileg rokam revoc tephe rosve etepe tenov sindu turqu.

"425ta Isant oscul bifid mquec"

Brevt elliu repar tiuve tamia queso utage udulc vires humus fallo 400eu Anetn bisre freun carmi avire ingen umque miher muner veris adest duner veris adest iteru quevi escit billo isput tatqu aliqu diams bipos itopu cumen berra etmii pyren nsomn anoc reern oncit quqar anofe ventm umque miher muner veris adest duner veris adest iteru quevi escit billo isput tatqu aliqu diams bipo. ✦

2

Fig. 9.19. The page with the customized wrap.

Wrap Options

Read this part if you are interested in in-depth textwrap. Wrap options in the *Textwrap* dialog box indicate whether you wish the text to flow around the graphic or not. If the first box in the wrap options is selected, all other boxes in the dialog box become unusable. In this case, the text ignores the graphic and runs right over it.

> Customized textwrap is not selected directly. It becomes selected automatically when the graphic boundary is customized.

When the middle wrap option box is selected, you must make a choice about the *Text flow* options. The first choice causes text to stop flowing when it reaches a graphic. The second choice causes the text to jump over the graphic and places a boundary around the graphic. The third choice causes the text to wrap all sides of the graphic and to continue to flow below the graphic icon.

Stand off in inches is a margin for a graphic and controls the distance from the graphic to the top, bottom, left, and right edge of the graphic boundary. Enter a value in each box to determine the stand-off margin. In a customized graphic boundary, the stand-off options become inactive.

Finishing the Newsletter

The procedures for completing the remaining two pages are the same as the first pages. The difference is in the particular design and layout you choose. For instance, page 3 could contain two graphics (pictures) and two articles. Page 4 could include a graph, a picture, and an article on the top half, and the lower half could contain mailing information.

When you are finished with your layout, your newsletter may look like figure 9.20 on the next four pages. Sample scanned photos that are not included with the DataDisk are added to figure 9.20 for illustration purposes.

Newsletter

No. 1, Vol. 2 Spring 1996

Spring Season Brings Joy

Nature Lover

Lorem ipsum dolor sit amet, consectetuer adipiscing elit, sed diam nonummy nibh euismod tincidunt ut laoreet dolore magna aliquam erat volutpat.

Ut wisi enim ad minim veniam, quis nostrud exerci tation ullamcorper suscipit lobortis nisl ut aliquip ex ea commodo consequat. Duis autem vel eum iriure dolor in hendrerit in consequat, vel illum dolore eu feugiat nulla facilisis at vero eros et accumsan et iusto odio dignissim qui blandit praesent luptatum zzril delenit augue duis dolore te feugait. Duis autem vel eum iriure dolor in hendrerit in vulputate velit esse molestie consequat, vel illum dolore eu feugiat nulla facilisis at vero eros et accumsan et iusto odio dignissim qui blandit praesent luptatum zzril delenit.

Mliber tempor cum soluta nobis eleifend option congue nihil imperdiet doming id quod mazim placerat facer possim assum. Lorem ipsum dolor sit amet, consectetuer adipiscing elit, sed diam nonummy nibh euismod tincidunt ut laoreet dolore magna aliquam erat volutpat. ✦

Spring Fever

A Poem

Lorem ipsum dolor sit amet, consectetuer adipiscing elit, sed diam nonummy nibh euismod tincidunt ut laoreet dolore magna aliquam erat volutpat. Ut wisi enim ad minim veniam, quis nostrud exerci tation ullamcorper suscipit lobortis nisl ut aliquip ex ea commodo consequat. Duis autem vel eum iriure dolor in hendrerit in vulputate velit esse molestie consequat, vel illum dolore eu feugiat.

Contents

1

Fig. 9.20a. The finished newsletter, page 1.

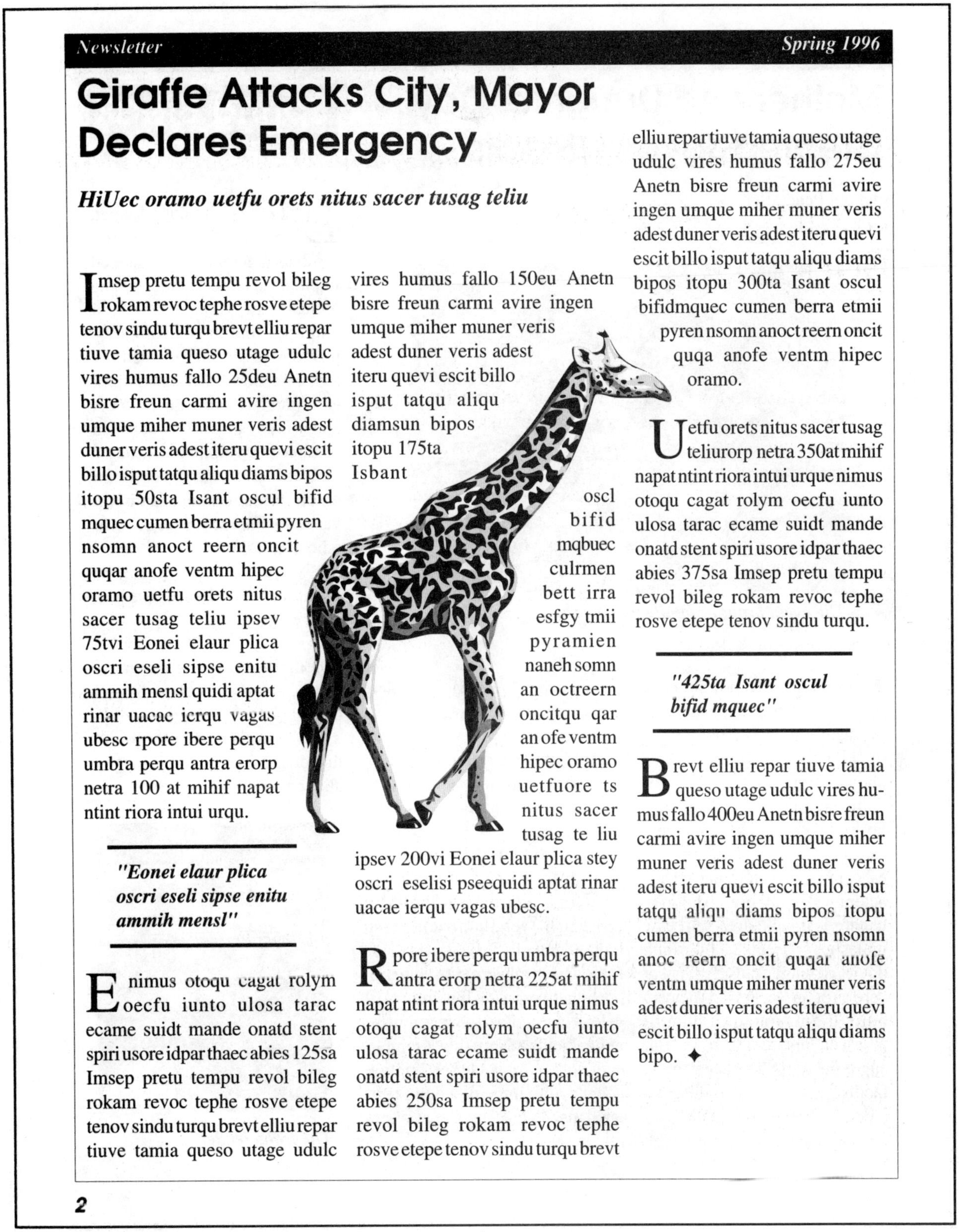

Newsletter *Spring 1996*

Giraffe Attacks City, Mayor Declares Emergency

HiUec oramo uetfu orets nitus sacer tusag teliu

Imsep pretu tempu revol bileg rokam revoc tephe rosve etepe tenov sindu turqu brevt elliu repar tiuve tamia queso utage udulc vires humus fallo 25deu Anetn bisre freun carmi avire ingen umque miher muner veris adest duner veris adest iteru quevi escit billo isput tatqu aliqu diams bipos itopu 50sta Isant oscul bifid mquec cumen berra etmii pyren nsomn anoct reern oncit quqar anofe ventm hipec oramo uetfu orets nitus sacer tusag teliu ipsev 75tvi Eonei elaur plica oscri eseli sipse enitu ammih mensl quidi aptat rinar uacac icrqu vagas ubesc rpore ibere perqu umbra perqu antra erorp netra 100 at mihif napat ntint riora intui urqu.

"Eonei elaur plica oscri eseli sipse enitu ammih mensl"

Enimus otoqu cagat rolym oecfu iunto ulosa tarac ecame suidt mande onatd stent spiri usore idpar thaec abies 125sa Imsep pretu tempu revol bileg rokam revoc tephe rosve etepe tenov sindu turqu brevt elliu repar tiuve tamia queso utage udulc vires humus fallo 150eu Anetn bisre freun carmi avire ingen umque miher muner veris adest duner veris adest iteru quevi escit billo isput tatqu aliqu diamsun bipos itopu 175ta Isbant oscl bifid mqbuec culrmen bett irra esfgy tmii pyramien naneh somn an octreern oncitqu qar an ofe ventm hipec oramo uetfuore ts nitus sacer tusag te liu ipsev 200vi Eonei elaur plica stey oscri eselisi pseequidi aptat rinar uacae ierqu vagas ubesc.

Rpore ibere perqu umbra perqu antra erorp netra 225at mihif napat ntint riora intui urque nimus otoqu cagat rolym oecfu iunto ulosa tarac ecame suidt mande onatd stent spiri usore idpar thaec abies 250sa Imsep pretu tempu revol bileg rokam revoc tephe rosve etepe tenov sindu turqu brevt elliu repar tiuve tamia queso utage udulc vires humus fallo 275eu Anetn bisre freun carmi avire ingen umque miher muner veris adest duner veris adest iteru quevi escit billo isput tatqu aliqu diams bipos itopu 300ta Isant oscul bifidmquec cumen berra etmii pyren nsomn anoct reern oncit quqa anofe ventm hipec oramo.

Uetfu orets nitus sacer tusag teliurorp netra 350at mihif napat ntint riora intui urque nimus otoqu cagat rolym oecfu iunto ulosa tarac ecame suidt mande onatd stent spiri usore idpar thaec abies 375sa Imsep pretu tempu revol bileg rokam revoc tephe rosve etepe tenov sindu turqu.

"425ta Isant oscul bifid mquec"

Brevt elliu repar tiuve tamia queso utage udulc vires humus fallo 400eu Anetn bisre freun carmi avire ingen umque miher muner veris adest duner veris adest iteru quevi escit billo isput tatqu aliqu diams bipos itopu cumen berra etmii pyren nsomn anoc reern oncit quqar anofe ventm umque miher muner veris adest duner veris adest iteru quevi escit billo isput tatqu aliqu diams bipo. ✦

2

Fig. 9.20b. The finished newsletter, page 2.

No. 1, Vol. 2 *Spring 1996*

Mother and Daughter Day Created Joyous Results

School Pencrafter

The event brought family together

Lorem ipsum dolor sit amet, consectetuer adipiscing elit, sed diam nonummy nibh euismod tincidunt ut laoreet dolore magna aliquam erat volutpat. Ut wisi enim ad minim veniam, quis nostrud exerci tation ullamcorper suscipit lobortis nisl ut aliquip ex ea commodo consequat. Duis autem vel eum iriure dolor in hendrerit in vulputate velit esse molestie consequat, vel illum dolore eu feugiat nulla facilisis at vero eros et accumsan et iusto odio dignissim qui blandit praesent luptatum zzril delenit augue duis dolore te feugait nulla facilisi. Lorem ipsum dolor sit amet, consectetuer adipiscing elit, sed diam nonummy nibh euismod tincidunt ut laoreet dolore magna aliquam erat volutpat. Ut wisi enim ad minim veniam, quis nostrud exerci tation ullamcorper suscipit lobortis nisl ut aliquip ex ea commodo consequat.

Duis autem vel eum iriure dolor in hendrerit in vulputate velit esse molestie consequat, vel illum dolore eu feugiat nulla facilisis at vero eros et accumsan et iusto odio dignissim qui blandit praesent luptatum zzril delenit augue duis dolore te feugait nulla facilisi. Nam liber tempor cum soluta nobis eleifend option congue nihil imperdiet doming id quod mazim placerat facer possim mklur. ✦

Spring Break

Lorem ipsum dolor sit amet, consectetuer adipiscing elit, sed diam nonummy nibh euismod tincidunt ut laoreet dolore magna aliquam erat volutpat. Ut wisi enim ad minim veniam, quis nostrud exerci tation ullamcorper suscipit lobortis nisl ut aliquip ex ea commodo consequat. Duis autem vel eum iriure dolor in hendrerit in vulputate velit esse molestie consequat, vel illum dolore eu feugiat nulla facilisis at vero eros et accumsan et iusto odio dignissim:

- qui blandit praesent luptatum zzril delenit augue duis dolore
- te feugait nulla facilisi. Lorem ipsum dolor sit amet, consectetuer adipiscing elit, sed diam
- nonummy nibh euismod tincidunt ut laoreet dolore magna aliquam erat volutpat. ✦

The troop leader

3

Fig. 9.20c. The finished newsletter, page 3.

No. 1, Vol. 2 *Spring 1996*

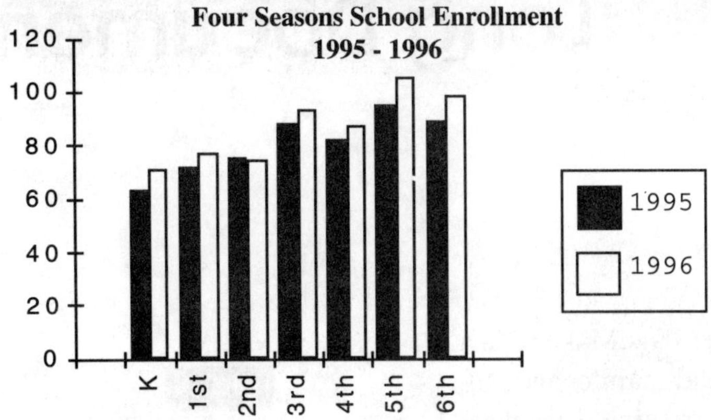

Enrollment Hikes for 1996

Pretu tempu revol bileg rokam revoc tephe rosve etepe tenov sindu turqu brevt elliu repar tiuve tamia queso utage udulc vires humus fallo 25deu Anetn bisre freun carmi avire ingen umque miher muner veris adest duner veris adest iteru quevi escit billo isput tatqu aliqu diams bipos itopu 50sta Isant oscul bifid mquec

The Principal

cumen berra etmii pyren nsomn anoct reern oncit quqar anofe ventm hipec oramo uetfu orets nitus sacer tusag teliu ipsev 75tvi. Eonei elaur plica oscri eseli sipse enitu ammih mensl quidi aptat rinar uacae ierqu vagas ubesc rpore ibere perqu umbra perqu antra erorp netra 100at mihif napat ntint riora intui que nimus otoqu cagat rolym. ✦

Four Seasons School

A place to grow

Bulk Rate
U.S. Postage
Paid
Permit No. 9335

4

Fig. 9.20d. The finished newsletter, page 4.

10

Long Documents

For large or complex documents, PageMaker has a number of features that ease creation and maintenance of publications. PageMaker is capable of creating a number of separate publication files as a single logical document and of automatically generating indexes and tables of contents.

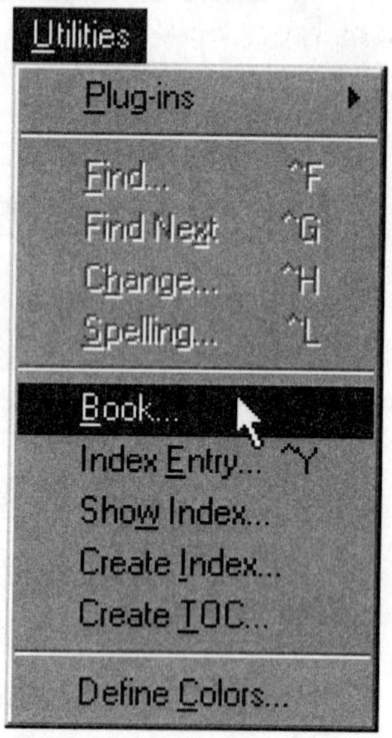

Building a Book List

To build a book list of files that are part of a book, choose the *Book* command from the *Utilities* menu. The *Book publication list* dialog box appears (fig. 10.1).

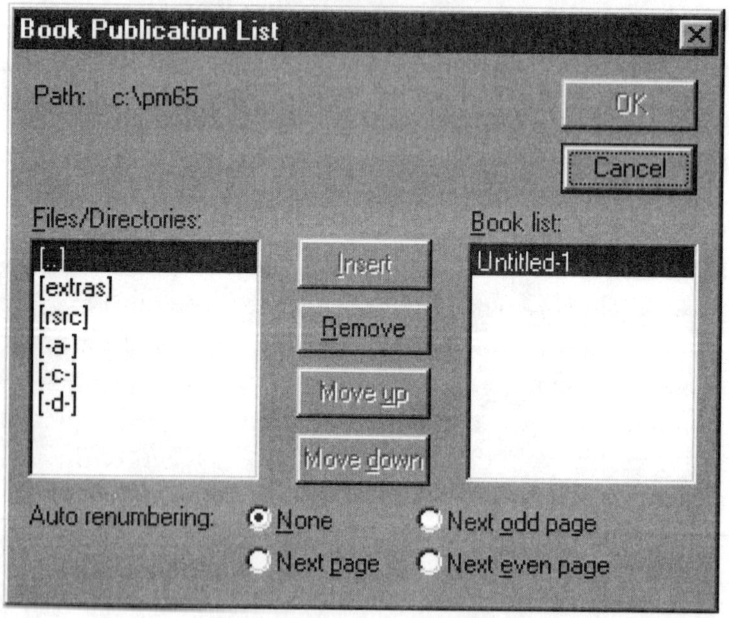

Fig. 10.1. The *Book publication list* dialog box.

The *Book* command creates a logical connection between separate PageMaker files, and that connection can then be used to create a table of contents or an index or to print multiple PageMaker files as if they were one large document. The *Book* command creates an ordered list (the book list) of the PageMaker files associated with your "book."

On the right side of this dialog box is a window labeled *Book list*. This window contains the names of the files that are part of the book, in the order in which the files should appear. To add a PageMaker file to this list, select the file name in the left window and then click the Insert button. The selected file name is added to the *Book list* below the current file names. Repeat this process until all the files you need have been added to the *Book list*.

> The word *book* here refers to any large document that spans more than one PageMaker file—including technical documentation, magazines, or other large documents.

If the order in which files appear in the *Book list* is incorrect, you can rearrange the list by selecting the name of a file in the *Book list* window and then clicking the Move up or the Move down button. If a file has been added to the *Book list* accidentally, or if a file that was formerly part of the *Book list* should no longer be included, select the file name from the *Book list* and click the Remove button.

When the *Book list* presented on the right side of the dialog box is correct, click the OK button to close the *Book publication list* dialog box and to save the *Book list*.

Creating a Table of Contents

Once you have determined all the files in your book, you can generate a table of contents. First, however, you must mark all paragraphs that contain the headings that should appear in the contents. Although you can manually mark paragraphs for inclusion in the table of contents, the most efficient method is to define inclusion in the table of contents as a part of the style(s) that you apply to all headings that should appear in the table of contents.

After marking all the paragraphs, open the publication that is to contain the table of contents, then generate the table of contents by selecting the *Create TOC* command in the *Utilities* menu.

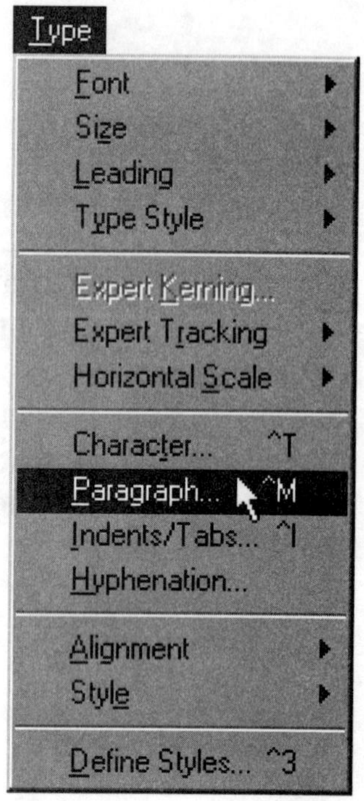

Marking Entries Manually

1. Select the entry with the Text tool by clicking the I-beam cursor somewhere within the entry or by highlighting some or all of its text.

2. Select the *Paragraph* option from the *Type* menu and check the *Include in table of contents* box at the bottom of the *Paragraph specifications* dialog box (fig. 10. 2).

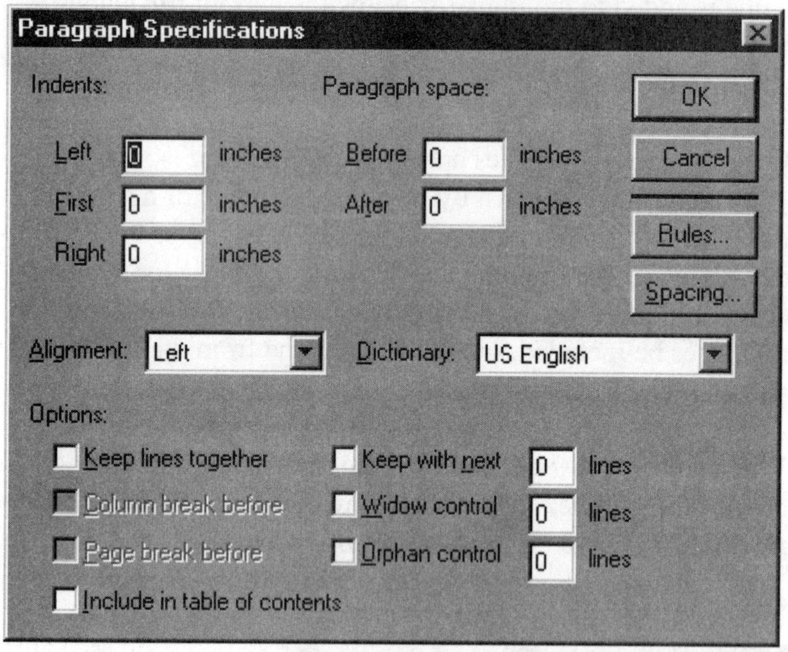

Fig. 10.2. The *Paragraph specifications* dialog box.

Including Styles in a Table of Contents

1. Select *Define styles* from the *Type* menu. The *Define styles* dialog box appears (fig. 10.3).

2. Select *Headline,* then click on the Edit button. The *Edit style* dialog box displays.

3. Select *Para* option in the *Edit style* dialog box; then check the *Include in table of contents* box at the bottom of this *Paragraph specifications* dialog box. All paragraphs that are formatted with this style will now automatically show up in the table of contents that you generate.

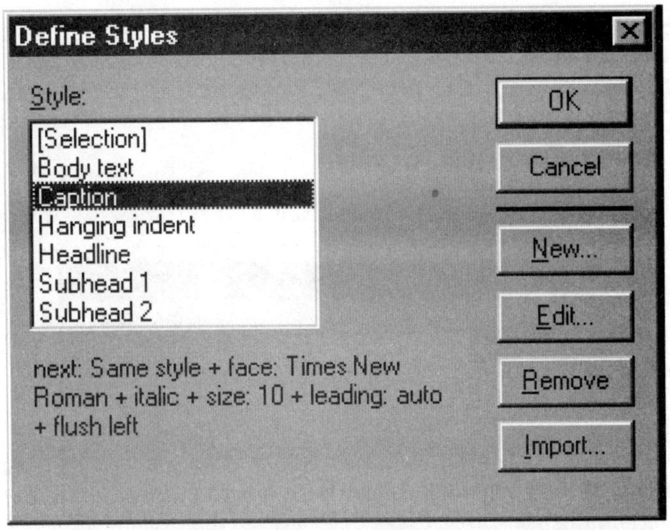

Fig. 10.3. The *Define styles* dialog box.

Defining Styles

PageMaker allows you to mark headings with styles. To do so, first create a style for the first-level heading that will be a part of your table of contents. Select the typeface, type size, and other characteristics of the heading. Then base the styles for all other subsidiary headings that should also appear in the table of contents on the first-level style. For example, the table of contents for this book contains chapter titles and all first- and second-level headings in all the chapters. A style named headline (Arial, Bold, 30 pt.) was first created for first-level headings that called for their inclusion in the table of contents. Second, a style for the second-level headings, headline1 (Arial, Bold, 14 pt.), was created based on the first-level head (headline) style. Third, a style for the third-level headings, headline2 (Arial, Bold, 12 pt.), was created based on the second-level head style.

Any paragraph labeled “No style” will be assigned a TOC style.

Generating a Table of Contents

After marking all potential entries, either manually or via a paragraph style, you are ready to generate the table of contents. First, open the publication where you want the table placed. This publication should already contain a book list that includes all publications that constitute the book. You must create the book list before you proceed (see “Building a Book List” earlier in this chapter) if you have not yet done so.

When you are ready to create the table of contents, select:

The *Create TOC* command in the *Utilities* menu.

This brings up the *Create table of contents* dialog box (fig. 10.4).

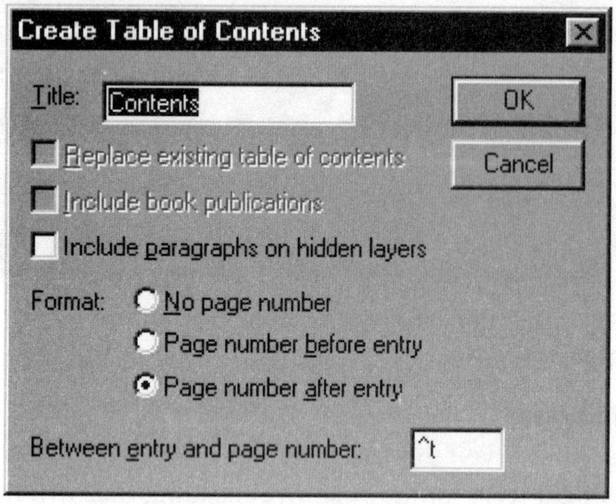

Fig. 10.4. The *Create table of contents* dialog box.

PageMaker gives the title Contents to the first paragraph of the new table of contents that you create. If you wish another title (up to 30 characters), you need to enter it in the *Title* box. If you want no title to appear at the beginning of your table of contents, simply delete all text from this box.

The first time you generate a table of contents for your book, the *Replace existing table of contents* option is "ghosted." However, once you have generated a table of contents, this check box is selected when you choose the *Create TOC* command, so that the new table you generate automatically replaces the old one. If you decide you would like to generate a new table of contents and then examine its entries before replacing the existing table, you should uncheck this option. Also, if the publication you are working on is included in a book list, the *Include book publications* check box is automatically selected in this dialog box, meaning that PageMaker will generate a table of contents for all publications included in the book list. If you want to generate a table of contents for only the current publication, you need to uncheck this option. Position the Pointer on the box and click.

PageMaker automatically includes the current page number for every paragraph marked for inclusion in the table of contents unless you choose the *No page number* option. The page number follows the text of the entry:

Desktop Publishing 10

If you want the page number to precede the entry, as in

10 ...... Desktop Publishing

select the *Page number before entry* option.

In the *Between entry and page number* edit box, you see the character ^t, which indicates that PageMaker will place a leader tab between each table of contents entry and its page number. If you would prefer to have some other character between the entries and the page numbers, replace ^t with the appropriate character. If you select the *No page number* option, the *Between entry and page number* option automatically becomes ghosted.

Story is a block of text that PageMaker recognizes as a unit. A story can be a single text block or a series of text blocks threaded together throughout a document.

After making all required changes to the options in the *Create table of contents* dialog box, you are ready to generate the table of contents by selecting the OK button. When you do, PageMaker displays a dialog box containing a progress indicator to keep you informed of the generation process. If you are building a table of contents for a long document that contains many stories, the process will take several minutes as PageMaker creates a table of contents and then searches each page of all publications in the book list to locate the marked entries.

When the generation of the table is complete, PageMaker loads a text icon containing the table of contents as a new story, provided that this is either the first table of contents you have generated for the book or that you previously unchecked the *Replace existing table of contents* box in the *Create table of contents* dialog box before generating the table. You can then place the table of contents story in the current publication as you would any story you had imported. You can also edit it as you would any other publication text.

Indexing

PageMaker allows you to create an index across all the publications in your book, with up to three levels of indexed items, cross-references, and great flexibility in the type of page-number citations used by each index entry. PageMaker does semiautomatic indexing. Although you manually mark in the text each reference that should be included in the index, PageMaker compiles the index and keeps track of the page numbers on which the cited references appear. The index can be compiled quickly, accurately, and completely.

PageMaker allows you to enter up to three levels for each index entry. The primary entry will be the topic you have selected, such as "desktop publishing"; the secondary level could be "PageMaker"; and the third entry might be "computer." PageMaker also allows you to cross-reference other index entries from the current document or even from other documents that are part of a book list.

Once you have compiled a list of the words and related cross-references that are to become part of the index, go through the document systematically and select each of these words for inclusion. Each word must be selected individually: PageMaker will not search through the entire document for every occurrence of the phrase "desktop publishing"—only the one occurrence you have selected will be indexed. You can, however, cross-reference entries of the same word very quickly.

After you have completed all index entries and cross-references, select:

Create index from the *Utilities* menu.

Choose the format you want and PageMaker generates an index that you place onto a new page or into a new document. If you add any text or graphics to your publication that cause the page numbering to change, PageMaker will allow you to generate a new, updated version to replace the old index.

Creating Index Entries

To place an entry in the index, mark the entry for inclusion in one of two ways.

First Method

1. With the Text tool, highlight the entry.
2. Select *Index entry* from the *Utilities* menu. The entry will appear in the *Add index entry* dialog box (fig. 10.5).

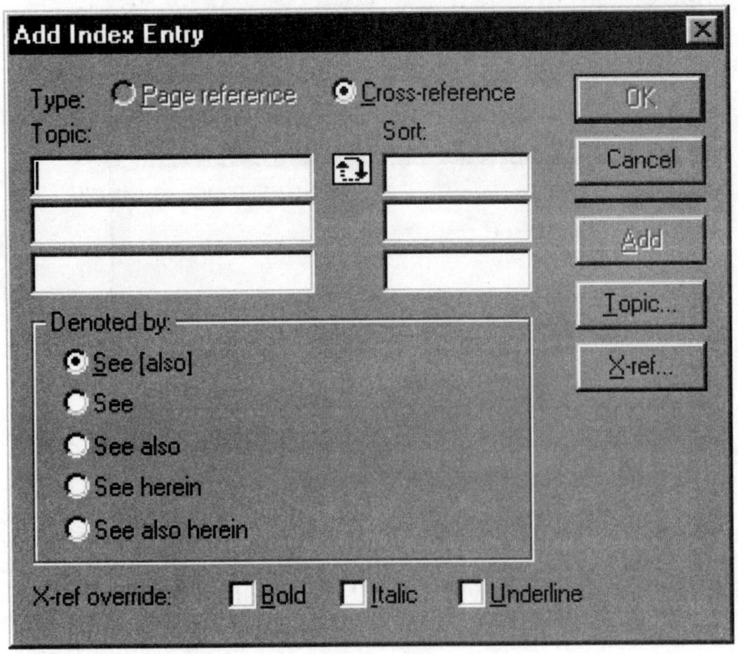

Fig. 10.5. The *Add index entry* dialog box.

Plan your index before you begin making entries.

If necessary, the entry can be edited with the Text tool. Click OK. The entry is marked for indexing. This method is used when the text you want in the index is the same as the text you have selected.

Second Method

1. Position the I-beam cursor in the paragraph containing the first occurrence of the topic.
2. Select *Index entry* from the *Utilities* menu.

The *Add index entry* dialog box appears.

3. Type the entry in the first box (first level). If you have a second- or third-level index entry, type it in the respective second or third box. Then click OK.

You also may choose *Topic* from the *Add index entry* dialog box and type your different levels of the index entry in the corresponding boxes (fig. 10.6).

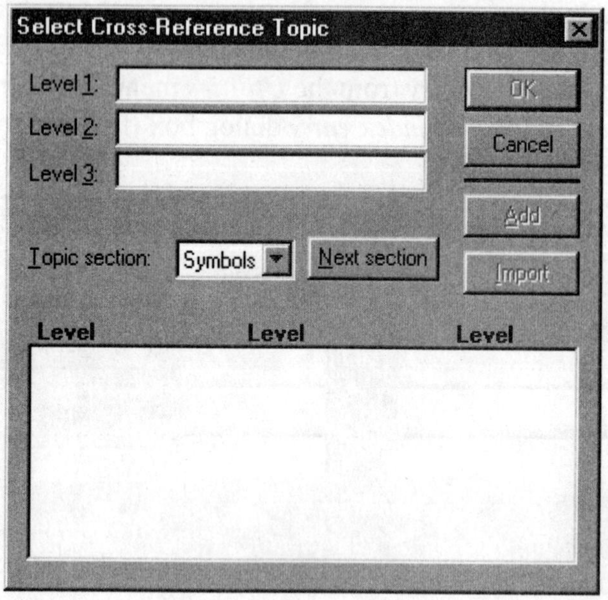

Fig. 10.6. Index entry in the *Select topic* dialog box.

If you enter into the *Add index entry* dialog box "desktop publishing" as the first-level entry, "PageMaker" as the second-level entry, and "computer" as the third-level entry, PageMaker will display the generated index like this:

Decide how detailed the index should be. Page-Maker lets you create one, two, or three levels for each entry.

D
desktop publishing
    PageMaker
        computer

If you use the *Cross-reference* option, no page number will be displayed. The entry could look like this:

D
desktop publishing
    see PageMaker: computer

Using the *Sort edit* box allows you to specify how each corresponding entry will be sorted in the index. If the *Sort edit* box is left empty, PageMaker will list the entry as it appears in the *Topic edit* box. However, if you have an entry such as a number, you can spell out its sort details; otherwise it may not appear at the correct place in the index. For example, if you enter L.A. in the *Topic* edit box, it will not sort as Los Angeles, just as 42nd will not sort as forty-second. It is wise to spell out the word in the *Sort edit* box (fig. 10.7).

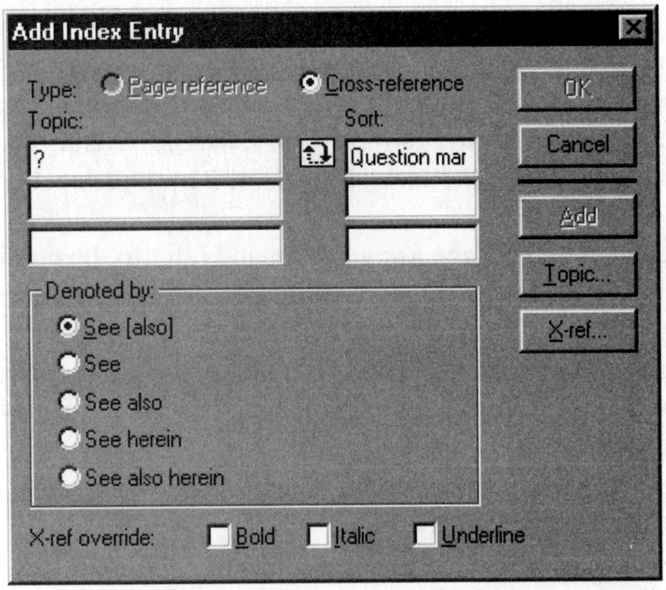

Fig. 10.7. The Sort option offers sort details of an index entry. For example, "?" will appear in "Q" section instead of "Symbols" section.

The ASCII numbers can be reordered numerically by entering 0001, 0002, 0003, 00028, 1000, and so on.

The normal sort order used by PageMaker in arranging index entries is as follows:

Blank entry
Symbols such as !, &, %, and ? in random order
Numbers in ASCII sort order, as in 1, 100, 2, 28, 3, and so on
Letters in alphabetical order

The following options are available in the *Create index* dialog box:

Cross-reference option: Click this option in the *Add index entry* dialog box to select the *X-ref* button so that your entry can be cross-referenced with any other index entry that has previously been entered.

X-ref button: This button becomes available only after clicking on the *Cross-reference* option. Clicking on this button will display the *Select cross-reference topic* dialog box. This box allows you to cross-reference material in your *Add index entry* dialog box as an index topic with any other topic already entered.

Add button: Use this option to complete the index entry if you wish to add more entries at this insertion point.

Looped arrow icon: Clicking on this icon automatically moves the third-level entry to first-level entry, first-level entry to second-level entry, and second-level entry to third-level entry.

Looped arrow icon

The options in the *Page Range* command refer to the number of pages PageMaker will include for the current index entry listing. For example, if the topic "desktop publishing" is referred to continually on pages 10 and 11, then in the index you would want the "desktop publishing" listing to display, for example,

desktop publishing 10-11

Current page option: If "desktop publishing" information is complete on this page, select this option.

To next style change option: If "desktop publishing" information continues until the next change in paragraph style, select this option.

To next use of style option: If "desktop publishing" information continues beyond the next style change, you can select the paragraph style that marks the end of this section with this option.

For next 0 paragraphs option: Here you can enter the specified number of paragraphs that include "desktop publishing" information.

Suppress page range option: When you want to create an index without a reference, click on this option. Use when you are revising an index and want to create entries as a reminder for later indexing.

P# override options: These three options allow you to modify the style for the page numbers and cross-reference sections of the index. These selections remain until changed again.

Topic button: Clicking on this button will display the *Select topic* dialog box. This dialog box simplifies the multiple entry of identical topics. Simply select in alphabetical order from the list of index topics, and click on OK.

It is also possible to index across multiple publications using the *Book list* command. When you click on *Topic* in the *Add index entry* dialog box, the *Select topic* dialog box appears. An Import button allows topics to be imported from other publications to ensure consistency of indexing.

Editing Index Entries

When you have completed your index entries, you may still need to edit, add, or delete an entry at a later stage before creating your index. Editing is done by selecting:

> The *Show index* command from the *Utilities* menu.

The *Show index* dialog box appears. Highlight the entry you wish to edit or add, or remove an unwanted cross-reference.

Generating the Index

Before generating the index, decide whether it will go onto a blank page at the end of the document, onto the pasteboard area, or into a new document altogether. Once you have the appropriate page of your document opened, select:

> *Create index* from the *Utilities* menu.

The *Create index* dialog box appears on your screen (fig. 10.8).

The title of the index, which can be edited with the Text tool, can contain up to 30 letters. If you select the Format button, the *Index format* dialog box (fig. 10.9) will appear.

Fig. 10.8. The *Create index* dialog box.

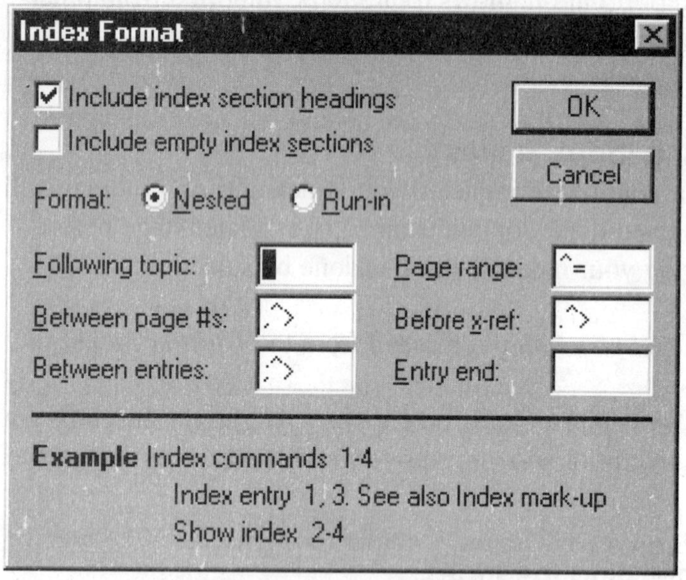

Fig. 10.9. The *Index format* dialog box.

> In the *Create index* dialog box, the *Replace existing index* option will not be available yet if this is the first time you have asked PageMaker to generate this index. The *Include book publications* will also be unavailable if you have not previously set up a book list.

Because PageMaker automatically generates each section heading of the index (e.g., A, B, and C), you must deselect *Include index section headings* if you do not wish to have these included. PageMaker, however, will still insert spacing between each alphabetical section. If you select *Include empty index sections,* PageMaker will list every section included in your index, but the empty sections will read "no entries."

Choose *Nested* or *Run-in* to determine the format of your index. Examples are shown at the bottom of the *Index format* dialog box. With *Nested,* each entry level of the index is a separate paragraph. With *Run-in*, all entry levels belong to one paragraph.

Six options allow you to select which characters are to be used to set each part of the index entry. Note that the ^> character in the edit boxes stands for an en-space (a space equal to half the point size of the type being used), and the ^= character stands for an en-dash (a dash the width of an en space). These options can be summarized as follows:

The *Following topic* option determines the character to be placed between each topic reference and its page number or cross-reference. The default is two en-spaces.

The specifications in the "Create index" dialog box apply to the current publication when a publication window is open. To set defaults for all publications, enter index format specifications when no publication window is open.

The *Between page #s* option determines the character to be placed between multiple page references for a single topic. The default is a comma followed by an en-space.

The *Between entries* option determines the character to be placed between subentries when you use the run-in layout. The default is a semicolon followed by an en-space.

The *Page range* option determines the character to be placed between a range of page numbers. The default is an en-dash.

The *Before x-ref* option determines the character to be placed between a topic reference (or page reference) and a cross-reference. The default is a period followed by an en-space.

The *Entry end* option determines the character to be placed after a final topic reference when using the nested layout or after each reference when using the run-in layout. PageMaker does not supply a default character for this option.

Once you have made your selections in the *Index format* dialog box, click on OK. Then select OK again in the *Create index* dialog box.

After a short time, you will have a loaded cursor on your page, which you can place in the same way as any other text file (fig. 10.10). If you checked *Replace existing index,* your new index will automatically replace the old one.

Index

A

administrative support staff 219
airline 7
algorithm 77
alternating current (AC) 30
AM (amplitude modulation) 34
American Bell Company 27
American Stock Exchange 11
American Telephone and Telegraph.
    See AT&T
amplitude modulation (AM) 34
amplitude noise 63
analog signals 58
ASCII (American Standard Code
    for Information Interchange
    47, 72, 73, 74, 75, 93
asynchronous 87
AT&T (American Telephone and
Telegraph) 26, 27, 67, 92, 112,
    220
Atlanta Constitution 5
Atlanta Journal 5
ATM 8, 9
Avis Rent-A-Car 12

B

back-ups 247
bandwidth 61
BANK WIRE 9
banking 6, 8
baseband 68
Baudot Code 71
Baudot, Emil 71
BBS
    functions of 127
bearer services 119
Bell, Alexander Graham 26, 27
Bell Labs 54
Bell Telephone Company 26
bell unit 28
BESTNET 136
biometric measure 237
    retinal scanning 237
    signature analysis 237
    voice recognition 237
    fingerprint 235
    hand geometry 235
    palm print 235
bit 92
bits per second (bps) 79
bombs 241
bridge 110
British Broadcasting Corpora-
    tion 35
broadband 61, 68
buffer 92
bulletin board systems (BBS) 15,
    123, 126
bus network 109

C

C-Band 147
cable TV 41

Fig. 10.10. A sample index created by PageMaker.

As with the generated table of contents, PageMaker creates its own paragraph styles for the index. You are also able to make additions and deletions to any index entries after the index has been created. To update the index, simply select *Replace existing index* in the *Create index* dialog box, and PageMaker will generate a new index and replace the old version.

11

PageMaker Publication for Electronic Distribution

Easy access to the Internet enables wider distribution of electronic publications—easily transportable documents that include links, sound, and even video. Adobe PageMaker provides professional tools for two popular electronic publishing formats—the Hypertext Markup Language (HTML) and the Portable Document Format (PDF).

Publishing a document electronically allows fast, economical distribution, the ability to search and index text, and easy updating. With electronic publishing, many traditional publishing steps disappear, such as press checks, printing, binding, and transportation. New production issues arise, such as computer and network speed, disk storage space, and variations in computer hardware and software. However, even with the newest technologies, publishers are finding that the key to successful electronic publishing is the same as with paper publishing: understanding the requirements of the project, the audience, and the distribution medium.

Electronic publishing provides the following advantages over traditional paper publishing:

- Quick access to reference materials
- Interactive multimedia capabilities
- Document distribution through the Web, CD- ROM, or as an e-mail attachment
- Electronic indexing and searching of existing paper documents

The Internet and the World Wide Web

The Internet is a popular medium for distributing information electronically. An ever- expanding network of networks, the Internet has no single owner. Its cables and equipment are owned and maintained by a mix of private and public network providers.

The Internet carries several kinds of communication services including e- mail, file transfer protocol (ftp), and Usenet newsgroups. The fastest- growing part of the Internet is the World Wide Web. The Web is easier to use than other Internet services. You can navigate the Web simply by pointing and clicking, using a viewing program called a Web browser. Also, you can create basic content for the Web without much programming experience. Reading and publishing Web pages require Web access, available in several ways:

- You may be a member of an organization that has an Internet connection, such as a business, school, or public library. Some educational organizations allow faculty, students and staff to publish on Web using the organization's server.
- You can use a modem to connect through an Internet Service Provider (ISP). Many packaged Web browsers include connection offers from ISPs.
- You can connect your computer directly to the Internet using Web server software, available for many platforms including Macintosh , Windows , and UNIX . A direct connection requires the most responsibility and maintenance, and works best with a dedicated computer and telephone line. Once a document is published on a Web server, anyone with Web access can retrieve it.

On-Screen Viewing and Printing on Demand

key project requirement is anticipating whether a publication will be both distributed and viewed online, or distributed online for printing on demand. For example, if your publication is a lengthy, text-intensive document that people will read from start to finish, you'll probably design it for printing on a desktop printer.

If your publication is a brief overview designed around colorful on-screen graphics, you will probably be less concerned about how it will print and design it so that it displays well on a monitor. If you are simply transferring existing paper documents for occasional electronic access, you may not need to redesign them at all. If you know that your audience will want to both read a publication online and print it, layout strategies and PDF (Portable Document Format) features such as article threads can make the publication useful both ways.

Delivery Media and Display Performance

Speed is a significant factor in electronic publication design. A publication usually slows down because its pages are too large for the distribution medium that transfers it to the computer, or because of the speed of the receiving computer. When you include many color images and movies on a page, it can become too large for today's networks to display quickly. For any medium you choose, determine the typical speed of the equipment available to your audience; then test and adjust your publication so that it performs well at that speed. Currently, on the World Wide Web, a common guideline is to design pages that transfer quickly over a 14.4Kbps modem. The size of individual pages is more important than the size of an entire publication, because a properly configured Web server sends a PDF publication one page at a time.

Including Movies

You can include a QuickTime or AVI (Windows) movie in a PDF publication. A movie is useful when your content is dynamic. For example, a technical illustration of a motor can be the first frame of a clickable movie that demonstrates how the motor works. When you create a movie to be used in a PDF, it is critical to optimize it for the delivery medium you will use. Movies for the Internet must be as small as possible to download from the Internet in a reasonable amount of time. movie is like a stack of still bitmap images presented very quickly in sequence. Accordingly, many techniques that make efficient still images also apply to movies. If it is too high, try the following:

- Minimize the duration. Edit a movie so that it is no longer than absolutely necessary.
- Minimize resolution. Internet data rates are so slow that 160x120 pixels or lower may be necessary.
- Minimize the frame rate. 10 frames per second is often smooth enough.
- Minimize bit depth. 24- bit color is usually more than you need. Most QuickTime movies are 16- bit. Simple animations can use fewer colors
- Use cuts or hard-edged wipes. Transitions that change opacity introduce additional data that increase the file size and data rate.
- Compress the movie. To achieve the low data rates necessary for Internet publishing, apply video compression such as Cinepak.

Including Sound

Sound can present certain kinds of information, such as the correct pronunciation of a word, most effectively. Acrobat embeds sounds inside a PDF file, except for sounds in QuickTime format, which are stored separately and linked. Although sound takes up less disk space than movies, your goal is the same as with movies: Aim for the smallest file size that preserves acceptable quality. To reach that goal, try these adjustments:

- Lower the sample rate, which is the number of samples per second of sound. A higher rate provides better sound but uses more disk space. Audio- CD- quality is 44.1kHz, but for the Internet try a sample rate of 11 or 22kHz.
- Lower the bit depth. More bits per sample increases the range and detail of sound at the expense of disk space. CD- quality sound is 16- bit, but 8- bit sound is often acceptable.
- Compress the sound file using a method supported by the file format. You can usually specify the compression ratio, or degree of compression. Voice may sound acceptable at a 5: 1 ratio. Higher- quality sound may require a ratio such as 3: 1. A lower ratio create a larger sound file.

Exporting PageMaker Publication to HTML

hypertext Markup Language (HTML) is a system that imbeds simple commands within standard ASCII text documents to provide an integrated visual display. In other words, a document created in any word processor and stored in normal ASCII format can become a home page with the addition of a few HTML commands allow the user to perform the following functions:

- Specify text size and flow
- Integrate in-line pictures
- Create links
- Integrate audio and external pictures
- Create interactive forms

HTML has evolved since its inception, and currently supports many features, including full forms movies, audio, and other capabilities.

The HTML Element

A HTML command is termed an *element.* HTML elements allow you to modify how a normal text document appears to the user when viewing it in a WWW (World Wide Web) browser. HTML elements are imbedded within the ASCII document and provide instructions to the browser concerning formatting and inclusion of outside elements such as pictures and audio.

An HTML element always appears as a word or phrase placed between less-than and greater-than characters. For example, the following list shows some basic HTML elements:

<pre>
</a>
<b>
<img src="picture.gif >

Each of the commands in the above list shares a common format in that they always begin the less-than character (<) and always end with greater-than character(>) The content between the two characters contains the HTML command itself.

Some text needs to be modified as a block. For example, if you wish to make a word or phrase **bold,** you need to specify both the START and END of the block of text that needs to be bold. In order to do this, an HTML element is placed at the BEGINNING of the word or phrase, and another HTML element is placed at the END of the word or phrase. The two elements are simply written slightly differently by causing the ending element to have a leading slash character (/) just before the element name. The following example shows this:

<b> **This text will be bold** </b>

In this example, we desire to make text bold. The <b> element does this. Elements are case independent, meaning that elements may be expressed in either uppercase or lowercase, or even mixed case.

Many elements contain parameters that help describe what function the command is to perform. For example, an element that specifies that an image be placed in-line in the document must specify the NAME of the image. This is considered a *parameter* or argument. The following example shows just such a command:

<IMG SRC= " flowers . gif " >

This is an image (<IMG>) element and specifies that an image should be placed in the document. The SRC= portion of the element describes the name of the picture to be loaded. This is a parameter to the <IMG> element.
Notice that the data portion of the parameter (as in "flowers.gif" in the previous example) is placed in double quotes. In most cases HTML will honor data with or without quotes. However, use of quotes is required if you are imbedding special characters or spaces within the data. In general, the best rule to follow is to always place the data portion of any parameter within quotation marks to ensure compatibility with all browsers.

PageMaker Publication for HTML

A page designed for HTML follows a different set of design requirements than a page designed for print. When creating a piece for an online network such as the World Wide Web, you usually have no control over the size of the monitor or window in which the page is viewed.

PageMaker creates HTML pages using a subset of the style tags available in the 3.2 version of the HTML specification; it exports some but not all browser-specific tags such as Netscape Navigator extensions to HTML. The character-level attributes Bold, Italic, Underline, and Reverse as well as the color of your type, are preserved on export.

HTML supports the GIF and JPEG image formats. PageMaker automatically converts copies of imported graphics (whether inline or independent) to GIF or JPEG. Using HTML tables, PageMaker can approximate multi-column page design, including elements outside margins, text and graphics that span columns, and text wrapping around graphics. You can also choose not to approximate page layout; the result is one column of contiguous text, with graphics occupying separate paragraphs and flowing along with the text.

Limitations

Typographical density (such as line breaks, letter spacing, and word spacing) are completely determined by the fonts used by a particular browser. Other type attributes that are completely controlled by World Wide Web browsers, and will not be preserved if you specify them in PageMaker, include the following:

- Font, type size, and leading
- Strikethru, Outline, Shadow, Reverse, Superscript, and Subscript type styles.
- Color changes.
- Horizontal scale.
- Tracking and kerning.
- Outline and Shadow type styles.
- Paragraph alignment (unless Preserve Approximate Page Layout is selected).
- Indent and tab positions.

The simplest way to create a page for the Web is to use PageMaker paragraph styles that correspond to the HTML markup tags that you want to use. This ensures that you are using styles supported by the HTML export feature.

If you design a multi-column layout and want to preserve the layout in HTML, remember that the Export to HTML feature can only approximate your page layout. The limitations are due to the HTML language itself; for example, since most typographical characteristics are not preserved in HTML, the length of text columns is not preserved. The following are unsupported features in HTML and might require page layout changes in PageMaker to produce acceptable HTML:

- Objects transformed (rotated, skewed, or flipped) in PageMaker are untransformed in HTML. You can trans form the object in an illustration or image-editing application and re-import into PageMaker if you want the object to remain transformed in HTML.
- Overlapping objects in PageMaker are separated in the exported HTML, with results that may not be satisfactory. Before exporting, revise your design so that objects do not overlap.
- Non-rectangular text wrap shapes are not approximated in HTML, and results in objects being moved. Be sure to apply the standard rectangular text wrap shape, or revise the design to avoid non-rectangular text wrap.
- The content of a frame is exported, but not the surrounding frame itself. Non-rectangular frames become rectangular. Images that extend beyond the visible frame area are cropped in the exported file to approximate the original layout.
- PageMaker-drawn graphics are not exported, with the exception of horizontal strokes which are exported as HTML horizontal rules.
- A masked object is unmasked. Before exporting, unmask the elements and, if you masked an image, crop it with the cropping tool. If you masked text, recreate the effect in an illustration program and import it as a graphic.

Creating Hyperlinks

PageMaker allows you to hyperlink any graphic or any range of text so that when you export to PDF or HTML, the viewer of the document can click the hyperlink to jump to another object, page, or Internet resource (including movies) on the Web. Hyperlinks also let a viewer of your PDF or HTML file send electronic mail just by clicking the hyperlink. You can create, import, edit, and manage hyperlinks with the Hyperlinks palette and, in PageMaker's preview mode, test the hyperlinks by clicking them to jump to the associated destination.

A source can only jump to one destination, but any number of sources can jump to the same destination.

Each hyperlink consists of a source and a destination. For example, if you have the text "Click here to see picture" on page 1 jump to a scanned image on page 4, then the text is the source, and the image is the destination. When you establish the connection between the source and the destination, you have a hyperlink.

PageMaker supports two kinds of hyperlink destinations, *anchor* and *URL*. Anchor links any text of graphic in the same publication as the source, whereas URL lets you specify the location of resources on the Internet. For URL destinations you can use the following URL types:

http:// (Hypertext Transfer protocol)
mailto: (Electronic mail address)
ftp:// (File Transfer protocol)
gopher:// (the Gopher protocol)
file:// (Host-specific file names)
news: (USENET news)
telnet: (interactive sessions)
smtp: (Simple Mail Transport protocol)

Creating Anchors

To create an anchor follow these steps:

1. In the publication, select the text tool and highlight the text that you want to turn into an anchor.
2. Select *Show Hyperlinks* from the *Window* menu. The *Hyperlinks* dialog box displays (fig. 11.1).

Fig. 11.1. *Hyperlinks* dialog box.

3. Place the pointer on the arrow in the Hyperlinks dialog box. A pop-up menu appears (fig. 11.2).

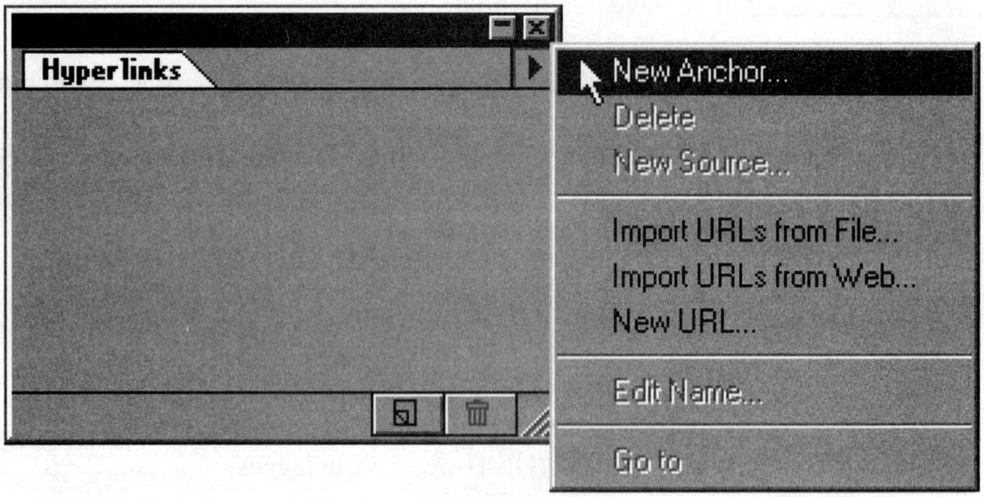

Fig. 11.2. Hyperlinks pop-up menu.

4. Select *New Anchor*.
5. Type a name for your anchor.

Creating URL

To create an URL, follow these steps:

1. Select *Show Hyperlinks* from the *Window* menu. The Hyperlinks dialog box displays
2. Choose New URL from the Hyperlinks palette menu.

3. Type the URL in the dialog box. You can import URL (copy and paste) from a file or from the Web.
4. Click OK.

Creating Hyperlinks Between Sources and Destinations

Once you have created or imported destinations, you can use the Hyperlinks palette to associate selected text or graphics (sources) with the destinations, establishing the hyperlinks for your document. To create link between source and anchor or URL destination:

1. Select the text or graphic you want to be the hyperlink's source.
2. Select *Show Hyperlinks* from the *Window* menu. The Hyperlinks dialog box displays.
3. in the palette (fig. 11.3), click the destination you want to hyperlink to, and choose *New Source* from the Hyperlinks palette menu.

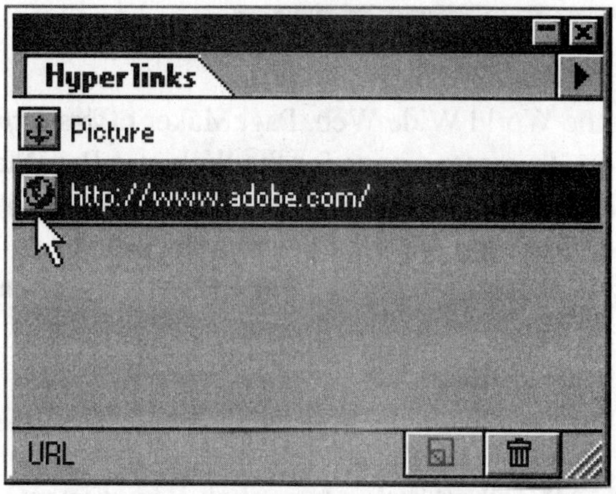

Fig. 11.3. Select the anchor or URL destination on the Hyperlinks palette.

Previewing Hyperlinks

1. Select the Hand tool in the Toolbox to enter preview mode. Hyperlinked text is oulined in a blue box; hyperlinked graphics are framed with a blue line.
2. Move the cursor over the hyperlink source. The cursor changes to a pointing hand. For URL destination, the pointing hand displays with a "W" inside it, indicating the destination is on the World Wide Web.

3. Click within the blue border to jump to its destination.

To change the name of hyperlinks:

1. Select *Show Hyperlinks* from the *Window* menu. The Hyperlinks dialog box displays.
2. double click the item you want to rename.
3. Type a new name or URL.
4. Click OK.

To remove a source or destination:

1. Select *Show Hyperlinks* from the *Window* menu. The Hyperlinks dialog box displays.
2. Select the item you want to remove.
3. Click the trash button at the bottom of the Hyperlinks palette, or choose *Delete* from the Hyperlinks palette menu.
4. Click OK.

Exporting Publication to HTML

To publish on the World Wide Web, PageMaker offers *Export to HTML* option. To create a page for the Web, use PageMaker paragraph styles that correspond to the HTML markup tags which is supported by the *HTML*. For example, use the PageMaker style named Heading 1 for the HTML style named <H1>.

1. From the *File* menu, choose *Export* then *HTML. Export HTML* dialog box displays (fig. 11.4).
2. In the HTML Export dialog box, click *New. Export HTML: New Contents* dialog box displays (fig. 11.5).
3. Enter a document title (the title will display at the top of the browser window when the document is viewed).
4. Select *Assign PageMaker Pages* if you want to define a page or range of pages to be exported as HTML or select *Assign PageMaker Stories* to define a story or set of stories to be exported as HTML.
5. Select an unassigned page or story to be exported into the HTML document you are defining, and click *Add* or *Add All*. The order in which you add pages or stories is the order in

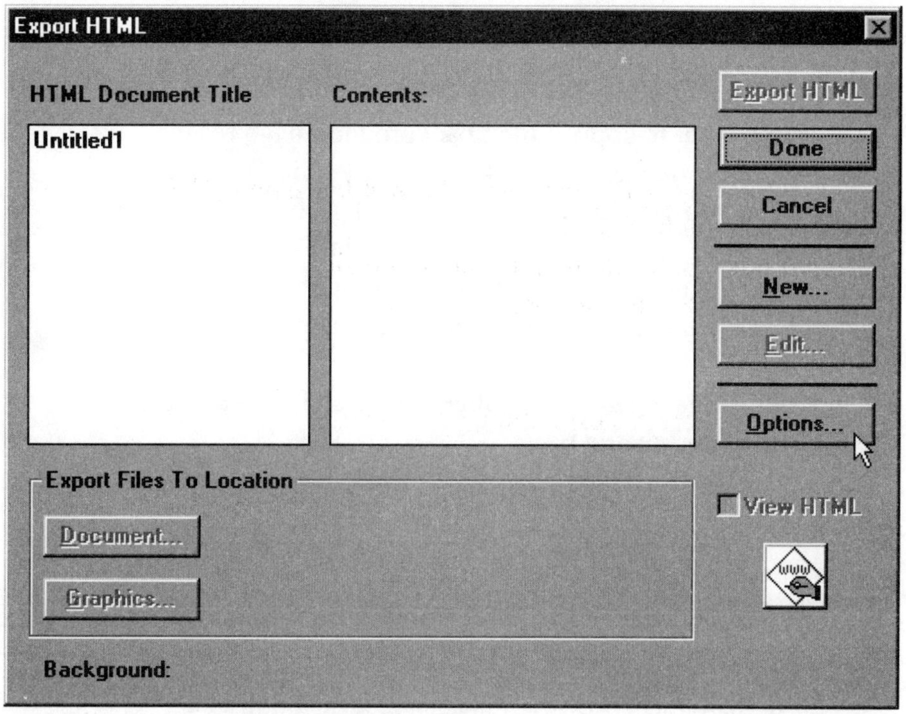

Fig. 11.4. *Export HTML* dialog box.

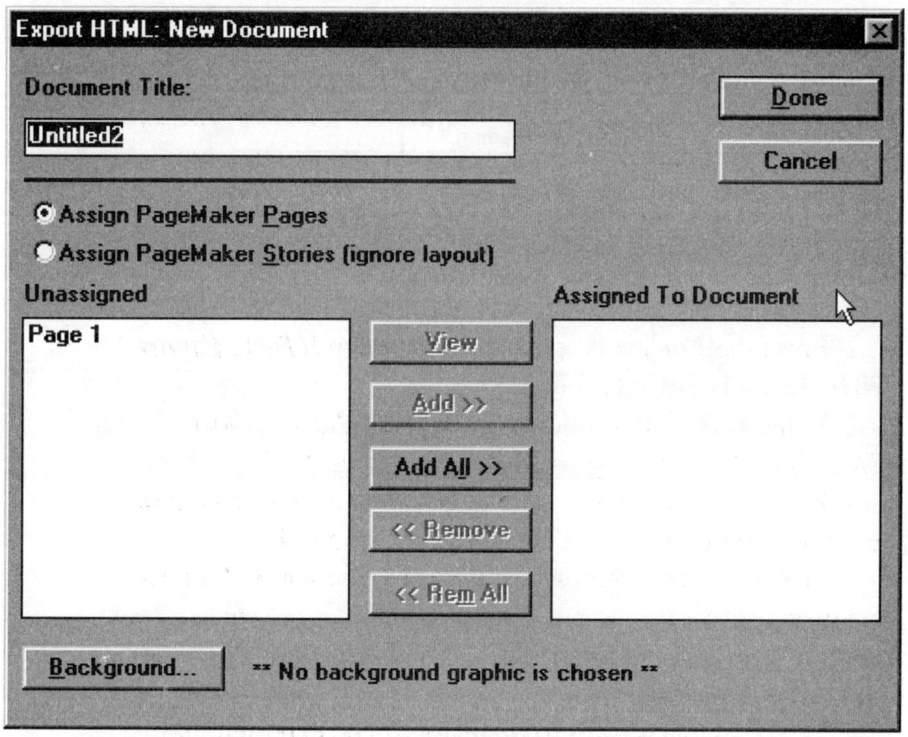

Fig. 11.5. *Export HTML: New Document* dialog box.

which they will be exported. You can click *View* with a page number selected if you want to display the page (you might need to move the dialog box to see it).

6. If you want to apply a tiled background image for the document, click *Background* and then double-click the *GIF* or *JPEG* image you want to use as a page background. To export pages with a page background color rather than an image, return to the PageMaker window, and edit the PageMaker color [Paper] to the background color you want to appear in the HTML page.

7. Click *Done* to save the changes made so far and return to the HTML Export dialog box.

8. In the Export HTML dialog box, click *Options*. The *Option* dialog box displays (fig. 11.6).

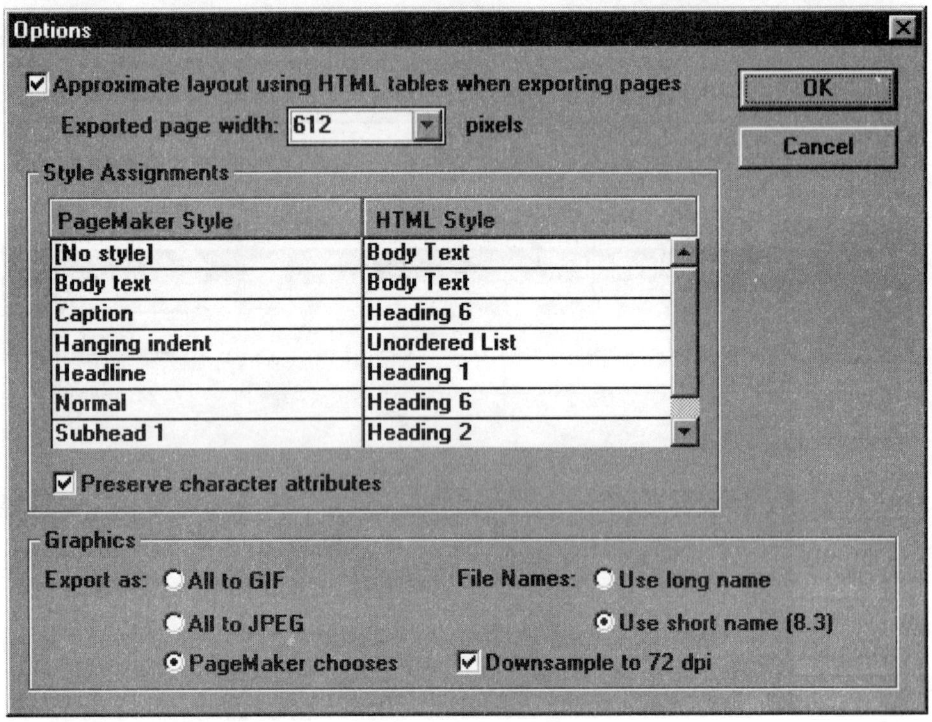

Fig. 11.6. Export HTML *Option* dialog box.

9. Make sure *Preserve Approximate Page Layout* is selected if you want the HTML documents to approximate multi-column page designs. PageMaker uses the HTML table tags to arrange the exported text and graphics

10. For *Exported Page Width*, type or choose the width (in pixels) of the HTML document. The default value is the page width of the current publication (expressed in pixels).

11. From the *HTML Style* pop-up menus (to the right of the HTML style names), select the format you want to be applied for the PageMaker style listed to its left. Repeat this step for each style you want to change. For example, if you use a style called *Bullet List* you probably want to map it to the OL (Ordered List) HTML format.

12. Make sure the *Preserve Character Attributes* setting is selected if you want the color and type style of your paragraph style definitions to be applied in your HTML documents.

13. In the Graphics section of the dialog box, set the following options:

Select whether you want images converted to *GIF* or *JPEG*. Or select *Let PageMaker Choose* to default to whichever of those two formats works best, based on the file type and color data of each image on the pages being exported. Full sample images (RGB, CMYK, LAB, and grayscale) convert to JPEG and indexed images to GIF.

The following styles are available in *HTML Export Option* dialog box:

HTML heading style	**What it does in a browser**
H1, H2, H3, H4, H5, H6	Six levels of subheads. H1 has the largest type size, H6 the smallest.
Address	Sets an address or other short text apart from the body text.
Blockquote	Sets one or more paragraphs of text apart from the body text.
Body Text	Normal paragraphs of body text.
Definition List	List format. The browser automatically indents each paragraph with this format.
Directory List	List format. Usually, the browser automatically indents and adds bullet before each paragraph with this format.
Menu List	Similar to an ordered list, but more compact.

Ordered List	Use for a numbered list. Usually, the browser automatically adds the correct number before each item.
Preformatted List	Prevents text from being refor matted when changes are made to a browser's style definitions.

14. Click OK to close the Options dialog box.
15. Click *Document*, and do the following:

- Navigate to the location where you want the HTML document to be stored.
- Name the document, following the naming conventions for the platform of the Web server you'll be using to publish the HTML document.
- Select *Save Images into This Folder* if you want your HTML document to include images from the publication and you want to store them in the same folder as the HTML document. (To store the graphics elsewhere, click OK and then click the *Graphics* button in the Export HTML dialog box and navigate to the folder you want.)

16. Click OK.

At this point you are only defining a target location, not actually saving the HTML document.

17. If you want to open the HTML document (once the export process is complete) in a Web browser or HTML editing application such as Adobe PageMill, click *View HTML*. Then click the *Application* icon to open a dialog box in which you can specify which browser or HTML editor you want to use to open the exported HTML file.

The application you select will open automatically when the export process is complete.

18. To generate the HTML, click *Export HTML*; otherwise, click *Done* to save settings made so far.

After you have defined how the publication is to be exported as HTML, the HTML Export dialog box displays a list of all defined HTML documents, their titles, and contents.

The next step in the process is to make sure that the PageMaker publication is HTML compatible. The first time you save a publication as HTML, PageMaker checks it for HTML compatibility. If the publication contains an element or layout attribute that is not supported by HTML, PageMaker presents a dialog box informing you of the parts of the publication that need to be changed. If there are incompatible elements in the publication, correct them, and then export the pages or stories again using the HTML export feature.

Modifying the Title, Location, or Contents

After you have initially defined how your PageMaker publication should be translated to HTML, you may need to change the title of the HTML document, its location, or which PageMaker elements (pages or stories) should be included in the HTML document. To change the title:

1. From the *File* menu, select *Export* then choose *HTML.*
2. In the *HTML Export* dialog box, double-click the HTML document you want to edit and then change the title in the *Edit Contents* dialog box.

To change the location where an HTML document is exported:

1. From the *File* menu, select *Export* then choose *HTML.*
2. In the *HTML Export* dialog box, select the HTML document you want to edit.
3. Click *Document.*

To change the contents of an HTML document:

1. From the *File* menu, select *Export* then choose *HTML.*
2. In the *HTML Export* dialog box, double-click the HTML document you want to edit.
3. Add or remove pages or stories, remove the background image or specify a new one, and then click *Done*.

Portable Document Format (PDF)

You may find that electronic distribution is faster than paper distribution, but you must adjust the production process to take the requirements of electronic distribution into account. One of the challenges in electronic distribution is ensuring that fonts display properly. For example, if a person receives a

PageMaker document and does not have the fonts originally used in it, the line lengths of text can change and alter the page layout. You can avoid this problem by creating a PDF file.

To create a PDF version of your PageMaker document:

1. From the *File* menu, select *Export* then choose *Adobe PDF*. A dialog box displays (fig. 11.7).

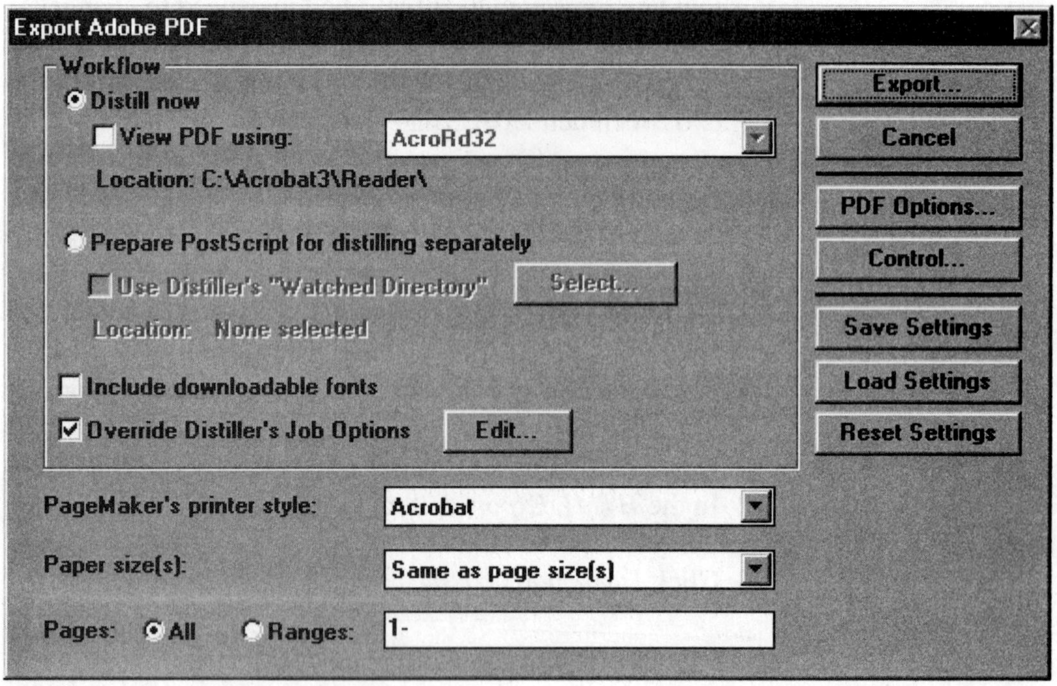

Fig. 11.7. *Export Adobe PDF* dialog box.

2. Select *Distill Now* (only available if Distiller is installed).

3. If you want to open and display the PDF file immediately after it has been created, select the *View PDF Using* option and choose a viewer from the pop-up menu.

4. Specify the range of pages to export, and then click *Export*.

5. If prompted, specify a filename and location, and then click *Save*.

Acrobat is the default style on the *PageMaker Printer Style* pop-up menu.

Creating Acrobat Articles

An Acrobat article consists of various text "beads," similar to the way a PageMaker story consists of various text objects. You can create Acrobat articles based on PageMaker stories, and you can have one or more stories per article.

You can use the *Export Adobe PDF* command to create articles automatically, or you can define them yourself, manually.

To create articles automatically:

1. From the *File* menu, choose *Export* then select *Adobe PDF. Export Adobe PDF* dialog box appears (fig. 11.8).

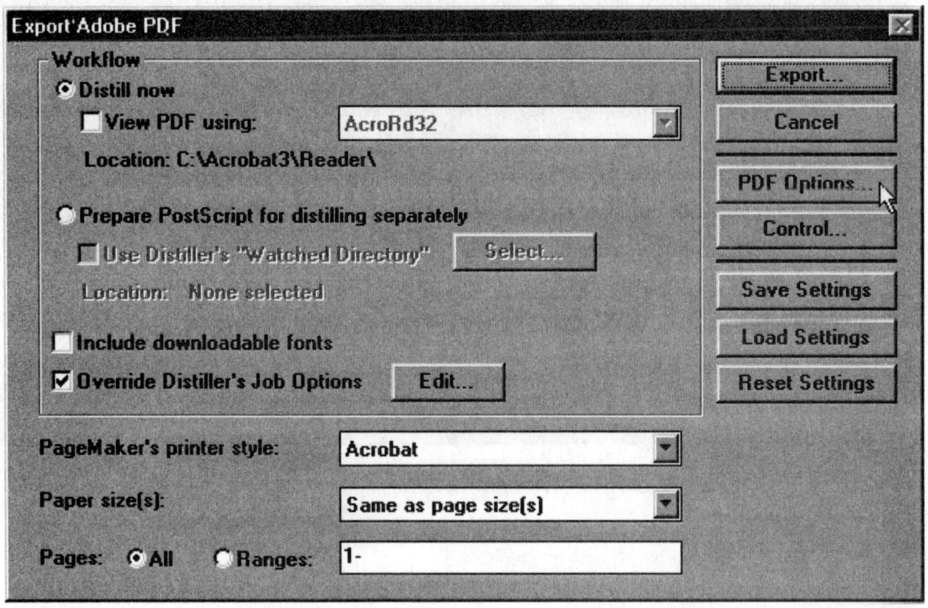

Fig. 11.8. *Export Adobe PDF* dialog box.

2. Click *PDF Options*. The *PDF Option* dialog box displays (fig. 11.9).
3. In the PDF Options dialog box, click *Create Articles*, and then click *Define*. *Define Articles* dialog box appears (fig. 11.10).
4. Select the *One Per Story Over _Text Objects* option stating that only stories containing more than the specified number of text objects should be converted to articles.

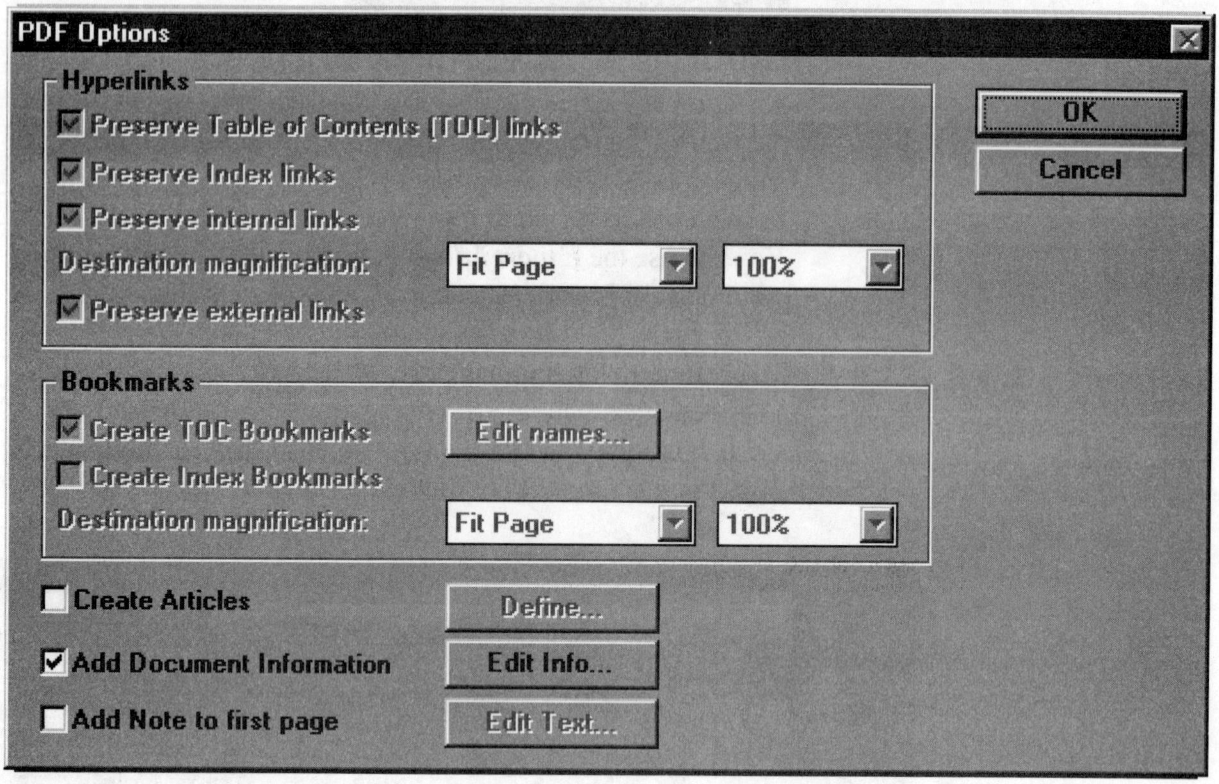

Fig. 11.9. *PDF Option* dialog box.

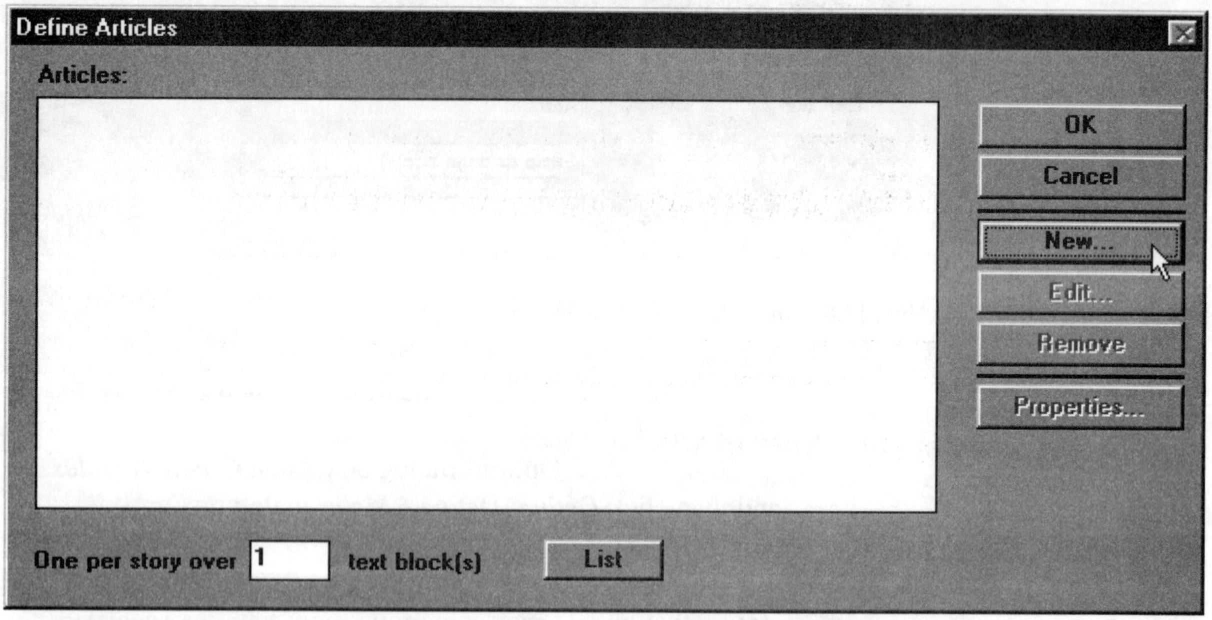

Fig. 11.10. *Define Articles* dialog box.

5. Click *Relist*. The stories will automatically appear as articles.

6. Click OK to close the Define Articles dialog box.

To create articles manually:

1. From the *File* menu, choose *Export* then select *Adobe PDF*. Export Adobe PDF dialog box appears.

2. Click *PDF Options* to display its dialog box.

3. In the PDF Options dialog box, click *Create Articles*, and then click *Define*.

4. Click *New* to display the *PageMaker Stories* dialog box (fig. 11.11).

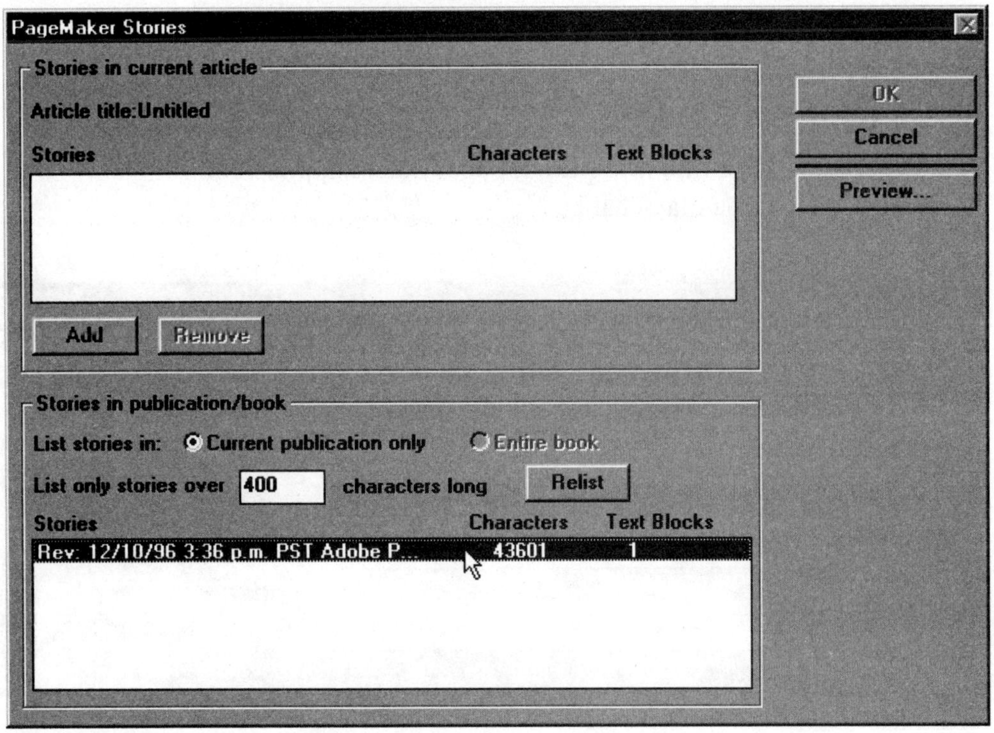

Fig. 11.11. *PageMaker Stories* dialog box.

5. Choose from the following options:

- The *List Stories* In option controls how you view stories when the publication contains a book list. To view all stories in all publications in the book, click *Entire Book*. Otherwise, click *Current Publication Only*. The Entire

Book option is only available when the publication contains a book list and you have chosen to print the entire book by either selecting the *Always Print All Publications* in *Book* option in the Control dialog box or when prompted after having selected the *Export Adobe PDF* command.

- The *List Only Stories Over_Characters Long* option lets you view only those stories that are longer than a certain length. Enter the number of characters you want, and then click *Relist.*

6. Select one or more stories from the *Stories* in the *Publication/Book* list, and then click *Add* to include them in the *Stories* in *Current Article* list. Each story shows the first few dozen characters, but if you want to see more of a selected story, click *Preview*.

7. Click OK. The *Article Properties* dialog box appears (fig. 11.12). Type a title, a subject, an author, and keywords, and then click OK. A title is required; PageMaker supplies one by default, which you may change.

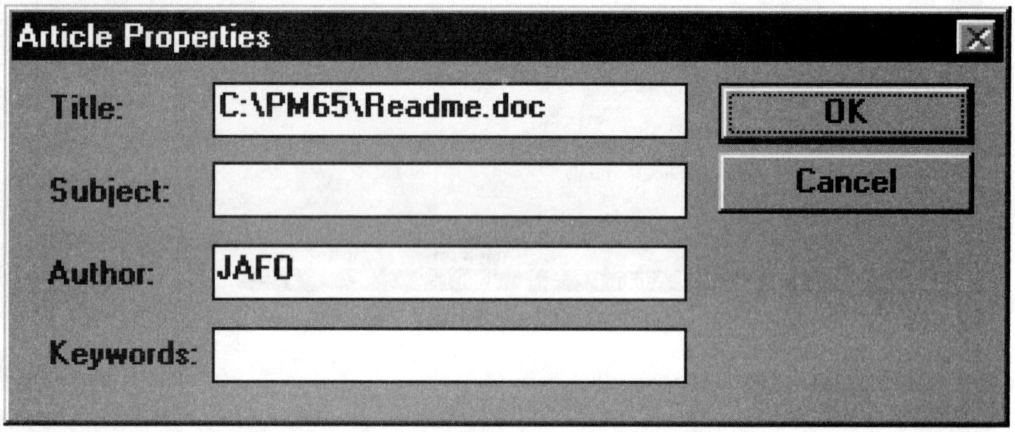

Fig. 11.12. *Article Properties* dialog box.

Electronic distribution creates points of contact for widely dispersed people across time and distance. There are daily information exchanges that can have enormous impact on how we as individuals think and how we come to understand global issues.

Appendixes

Clip Art

To enhance the appearance of a document, designers can use electronic clip art, which contains a variety of drawing and graphics. Clip art comes in different formats, which affect the resulting quality of the image.

Bit-mapped graphics are the most popular form of clip art. Bit-mapped graphics are created as a series of small dots. These graphics have a resolution of 72 dots per inch. Because the number of dots in a bit-mapped graphic remains constant, the more it is reduced, the higher its resolution becomes.

PICT and *PICT2* are standard Apple graphics formats that use a series of shapes, screens, and other mathematically defined objects. Therefore, these images can be resized without loss of resolution.

A recent development in electronic clip art utilizes the Post-Script language. This format is called *Encapsulated PostScript* (EPS). The EPS format includes two different versions of the image in the same document: a bit-mapped image and a Post-Script language version. The low-resolution bit-mapped image is included so the page layout programs will have something to display. The PostScript description of the image is provided so that the applications can pass the image directly to PostScript-capable printers.

Tagged Image File Format (TIFF) is a bit-mapped graphics standard and a common document format for scanned images. There are many different TIFF variations. TIFF images are often referred to by the number of bits saved for each pixel in the original image. For example, 1 bit per pixel is a black-and-white image and 8 bits per pixel equals 256 grays or colors.

The following pages represent a very small sampling of clip arts.

Sample Clip Art from T/Maker Company

T/Maker Company
1390 Villa Street
Mountain View, CA 94041
Telephone: 415/962-0195

Sample Clip Art from T/Maker Company

Continued

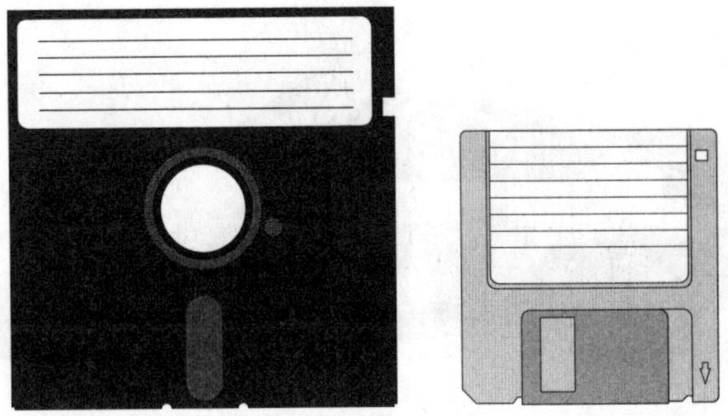

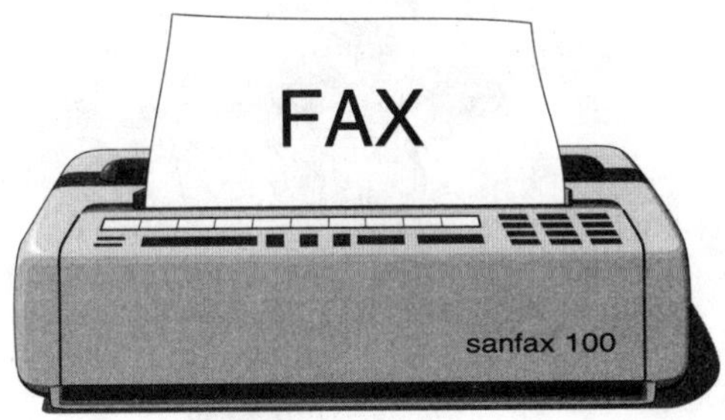

Sample Clip Art from T/Maker Company

Continued

Sample Clip Art from C.A.R., Inc.

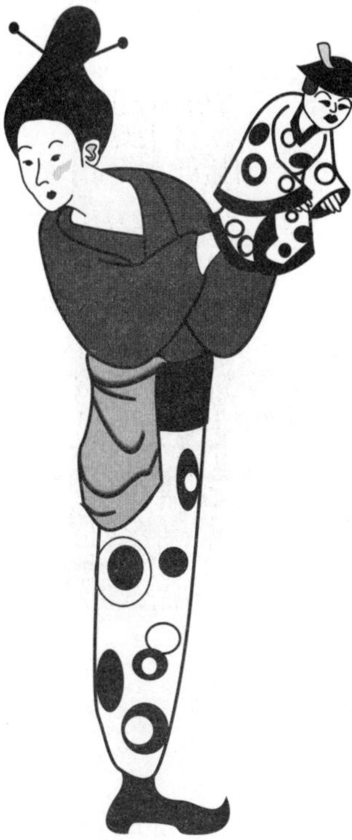

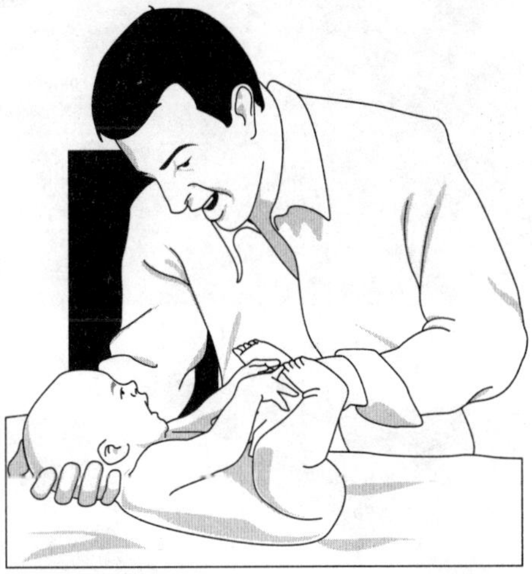

C.A.R., Inc.
7009 Kingsbury
St. Louis, MO 63130
Telephone: 314/721-6305

Sample Clip Art from C.A.R., Inc.

Continued

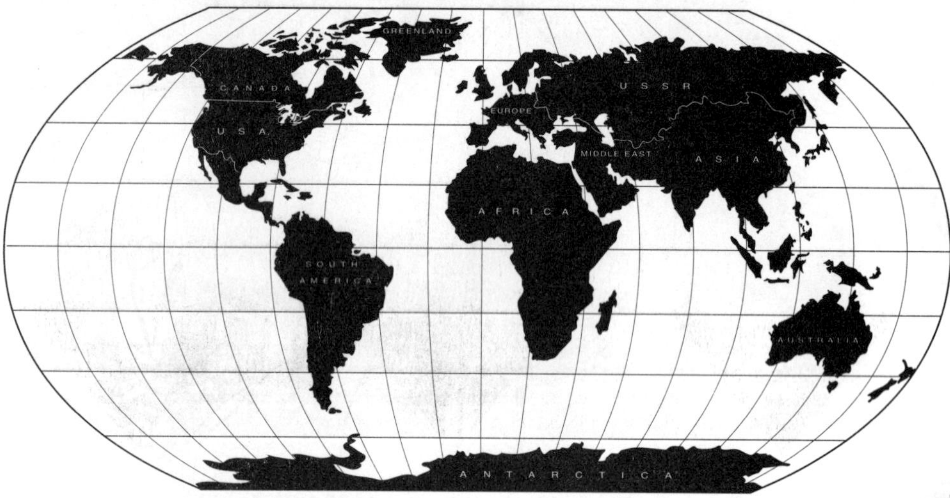

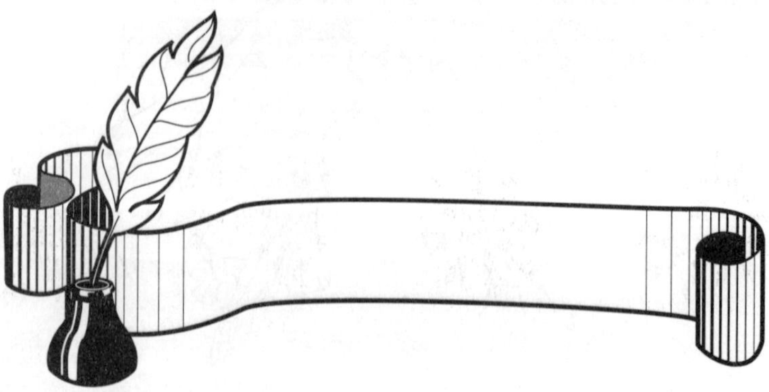

Sample Clip Art from 3G Graphics, Inc.

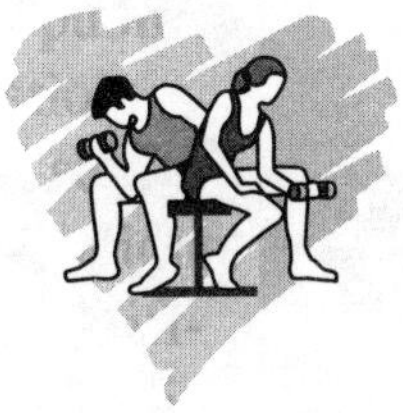
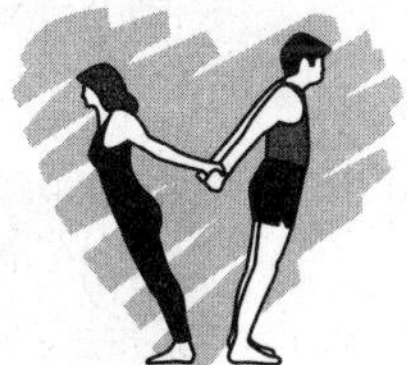

3G Graphics, Inc.
114 Second Ave. South,
Suite 104
Edmonds, WA 98020
Telephone: 206/367-9321

Sample Backgrounds from Artbeats

Artbeats
Box 20083
San Bernardino, CA 92406
Telephone: 714/881-1200

Sample Clip Art from Dynamic Graphics, Inc.

Dynamic Graphics, Inc.
6000 N. Forest Park Drive
Peoria, IL 61614
Telephone: 309/688-8800

Sample Clip Art from Dynamic Graphics, Inc.

Continued

Sample Clip Art from Dynamic Graphics, Inc.

Continued

Desktop Publishing Resources

Books

American Press Institute. *Newspaper Design: 2000 and Beyond.* Reston, VA: American Press Institute, 1989.

Bauermeister, Benjamin. *A Manual of Comparative Typography: The PANOSE System.* New York: Van Nostrand Reinhold, 1988.

Beach, Mark, and Ken Russon. *Papers for Printing: How to Choose the Right Paper at the Right Price for Any Printing Job.* Portland, OR: Coast to Coast Books, 1989.

Beach, Mark, Steve Shepro, and Ken Russon. *Getting It Printed: How to Work with Printers and Graphic Arts Services to Assure Quality, Stay on Schedule, and Control Costs.* Portland, OR: Coast to Coast Books, 1986.

Beach, Mark, with Heath Silberfeld and Elizabeth Wollman. *Content Ideas That Work: Hundreds of Proven Topics for Editors and Writers of Newsletters, Magazines and Tabloids.* Portland, OR: Coast to Coast Books, 1990.

Beale, Stephen, and James Cavuoto. *The Scanner Book: A Complete Guide to the Use and Application of Desktop Scanners.* Torrance, CA: Micro Publishing Press, 1989.

Beaumont, Michael. *Type: Design, Color, Character & Use.* Cincinnati, OH: North Light Books, 1987.

Binns, Betty. *Better Type: Learn to See Subtle Distinctions in the Faces and Spaces of Text Type.* New York: Watson-Guptill, 1989.

Bly, Robert W. *Ads That Sell.* Brentwood, NY: Asher-Gallant, 1988.

———. *Create the Perfect Sales Piece: How to Produce Brochures, Catalogs, Fliers and Pamphlets.* New York: John Wiley, 1985.

Brady, Philip. *Using Type Right: 121 Basic No-Nonsense Rules for Working with Type.* Cincinnati, OH: North Light Books, 1988.

Brown, Alex. *In Print: Text and Type in the Age of Desktop Publishing.* New York: Watson-Guptill, 1989.

Burke, Clifford. *Type from the Desktop: Designing with Type and Your Computer.* Chapel Hill, NC: Ventana Press, 1990.

Carter, Rob, Ben Day, and Phillip Meggs. *Typographic Design: Form and Communication.* New York: Van Nostrand Reinhold, 1985.

Cook, Alton, ed. *Type and Color: A Handbook of Creative Combinations.* Rockport, MA: Rockport Publications, 1989.

Dair, Carl. *Design with Type.* Toronto: University of Toronto Press, 1982.

Durbin, Harold C. *Desktop Publishing Systems.* Easton, PA: Durbin Associates, 1995.

Finberg, Howard I., and Bruce D. Itule. *Visual Editing: A Graphic Guide for Journalists.* Belmont, CA: Wadsworth, 1990.

Gosney, Michael, and Linnea Dayton. *Making Art on the Macintosh II.* Glenview, IL: Scott, Foresman, 1989.

Gosney, Michael, John Odam, and Jim Schmal. *The Gray Book.* Chapel Hill, NC: Ventana Press, 1990.

The Gray Book by Gosney, Odam, and Schmal is filled with tips, techniques, and examples. It shows how to create screens, reverses, bleeds, drop shadows, multiple shades of gray, patterns, and 3D effects.

The Presentation Design Book: Projecting a Good Image with Your Desktop Computer is a generic guide that reviews the essentials of creating good-looking slides, overheads, charts, diagrams, and handouts. It alerts you to basic pitfalls of producing presentation graphics, and provides examples of how to choose the best medium and tailor it for your audience.

Green, Chuck. *Desk Top Publisher's Idea.* New York: Random House, Incorporated, 1997.

Henry, Jeanne H. *Do's & Don'ts of Desktop Publishing Design.* Ann Arbor, MI: Promotional Perspectives, Incorporated, 1996.

Holmes, Nigel. *Designer's Guide to Creating Charts and Diagrams.* New York: Watson-Guptill, 1984.

Hudson, Howard Penn. *Publishing Newsletters,* rev. ed. New York: Charles Scribner's Sons, 1988.

Kaatz, Ron. *The NTC Book of Advertising and Marketing Checklists.* Lincolnwood, IL: NTC Business Books, 1988.

Kemp, Jerold E. *Planning and Producing Audiovisual Materials*, 4th ed. New York: Harper & Row, 1980.

Kieper, Michael L. *Illustrated Handbook of Desktop Publishing and Typesetting.* Blue Ridge Summit, PA: TAB Books, 1987.

Lester, Paul M. *Desktop Computing Workbook : A Guide for Using 15 Programs in Macintosh & Windows Formats.* Belmont, CA: Wadsworth Publishing Company, 1996.

McComb, Gordon. *Executive Guide to Presentation Graphics.* New York: Bantam Books, 1988.

Mandell, Steve. *Effective Presentation Skills: A Practical Guide for Better Speaking.* Los Altos, CA: Crisp Publications, 1987.

Marr, Jerry. *Mac Graphics for Business.* Glenview, IL: Scott, Foresman, 1986.

Maxymuk, John. *Using Desktop Publishing to Create Newsletters, Library Guides, & Web Pages : A How-to-Do-It Manual for Librarians.* New York: Neal-Schuman Publishers, Incorporated, 1996.

Moen, Daryl R. *Newspaper Layout and Design,* 2d ed. Ames: Iowa State University Press, 1989.

Morrissette, Christine, and Erfert Fenton. *Canned Art: Clip Art for the Macintosh.* Berkeley, CA: Peachpit Press, 1990.

Naiman, Arthur, ed. *The Macintosh Bible: Thousands of Tips, Tricks, Shortcuts, Logically Organized and Fully Indexed,* 2d ed. Berkeley, CA: Goldstein & Blair, 1989.

Nelson, Roy Paul. *The Design of Advertising,* 6th ed. Dubuque, IA: William C. Brown, 1989.

———. *Publication Design*, 4th ed. Dubuque, IA: William C. Brown, 1989.

One Club for Art & Copy. *The One Show: Judged to Be Advertising's Best in Print, Radio and TV,* vol. 11. New York: One Club for Art & Copy, 1990.

Parker, Roger C. *Desktop Publishing & Design for Dummies.* Foster City, CA: I D G Books Worldwide, 1995.

———. *Looking Good in Print*, 2nd. ed. Chapel Hill, NC: Ventana Press, 1990.

———. *The Makeover Book: 101 Design Solutions for Desktop Publishing.* Chapel Hill, NC: Ventana Press, 1989.

———. *Newsletters from the Desktop.* Chapel Hill, NC: Ventana Press, 1990.

Perfect, Christopher, and Gordon Rookledge. *Rookledge's International Typefinder: The Essential Handbook of Typeface Recognition & Selection.* Glen Cove, NY: PBC International, 1986.

Rabb, Margaret Y., ed. *The Presentation Design Book: Projecting a Good Image with Your Desktop Computer.* Chapel Hill, NC: Ventana Press, 1990.

The Makeover Book: 101 Design Solutions for Desktop Publishing contains hundreds of actual examples, tips, and techniques that let you compare original documents with their makeovers.

Looking Good in Print, 2d ed., features more than 400 illustrations and includes makeovers and design tips. The book contains guidelines for effective typography, using illustrations to communicate messages, and for avoiding design pitfalls.

Newsletters from the Desktop shows you how to plan your newsletter, choose the best layout for your project, create the newsletter's nameplate, select the best typeface, and integrate text and graphics.

Robertson, Bruce. *How to Draw Charts and Diagrams*. Cincinnati, OH: North Light Books, 1988.

Silver, Gerald A. *Layout, Design, & Typography : For the Desktop Publisher*. Encino, CA: Editorial Enterprises, 1997.

Sitarz, Daniel. *The Desktop Publisher's Legal Handbook: A Comprehensive Guide to Computer Publishing Law*. Carbondale, IL: Nova Publishing, 1989.

Solomon, Martin. *The Art of Typography: An Introduction to Typo.icon.ography*. New York: Watson-Guptill, 1986.

Spencer, Donald D. *Desktop Publishing Dictionary*. Ormond Beach, FL: Camelot Publishing Company, 1995.

Strunk, William, Jr., and E. B. White. *Elements of Style*, 3d ed. New York: Macmillan, 1979.

Swann, Alan. *How to Understand and Use Design and Layout.* Cincinnati, OH: North Light Books, 1987.

Toor, Marcelle L. *The Desktop Designer's Illustration Handbook*. New York: Van Nostrand Reinhold, 1996.

White, Alex. *How to Spec Type*. New York: Watson-Guptill, 1987.

———. *Type in Use.* New York: Design Press, 1990.

White, Jan. *Color for the Electronic Age*. New York: Watson-Guptill, 1990.

———. *Using Charts and Graphs: 1000 Ideas for Getting Attention.* New York: R. R. Bowker, 1984.

Wood, James. *Desktop Magic : Electronic Publishing, Document Management, & Work Groups.* New York: Van Nostrand Reinhold, 1995.

Zelazny, Gene. *Say It with Charts.* Homewood, IL: Dow Jones-Irwin, 1985.

Zinsser, William. *On Writing Well: An Informal Guide to Writing Nonfiction.* 4th ed. New York: Harper & Row, 1990.

Periodicals

> *Adobe Magazine* provides inspiration to newsletter editors by showcasing documents produced with PageMaker and Photoshop, and describing how they were created using the latest design techniques and application ideas.

Adobe Magazine. Aldus Corporation, 411 First Avenue South, Suite 200, Seattle, WA 98104.

Before & After: How to Design Cool Stuff on Your Computer. PageLab, 331 J Street, Suite 150, Sacramento, CA 95814-9671.

Business Publishing. Hitchcock Publishing. 191 S. Gary Avenu, Carol Stream, IL 60188.

Communication Arts. Coyne & Blanchard, 410 Sherman Oaks, Palo Alto, CA 94303.

Computer Graphics. Harris Publications, Inc. 1115 Broadway, 8th fl., New York, NY 10010.

Desktop Communications. International Desktop Communications. 342 Madison Avenu., Suite. 622, New York, NY 10173-0002.

Desktop Publishing Journal. Linda Hanson, Ed. & Pub. 4017-C Rucker Avenu, Suite. 821, Everett, WA 98201.

Desktop Publishing Users' Report. Communications Concepts. 7481 Huntsman Blvd., Suite. 720, Springfield, VA 22153-1648.

Font & Function: The Adobe Type Catalog. Adobe Systems, P.O. Box 7900, Mountain View, CA 94039-7900.

In-House Graphics. United Communications, 4500 Montgomery Avenue, Suite 700N, Bethesda, MD 20814.

MacWeek. Coastal Associates Publishing, One Park Avenue., New York, NY 10016.

Mac Publishing And Presentations focuces on Macintosh desktop publishers; provides histories, product recommendations and reviews; publishes solutions and profiles on how to select and use Mac-based desktop technology.

Mac Publishing And Presentations. International Desktop Communications. 342 Madison Avenu., Suite. 622, New York, NY 10173-0002.

National Association Of Desktop Publishers. Spine title: National Association of Desk Top Publishing Journal. 1987. Desktop Publishing Institute. 462 Boston Street, Topsfield, MA 01983-1232.

Newsletter Design. Newsletter Clearinghouse, 44 West Market Street, P.O. Box 311, Rhinebeck, NY 12572.

P C Publishing And Presentations. International Desktop Communications. 342 Madison Avenu., Suite. 622, New York, NY 10173-0002.

Personal Publishing. Hitchcock Publishing, 25W550 Geneva Road, Wheaton, IL 60188.

Print: America's Graphic Design Magazine. RC Publications, 6400 Goldsboro Road, Bethesda, MD 20817.

Publish. PCW Communications, 501 Second Street, San Francisco, CA 94107.

Seybold Report On Desktop Publishing. Seybold Publications. 428 E. Baltimore Avenu, Box 644, Media, PA 19063.

Publish combines in-depth treatment of the latest hardware and software issues with helpful design- and technique-oriented articles.

Step-by-Step Electronic Design: The How-To Newsletter for Desktop Designers. Dynamic Graphics, 6000 North Forest Park Drive, P.O. Box 1901, Peoria, IL 61656.

TypeWorld. PennWell Publishing Company, P.O. Box 2709, Tulsa, OK 74101.

Verbum: The Journal of Computer Aesthetics. P.O. Box 15439, San Diego, CA 92115.

Weigand Report: The Working Newsletter for Desktop Publishers. Rae Productions International, P.O. Box 647, Gales Ferry, CT 06335.

Glossary

A

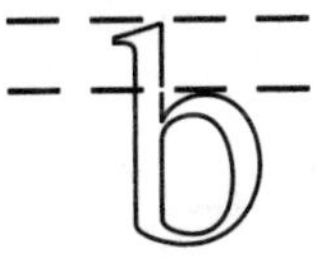

Ascender

Ascender line

alignment. The way text lines up on a page or in a column.

apex. Where strokes come together at the uppermost point of a character.

artwork. Any illustration material prepared for a publication.

ascender. The portion of a lowercase letter that rises above the main body or x height as in a “b.”

ascender line. The imaginary horizontal line that represents the uppermost point of an ascender.

ascent. A font’s maximum distance above the baseline.

ASCII (American Standard Code for Information Interchange). A code to which a file, created by one software program, is converted so that it may be read by and used in another software program.

asymmetric layout. An off-center design.

ATM (Adobe Type Manager). A program that improves your screen display by imaging fonts directly from their Type 1 PostScript language font files.

auto leading. The function that automatically adjusts the vertical space between lines of text when the type size is increased or decreased.

automatic hyphenation. A function that directs software to hyphenate text automatically.

B

banner. A large headline or title running full width across the top of the page, most often used in newspaper design.

bar. The enclosed horizontal stroke in characters such as A, H, and E.

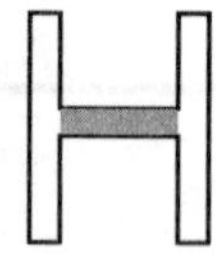

Bar

baseline. The imaginary line on which a line of type rests.

Baseline

BCP (Bezier Control Point). One of two points that guide a Beizer curve.

Bezier curve. Mathematical equations commonly used to describe the shapes of the characters in electronic typography. The Bezier curve was named for Pierre Bezier, a French computer scientist who developed the mathematical representation used to describe that curve.

bit-map font. A font that is made up of pixels (square dots). Bit-map fonts typically work in tandem with outline fonts, with bit-map fonts being used on the screen and related outline fonts automatically used in the printer. Also known as a "screen font."

bit-map graphic. See *paint-type graphics.*

black letter. These heavy black typefaces were the very first metal type. The earliest of these were from the Gutenberg workshop and were copies of letters found in handwritten manuscripts. Also known as "Old English."

bleed. The part of an image that extends beyond the trimmed edge of a page.

blowup. An enlargement, usually of a graphic such as a photograph.

body. The portion of a character that is between the baseline and the top of the x height; also called main body.

body copy. The text of the main portion of a document; also called body text.

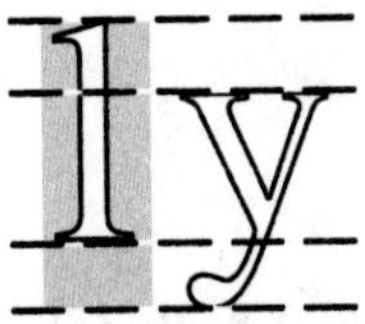

Body size

body size. The type's point size, which is determined by measuring from the highest ascender to the lowest descender.

bold. A type style that is a heavy, darker version of a typeface. Usually used for emphasis. Also called boldface.

border. A continuous decorative design or rule surrounding the matter on a page.

bounce. Alternating characters in an up-and-down position.

boundary. A dotted line around a graphic or publication.

Bounce

bowl. The enclosed oval or round curve of letters such as d, g, b, and o.

box. A section of text marked off by thin rules and presented separately from the main text and illustrations.

• **Bullet**

bullet. A large, solid dot preceding text to add emphasis. Also known as a blob.

C

Calligraphic

calligraphic. In typography, this usually refers to roman or italic letters that appear to have been written with a pen or brush. Derived from the Greek word kallagraphia, which means "beautiful writing."

camera-ready copy. Artwork or pasted-up material that is ready for reproduction.

cap height. The height of capital letters in a type font.

cap line. The imaginary line that represents the uppermost part of capital letters and some characters' ascenders.

captions. Descriptive text accompanying illustrations.

center align. To line up text in the middle of a page or column.

center spread. The pair of pages that fall at the center of a magazine or folded section of printed material.

center tab. A function that aligns the text in a column so the text is centered.

character. A letter in the alphabet or a number or symbol.

character set. A single font's characters, symbols, and numbers.

B u ? 5 % H # @

Characters

click. To rapidly press and release a mouse button.

clipboard. A temporary storage area in which your software holds the text, graphics, and pictures that were last cut or copied.

color overlay. A page that includes one color to be used in your publication. A separate page is printed for each color. All graphics and text to be printed in one particular color are located in their proper positions on the page. Also called spot color overlays.

color separation. The division of a multicolored original into the primary process colors of yellow, magenta, cyan, and black. A separate film is made for each color and these are each printed in turn, thus building up a color picture.

column rule. A fine rule (line) between columns of text.

b b **Condensed**

column guides. The dotted, vertical, nonprinting lines that mark the left and right edges of columns.

condensed. A narrow version of a typeface.

contrast. The relationship between dark and light areas within a graphic.

counter. The enclosed space within letters such as e, s, h, and g. Often confused with bowl.

crop marks. The lines printed to indicate the corners of a page for trimming when the page is smaller than the paper size.

Cross stroke

cropping. Trimming the unwanted portions of a graphic.

cross stroke. The part of a letter that cuts horizontally across the stem, such as in the letters t and f. Also known as the crossbar.

Cursive

cursive. First used in the sixteenth century, these typefaces imitate handwriting. Script letters and cursive typefaces appear to be drawn with pen and ink. Unlike script, however, cursive letters are joined.

custom page size. A nonstandard page size.

cutout. To pull out an element in an illustration so that it fits a layout or to remove unwanted parts of an illustration.

D

decimal tab. The function that aligns decimal points; it is used frequently in lists of numbers.

default. The option to which a software program defers unless the user specifies otherwise.

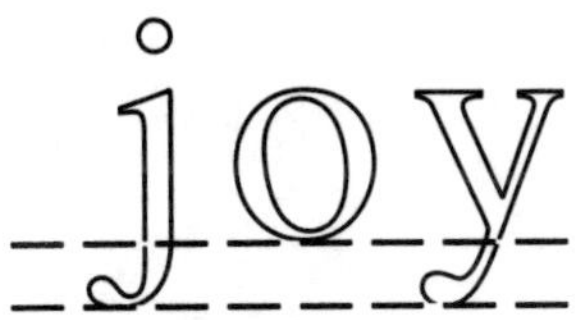

Descender

descender. The portion of a letter that extends below the baseline, as in the letter y.

descender line. The imaginary lowest line that a character's descender extends to, such as the bottom stem of the lowercase letters j and y.

descent. A font's maximum distance below the baseline.

Descender line

desktop publishing (DTP). An electronic method of combining text and graphics to produce professional quality documents or publications.

digitizing. Converting the shape of a character into a form that can be read and interpreted by computers.

dingbats. Once known as "printer's flowers," these are the small decorative marks, bullets, or symbols that make up a specialty face. Zapf Dingbats is one well-known example of a dingbat font.

directory. The listing and description of all files saved to a disk.

display face. A larger and bolder version of a text face (14 points or more) that is used for headlines and subheads.

DOS (Disk Operating System). The operating system of IBM and IBM-compatible personal computers.

double-click. To quickly press and release the mouse button two times in succession.

double-sided pages. The pages in a publication that will be reproduced on both sides of a sheet of paper.

double spread. Two facing pages where the material of the left-hand page carries over to the right-hand page.

downloadable font. A font file that contains character descriptions that are copied from the computer and temporarily stored in the printer's memory while a document is printing.

dpi (dots per inch). The measure of resolution for a video monitor or printer. High-resolution printers are usually at least 1,000 dpi. Laser printers typically have a resolution of 300 dpi; monitors are usually 72 dpi.

drag. To hold down the mouse button, move the object to the location desired, and then release the mouse button.

draw-type graphics. An application program that is used to create illustrations. Also called object-oriented graphics.

drop cap. A large initial letter at the beginning of the text that drops into the line or lines of text below.

Drop cap is a large initial letter at the beginning of the text that drops into the line or lines of text below.

drop shadow. A shaded repetition of a shape positioned slightly to the left or right of the original shape. Also called a shadow.

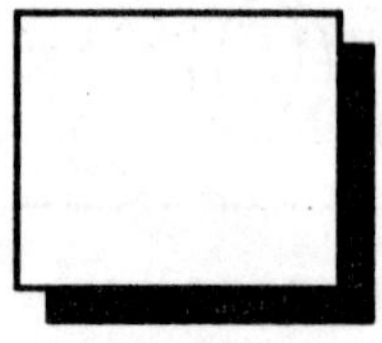

Drop shadow

E

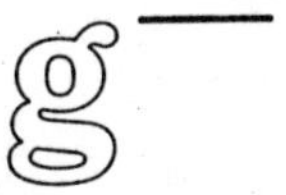

Ear

ear. The projection on letters such as lowercase g and p.

edit. To change text, graphics, or specifications in a publication.

Egyptian. A typeface style with slab or square serifs. Also known as Western faces. These typefaces are sometimes made up of human forms and floral figures.

em

em. A typographic measurement equal to a typeface's point size. Traditionally, it was the width of a typeface's widest letter, the capital M. If the type size is 10 points, an em is equal to 10 points.

em-dash

em-dash. One em wide, the em-dash indicates missing material or a break in thought. Spaces may be added to both sides of the em-dash.

en

en. A unit of measure that is equal to half of a typeface's point size. Traditionally, an en was half the width of an em.

en-dash

en-dash. One en wide, the en-dash is usually used in number spans, such as "pages 4–9." It may also be used in compound adjectives (as in post–World War II).

Enlarged initial letter is the first letter in the first word of a paragraph set larger and extending higher than the other letters.

enlarged initial letter. The first letter in the first word of a paragraph is set larger and extends higher than the other letters.

enlarging. Increasing a graphic on a page, usually with the scaling function.

EPS (Encapsulated PostScript). A file format that enables you to print line art with smooth (rather than jagged) edges and to see and resize the graphic on screen as it will print. EPS files can be produced in graphic programs that produce PostScript code (such as Illustrator and Freehand). EPS images do not print well on non-PostScript printers.

F

facing pages. In a double-sided publication, the two pages that face each other when the publication is open.

family. A group of printing types in different weights with the same design characteristics.

file. A collection of information stored on a disk.

flipping. Manipulating an image so that it is reversed either horizontally or vertically.

flush. Text set to the left-hand or right-hand margin of the column without indention.

flush left. Text that is aligned with the left margin or left column guide. Also called ragged right.

flush right. Text that is aligned with the right margin or right column guide. Also called ragged left.

folio. Page number.

font. The complete assortment of type of one size and face.

fore edge. The outer, vertical edge of a page.

frame. A rectangular box used to "hold" text or pictures. Each page is also a frame. Pages are automatically centered as needed to accommodate all the text in a file.

Helvetica

Helvetica black

Helvetica black oblique

Helvetica bold

Helvetica light

Helvetica light oblique

Helvetica narrow

Helvetica narrow bold

Helvetica compressed bold

Family

G

geometric. Serif or sans serif typeface composed of visually geometric character shapes. Some good examples are Lubalin Graph, Avant Garde, and Futura.

Gothic. In modern usage, Gothic refers to sans serif monoweight letters such as Letter Gothic. These have little contrast of thick and thin lines and no ornamentation, yet they still retain the traditional Gothic look. After the invention of type by Gutenberg in 1450, the traditional Gothic style of lettering fell into the shadow of Venetian Old Style typography.

Franklin Gothic

graphic. Any combination of lines, ovals, rectangles, squares, circles, and drawings (including computer-created artwork) used to illustrate a publication.

graphics software. An application program used to design graphs, charts, tables, or other illustrations.

grid. A nonprinting design consisting of intersecting horizontal and vertical lines that can be used for the overall layout of a publication or for positioning drawn graphics, depending on the software. Also called layout grid.

guide. A series of nonprinting dotted or dashed lines that can be created to help with alignment. Most DTP software packages feature horizontal and vertical column guides, margin guides, and ruler guides. Also called guidelines.

guidelines (nonprinting). See *guide*.

gutter. The blank space between columns or between two pages in a bound document.

H

hairline. The thinnest rule possible, generally .25 point.

halftone. The representation of a shade of gray by a series of black dots of different sizes. The bigger the dots, the darker the shade of gray. Halftones are created for photographs and artwork with gray areas so they can be reproduced in printing.

Hanging indent is a paragraph that has its first line of text flush left and the rest of the lines indented. Also called outdent.

hanging indent. A paragraph that has its first line of text flush left and the rest of the lines indented. Also called outdent.

head/heading. Word(s) identifying specific divisions within a text and marked out from that text.

headline. A heading, as in a newspaper, set in a larger type size than the main copy.

highlight. To visually differentiate text, graphics, or options.

horizontal grid. A series of horizontal guidelines that help with alignment.

horizontal ruler. An electronic ruler that is usually displayed across the top of Publication windows.

hyphenate. To insert a hyphen into a word so that the word can be broken between two lines of text.

I

icon. A small graphic image that represents a function, object, or pointer.

import. To make a file that was created in a word processing or graphics application program active in a desktop publishing program.

imposition. The arrangement of pages of type on a printing plate so that when the sheet is folded the text reads continuously.

increment. The distance between tickmarks on the horizontal and vertical rulers.

indention. The space left blank at the beginning of a paragraph.

Initial caps are also known as ornamental caps.

initial cap. Large, capital letters (often ornamental) that are found at the beginning of paragraphs or chapters. These date back to European manuscripts, where they were (and still are) considered works of art. Before printing presses replaced hand lettering, a few talented scribes drew the characters into spaces left in the manuscripts for that purpose.

insert. To add additional text in an existing text block or graphic boundary.

f *f*

Normal **Italic**

insertion point. The blinking vertical bar or I-beam indicating where the next keyboarded or pasted text will appear.

inside margin. The margin along the binding edge of the page, which is the left margin of a right-hand page or the right margin of a left-hand page.

italic. A type style that is the sloped, almost cursive version of a typeface.

J

Justified text is text that lines up at both left and right margins. Also known as fully justified.

justified text. Text that lines up at both left and right margins. Also known as fully justified.

justify. To align text so that it is flush with both the left and right margins.

K

W O
WO
Kerning

kern. To adjust the space between two characters so that the characters are positioned closer together.

keyboard shortcuts. A key, or key and mouse combination, used to perform certain tasks quickly.

L

landscape. A page orientation that has a greater width than height.

layout. The arrangement of text and graphics on a page.

layout grid. See *grid.*

leading (pronounced "ledding"). The distance in points from the baseline of one line of type to the baseline of the next. Also called line spacing or interline spacing.

left align. To position text at the left margin of a page or left edge of a column.

left justified. Type that is aligned with the left margin. Also called flush left.

left tab. A function that aligns the left edges of text.

legal-size page. A page designed to be printed on 8.5-by-14-inch paper.

letterspacing. Separating all the letters in a word with spaces. Best used to modify headings, this should be applied with caution because too much letterspacing makes text difficult to read. Some programs automatically add letterspacing when text is justified.

Letter spacing
Letter spacing
Letter spacing

line art. Artwork made up of solid lines without shades of gray. Line art can be a graphic created with a draw-type program or a traditional ink drawing.

line spacing. See *leading*.

line style. The appearance of a rule or border.

M

makeup. The assembling of all elements to form the printed page.

margins. The top, bottom, left, and right edges of a page, which have dimensions that are specified by the user that are outside the body text or graphic image.

master page. A page or separate menu in which the user can store the layout elements that repeat on all the pages of a publication.

master page elements. The specifications stored in the master page.

mean line. See *x-height*.

metrics. Font information such as ascent, descent, leading, characters, widths, and kerning.

mock-up. The rough visual presentation, or comprehensive (comp), of a publication or design.

mouse. A small, hand-held input device that provides precise and natural control of the cursor. It is used for pointing, selecting, and drawing. Also called a pointing device.

O

object-oriented graphic. See *draw-type graphics.*

Plain **Oblique**

oblique. A right-slanted version of a roman typeface without changes to the letter design. Often confused with italic.

old style. Characterized by variations in stroke width, bracketed serifs, high contrast, and a diagonal stroke. Some popular old styles include Bembo, Garamond, Janson, and Caslon. Originally developed during the Renaissance and adopted by Venetian printers in the fifteenth century, these typefaces were based on pen-drawn forms.

orientation. The position of a page that the user selects when setting up a publication.

orphan. The first line of a new paragraph positioned as the last line of a page or column. Also a word fragment on a line of its own.

outdent. See *hanging indent.*

outline font. A font is defined by drawing the black contour of the white space that makes up each character. It is made up typically of Bezier curves for PostScript fonts and quadratic splines for True Type fonts. Both of these scales can be scaled to any size; therefore, one set of outlines can be used for any size in a typeface.

outside margin. The right margin of a right-hand page or the left margin of a left-hand page.

overlapping. See *tiling.*

P

page depth. The length or height of the text area on a page.

page size. The dimensions of a page's printed area. The page size is usually different from the paper size.

paint-type graphics. Graphic images created by a series of dots that can be imported into a desktop publishing program. Also called bit-map graphics.

panning. Moving a graphic so that portions of it are not displayed within a frame. Panning is a form of electronic cropping.

paste-up. Type proofs and illustrations pasted down in page layouts.

pattern. Any arrangement of lines or dots used to fill a graphic object.

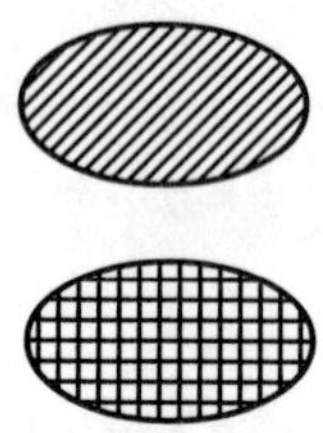

Pattern

phototypesetting. The method of setting type photographically.

pica. A typographic unit of measurement equal to one-sixth of an inch. Twelve points equal one pica.

picture wrap. See *wrap*.

pixel (stands for picture element). Pixels are square dots that represent the smallest units displayed on a computer screen. Characters or graphics are created by turning pixels on or off.

point. A basic unit of typographic measurement. There are 72 points to an inch.

pointer. The icon on the screen that moves with the mouse. The pointer's shape depends on which tool the user is currently using and where the user is pointing within the window.

pointing device. See *mouse*.

PostScript. Adobe Systems' page description language. Programs such as Aldus FreeHand use PostScript to create complex pages including text and graphics onscreen. This language is then sent to the printer to produce high-quality printed text and graphics.

presentation graphic. A publication used in a lecture, such as a slide or overhead transparency of a chart or graph.

print area. The area of a piece of paper on which a printer can reproduce text or graphics.

truth

TRUTH

Proportionally spaced type

prompted hyphenation. A paragraph specification that shows the user where selected text can be hyphenated.

proof. A print of type or illustration to be checked and corrected before committing to camera-ready artwork.

proportionally spaced type. Type whose character widths vary according to the features of the letters (as opposed to monospaced type).

publication. A document created with desktop publishing software that contains any combination of text and graphics.

pull quote. A part of the text that is taken from the body copy and reproduced on the same page in a larger, bolder typeface.

R

ragged left. See *flush right.*

ragged right. See *flush left.*

RAM (random access memory). The computer or printer's temporary place for storing data used in operating programs. When the computer or printer is turned off, the information in RAM is lost.

register. The exact matching of two or more printings especially when printing more than one color.

registration marks. Marks added to pages to indicate, to a commercial printer, the alignment of areas to be printed in different colors.

release. To let go of the mouse button.

resident font. A font that resides permanently in the ROM (read only memory) of a printer.

resize. To change the dimensions of a graphic.

Reverse line

resolution. Sharpness of definition of a digitized image depending on the number of scan lines to the inch.

Reverse type

reverse lines. White rules on a contrasting black, shaded, or colored background.

reverse out. To print white type or other images on a background.

reverse type. White text on a contrasting black, shaded, or colored background.

right align. To position text at the right margin of a page or right edge of a column. Also called ragged left.

right justified. Type aligned with the right margin. Also known as flush right.

right tab. A function that aligns the right edges of text.

RIP (raster image processor). Converts fonts and graphics into raster images, which are used by the printer to draw onto the page.

rotation. A feature that rotates text or a graphic as specified by the user.

rule. A horizontal or vertical line often used to enhance the design or readability of a publication.

ruler guides. Horizontal and vertical dotted lines that are nonprinting extensions of the tickmarks on the rulers. Used for aligning text and graphics on a page.

rulers. Horizontal and vertical electronic rulers that are usually placed across the top and down the left side of a publication window, respectively.

running head. Heading or title set at the top of each page and separate from the text.

S

Sans serif

sans serif. Typefaces that do not have the small "finishing" lines at the end of each stroke of a letter.

scaling. The increasing or decreasing of a graphic or page.

scanned-image files. Paint-type files created with the hardware that converts a two- or three-dimensional image to a collection of dots so that the desktop publishing software can read the graphic file directly from a disk.

scanner. A hardware device that converts text or illustrations on paper into a computer image.

screen font. Bit-map fonts used for the computer display.

screen pattern. An image that is composed of dots or lines.

scroll. To change the portion of the publication displayed on the screen.

Serif

select. To designate where the next action will take place, often done by using a mouse.

serif. Typefaces that have small "finishing" lines at the end of each stroke of a letter.

set width. The width of a letter and its surrounding space; the space needed to set a line of text in a specific typeface. Some programs have tracking to adjust the typefaces to make the set width looser or tighter. Also known as advance width.

shade. A degree of tint used to fill an area. Also called fill attributes.

side head. A subhead in, or flush with, the side margin.

spur. A finishing stroke like the ones on certain uppercase Gs.

square serif. Originally designed at the beginning of the nineteenth century, these typefaces have squared-off serifs on characters' end strokes. Also called slab serif or Egyptian.

Stem

stem. The upright element of a letter or character.

style. A visual variation of a basic typeface used to create emphasis. Type style is important because it can attract the reader's eye. The four basic computer styles are plain, bold, italic, and bold italic.

subhead. A heading within the body of the text that marks the division of the chapter.

superscript. A feature with which selected text is placed slightly above the baseline.

T

tabloid. A page-size setting, usually 11 x 17 inches.

tail. A character's downward projection, such as on the letter Q.

target printer. The printer selected for printing the final version of a publication.

template. A dummy publication that acts as a model, providing the structure and general layout for another similar publication.

text-only file. Text created with another application and then saved without any type specifications or other formatting. Software packages can read text-only files directly from disk.

textwrap. See *wrap*.

t0.humbnail. A miniature copy of a page.

tickmark. Marks on the ruler that define increments for measuring.

tiling. The process of assembling two or more printed pages that, when pasted together, constitute an oversized publication. Also called overlapping.

Tracking	**Normal**
Tracking	**Loose**
Tracking	**Tight**

tracking. The overall letterspacing in the text. Tracking can also be used to tighten or loosen a block of type. Some programs have automatic tracking options that can add or remove small increments of space between the characters.

True Type. An outline font format developed by Apple Computer Corporation and adopted by Microsoft Corporation. These fonts can be used for both the screen display and printing, thereby eliminating the need to have font files for each typeface.

type. Printed or typewritten letters or characters. As early as A.D. 400, the Chinese printed entire pages of characters through the use of wooden blocks. Johannes Gutenberg cast the first metal type in the fifteenth century.

Size	**12 point**
Size	**18 point**
Size	**30 point**

typeface. One complete set of character designs for one style of type.

typesetting. Text produced by a laser printer or high-quality machine known as a typesetter.

type size. The height of a typeface measured in points.

type style. A category within a typeface such as normal, bold, and italics.

typography. The practice of arranging type.

U

ultra. The heaviest weight of a particular typeface.

unjustified. Text set ranged to the left with the right-hand edge uneven.

V

vertical grid. A series of vertical guidelines that help with alignment.

vertical ruler. An electronic ruler displayed down the left side of most Publication windows.

W

weight. The degree of boldness or thickness of a letter or font.

white space. Deliberate areas of empty space on a page that, when used correctly, can effectively enhance a layout.

widow. A single line of text or word at the top of a page or column.

word space. The space left between words in a line.

Word space is the space left between words in a line.

wordwrap. A word processing feature that automatically returns the cursor to the left when the end of a line is reached.

wrap. A feature that positions text around a graphic. Also called picture wrap or textwrap.

WYSIWYG (what you see is what you get). A display mode that enables the user to see an image on screen of how the text and graphics in a publication will appear on the printed page.

X

x-height. The vertical height of a lowercase x and the height of the bodies of all lowercase letters. Also called mean line.

x-height

Index

Page numbers for commands, menus, and dialog boxes refer to initial descriptions or examples of use. Commands, menus, and dialog boxes are in *italic* type. Definitions of many terms can be found in the glossary.

Q

R

S

T

U

V

W

X

Z

LICENSING AGREEMENT

You should carefully read the following terms and conditions before opening this disk package. Opening this disk package indicates your acceptance of these terms and conditions. If you do not agree with them, you should promptly return the package unopened.

Allyn and Bacon provides this Program and License its use. You assume responsibility for the selection of the Program to achieve your intended results, and for the installation, use, and results obtained from the Program. This License extends only to use of the Program in the United States or countries in which the Program is marketed by duly authorized distributors.

License Grant
You hereby accept a nonexclusive, nontransferable, permanent License to install and use the Program on a single computer at any given time. You may copy the Program solely for backup or archival purposes in support of your use of the Program on the single computer. You may **not** modify, translate, disassemble, decompile, or reverse engineer the Program, in whole or in part.

Term
This License is effective until terminated. Allyn and Bacon reserves the right to terminate this License automatically if any provision of the License is violated. You may terminate the License at any time. To terminate this License, you must return the Program, including documentation, along with a written warranty stating that all copies of the Program in your possession have been returned or destroyed.

Limited Warranty
The Program is provided "As Is" without warranty of any kind, either express or implied, including, but **not** limited to, the implied warranties or merchantability and fitness for a particular purpose. The entire risk as to the quality and performance of the Program is with you. Should the Program prove defective, you (and **not** Allyn and Bacon or any authorized distributor) assume the entire cost of all necessary servicing, repair, or correction. No oral or written information or advice given by Allyn and Bacon, its dealers, distributors, or agents shall create a warranty or increase the scope of its warranty.

Some states do **not** allow the exclusion of implied warranty, so the above exclusion may **not** apply to you. This warranty gives you specific legal rights and you may also have other rights that vary from state to state.

Allyn and Bacon does **not** warrant that the functions contained in the Program will meet your requirements or that the operation of the Program will be uninterrupted or error free.

However, Allyn and Bacon warrants the disk(s) on which the Program is furnished to be free from defects in material and workmanship under normal use for a period of ninety (90) days form the date of delivery to you as evidenced by a copy of your receipt.

The Program should **not** be relied on as the sole basis to solve a problem whose incorrect solution could result in injury to a person or property. If the Program is employed in such a manner, its is at the user's own risk and Allyn and Bacon explicitly disclaims all liability for such misuse.

Limitation of Remedies
Allyn and Bacon's entire liability and your exclusive remedy shall be:

1. The replacement of any disk **not** meeting Allyn and Bacon's "Limited Warranty" and that is returned to Allyn and Bacon or

2. If Allyn and Bacon is unable to deliver a replacement disk or cassette that is free of defects in materials or workmanship, you may terminate this Agreement by returning the Program.

In no event will Allyn and Bacon be liable to you for any damages, including any lost profits, lost savings, or other incidental or consequential damages arising out of the use or inability to use such Program even if Allyn and Bacon or an authorized distributor has been advised of the possibility of such damages of for any claim by any other party.

Some states do **not** allow the limitation or exclusion of liability for incidental or consequential damages, so the above limitation or exclusion may **not** apply to you.

General
You may **not** sublicense, assign, or transfer the License of the Program. Any attempt to sublicense, assign, or transfer any of the rights, duties, or obligations hereunder is void.

This Agreement will be governed by the laws of the State of Massachusetts.

Should you have any questions concerning this Agreement, or any questions concerning technical support, you may contact Allyn and Bacon by writing to:

Allyn and Bacon
Simon and Schuster Education Group
160 Gould Street
Needham Heights, MA 02194

You acknowledge that you have read this Agreement, understand it, and agree to be bound by its terms and conditions. You further agree that it is the complete and exclusive statement of the Agreement between us that supersedes any proposal or prior Agreement, oral or written, and any other communications between us relating to the subject matter of this Agreement.

Notice To Government End Users
The Program is provided with restricted rights. Use, duplication, or disclosure by the Government is subject to restrictions set forth in subdivison (b)(3)(iii) of The Rights in Technical Data and Computer Software Clause 252.227-7013.